Praise for *Landed Jap*

"*Landed Japan* is an essential reference for anyone buying real estate in Japan. It is unbiased and full of practical, up-to-date information. Even Japanese buyers can learn a lot from this book."

Nobuo Takenaka
Chairman
Misawa Homes Co., Ltd.

"Dillon's book is so good that while reading it, I felt like I was an adult in a toy store: Envious of the stuff kids have now that I would have loved to have as a kid. If only I had the information in this book when I was building my house in the 1990s, I wouldn't have ended up with the financial albatross I have now! *Landed Japan* is required reading for anyone considering buying the most expensive consumer good in one of the most expensive (and tricky) housing markets in the world. It's even a good read!"

Dr. Arudou Debito
Author of *Embedded Racism: Japan's Visible Minorities and Racial Discrimination*

"*Landed Japan* not only answers the key questions and considerations for foreigners looking to buy, but also provides helpful examples of expats who've overcome the risks and obstacles. As Japan becomes a more popular destination for foreign buyers, *Landed Japan* is an indispensable resource."

Christopher Petersen
Managing Director, Asia
PEI Media

"When I bought a home in Tokyo in 2015, *Landed Japan* saved me time, money and effort. The second edition of *Landed Japan* is a major update, with information about Airbnb, the Olympics and dozens of other risks and opportunities. Read this book before you talk to a real estate agent."

Jay Bailey
MBA

"As an Airbnb Superhost, *Landed Japan* has been an indispensable resource that empowered me to purchase two investment properties in Tokyo, both of which earn respectable yields. The second edition of *Landed* has new information about choosing the best location given Japan's changing demographics. It also covers opportunities surrounding the latest megaprojects, Airbnb and short-term rentals. If you're excited about what the Japanese property market has to offer, this is truly an outstanding book that reads so well you'll have trouble putting it down."

Eric Anderson
Las Vegas, Nevada

"A must-read, not just for those considering buying a property in Japan, but also for individuals who are already homeowners, those who may be interested in refinancing, and there's even something to be learned by long-term residents who are renting. For those sourcing for non-owner-occupied properties and/or investment ideas including passive equity deployment, be sure to review *Landed*'s mini-section entitled 'Other Opportunities.'"

Steven Towns
Uguisu Research, LLC

"As a long-time resident of Tokyo and a property owner in Japan, *Landed* has proven to be an invaluable asset. A comprehensive study of the intricacies of the Japanese market, I found it not only extremely informative but also very readable; even entertaining. I haven't seen anything else out there with this depth of information."

Aiden Hopfner
Investment Banker

"My wife and I were looking at an investment property in Tokyo, a city we know very well socially but not commercially. Christopher's advice helped us avoid a mistake that could have cost us several hundred thousand dollars."

David Armitage
Hong Kong

L**A**NDED
JAPAN

Christopher Dillon

For James and Patricia Dillon

Dillon Communications Ltd.
G.P.O. Box 9339, Hong Kong, China
www.dilloncommunications.com

© Dillon Communications Ltd.
First published in 2010 as *Landed: The guide to buying property in Japan*
Second edition 2018

ISBN 978-988-14790-0-6

The author and publisher have made every effort to ensure the accuracy and completeness of the information in this book but assume no responsibility for errors, inaccuracies or omissions.

This book is published as a general reference and is not intended to be a substitute for professional legal, investment or tax advice.

CONTENTS

ACKNOWLEDGEMENTS

For generously sharing their time and expertise, I would like to thank Jake Adelstein, Toshihiro Ado, Paul Allen, Doris Castagno, Tony Collins, Mark Darbyshire, Matt Dening, Mark Dytham, Kenji Fujii, Mifuyu Hara, Richard Henderson, Steven Herman, Arisa Homma, Jun Honma, Emi Islam, John Kirch, Mark Kitabayashi, Astrid Klein, Masanori Kobayashi, KS Koh, Hidefumi Komiya, Grzegorz Laszczyk, Rickie Lo, John Mader, Ziv Nakajima Magen, David Markle, Nobuhiko Matsuoka, Jamie Miyazaki, Hank Mori, Shoichi Muromura, Yoko Nishi, Yusuke Ohue, Lily Ono, Erik Oskamp, Toshio Ota, Noriko Oyama, Dean Page, Paul Previtera, Jean-Guy Rioux, Jr., Jonathan Sharp, Greg Story, Hayaki Sugiura, Hideki Takahashi, Yutaka Takeda, Carrie Tan, Riccardo Tossani, Hirotoshi Toudou, Phoenix Tsang, Dale Willets and Steven Windholz.

I would also like to thank the Canadian Academy of Independent Scholars for their support.

Photo credits

The author's photo is by Idalina Silva. All other photos were taken by the author.

PREFACE

This is the sixth volume in the *Landed* series of real estate books.

In 2008, I wrote *Landed: The expatriate's guide to buying and renovating property in Hong Kong* after buying and renovating an office, an apartment and half a floor in a factory building. There were no English-language books explaining how to buy property in Hong Kong, so I wrote one in the hope my experience would help others. To my surprise, the book became a local bestseller.

Two years later, I published the first edition of this book. Unlike the Hong Kong book, *Landed: The guide to buying property in Japan* was written before I had purchased local property. As a result, I extended my research methods. I interviewed architects, builders and agents. I wrote case studies about foreigners who had successfully bought and built homes in Japan. I read trade magazines to learn about trends shaping the market. And I scoured academic journals for practical information about subjects ranging from asbestos to zoning.

The Japan book included several improvements. I added endnotes and a "Useful Information" section where readers could find additional resources. I also included a "Risk Factors" chapter that highlighted several concerns, including Japan's troubled nuclear industry. And I continued to focus on making the book clear, accessible and useful.

This model was refined in *Landed China* (2013), *Landed Global* (2014) and a second edition of *Landed Hong Kong* (2015). I shortened the name and commissioned a new design to reflect the fact that *Landed* was now a series, added checklists and began producing ebooks. I also incorporated lessons I had learned buying and selling property in Hong Kong and Japan, serving on the owners' committee of a 210-unit residential complex, and dealing with repairs, renovations and tenants.

From Abenomics to Airbnb and from the Olympics to Fukushima, Japan has experienced great change since the first edition of this book was published in 2010. But one thing remains constant: I hope *Landed Japan* helps you make informed, profitable and satisfying decisions about real estate in Japan.

INTRODUCTION

This book was written for anyone buying—or thinking of buying—a residential, recreational or investment property in Japan.

Landed Japan focuses on practical information. It explains the sales process, how to avoid common problems and where to find essential information. It doesn't include statistics, economic analyses or cultural background, except as they relate to real estate.

In writing *Landed Japan*, I have omitted the sales pitch. I assume that, whether for family, lifestyle or financial reasons, you want to buy real estate in Japan.

Information asymmetry

For most people, buying real estate is a textbook case of information asymmetry. You might buy one or two properties in your lifetime. When you do, you use an agent with intimate knowledge of the local market. You work with a lender who knows the mortgage market. And you buy from a vendor who is aware of her property's flaws. In short, everyone in the process knows more than you do. That puts you at a disadvantage, especially if you are operating in a second language and with laws and customs that are different from those at home. *Landed Japan* addresses these issues.

This book will aid couples in which one partner is fluent in Japanese and the other is not. Often, this leaves one party underinformed and puts the burden of translation and interpretation on the other person, whose property and financial knowledge may not match their language skills.

Inside Landed

Landed Japan opens with "People," which looks at the demographic trends shaping Japanese society.

"Your New Home" examines the process of buying real estate. It includes information about the things that make Japan's property market unique and the risks that accompany a real estate purchase.

"Locations" explains the trade-offs between the city center and the suburbs, and what makes a desirable neighborhood. This section features chapters on Hokkaido, Greater Tokyo, Nagoya, Kansai, Fukuoka and Okinawa. Each chapter describes the market's history, demographics and economics, as well as infrastructure projects that are under development.

"Finance" explains how and where to get a mortgage, Japan's earthquake insurance system and the tax implications of buying, holding, renting and selling property.

"Special Cases" explores the process of custom-designing a home as well as the opportunities available to landlords and Airbnb hosts. This section also covers foreclosed homes, recreational property and less conventional investments, such as share houses, homes for the elderly and love hotels.

The final section, "Resources," shows you where to find information about topics ranging from architects and real estate agents to earthquakes and termites. A series of checklists ensures you don't miss anything when inspecting a home or negotiating a purchase. Endnotes are included for readers who want to learn more about the topics covered in *Landed Japan*.

A final note

To make the most of *Landed Japan*, keep the following in mind:

▲ Japanese tax law is complicated, especially when multiple jurisdictions are involved. If you own property in Japan, get professional tax and estate planning advice.

▲ Government policies, lending practices and market conditions can change quickly. Use the "Resources" section to ensure your decisions are made with up-to-date information.

▲ Inclusion of an organization in *Landed Japan* should not be taken as a recommendation. And if I have omitted a company, it does not mean you should avoid them.

▲ Unless otherwise noted, all dollar figures are expressed in United States dollars.

▲ Prices fluctuate and are included in *Landed Japan* for illustrative purposes only.

▲ The Japanese fiscal year runs from April 1 to March 31. So, fiscal 2018 ends on March 31, 2019.

▲ With the exception of Dr. Arudou Debito, a naturalized Japanese citizen who has stated a preference for his name to appear in the Japanese order, Japanese names in this book are shown in Western order (first name followed by family name).

▲ To avoid using "he or she" and "s/he," I alternate between male and female pronouns throughout the book.

▲ Videos about Japanese real estate and a range of free information and resources are available at www.landedbook.com.

I look forward to including your comments and suggestions in the next edition of the book.

PEOPLE

DEMOGRAPHICS

Japan's population is aging and shrinking. Young people are moving from rural areas and small towns to Tokyo, Osaka and Nagoya, and households are becoming smaller. Each of these trends has long-term implications for the nation's economy and property market and for your investment in Japanese real estate.

Aging

Japan is demographically unique. In no other country do the elderly comprise such a large proportion of the population. From an aging society, with 7% of its population over 65 in 1970, Japan became an aged society (14% over 65) in 1995 and a hyper-aged society (21% over 65) in 2008. By 2010, seniors comprised 23% of the Japanese population, versus 13% in the United States and 20% in Italy and Germany.[1]

Rapidly aging population

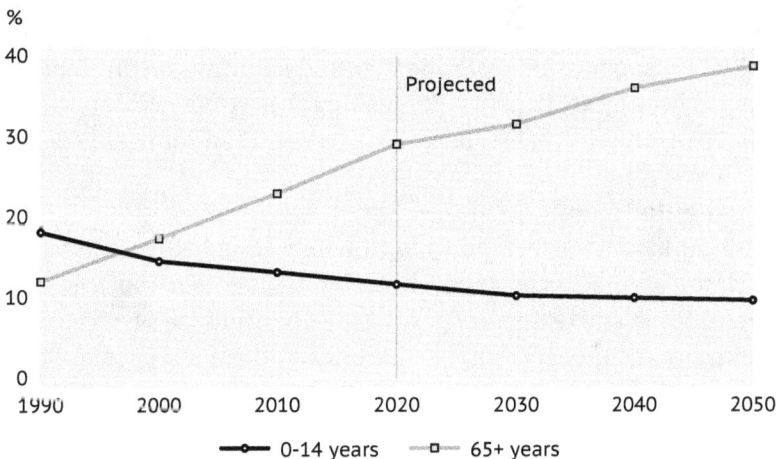

Source: Japan Statistical Yearbook 2017, Government of Japan.

The surge in Japan's elderly population has not peaked. Baby boomers, known as *dankaisedai*, began turning 65 in 2012. By 2060, 40%

of the population will be over 65, and one person in four will be over 75 by 2025.[2] The Japanese people's longevity fuels this trend. Girls born in 2015 are expected to live 86.8 years—the world's longest life span—while boys have a projected life span of 80.5 years, the world's sixth longest.

Social security expenditures

Longer life spans mean more government spending on senior citizens. In fiscal 2014, ended March 31, 2015, the national government spent ¥112 trillion on social security benefits. About 70% was directed to the elderly, with pensions representing over ¥54 trillion. Social security spending is expected to reach ¥149 trillion in fiscal 2025.[3]

With the aging of Japan's population, social security spending is rising as the number of working people is declining. Japan's old-age dependency ratio (calculated by dividing the population aged 65 and above by the population aged 15–64) is expected to rise from 36% (i.e. 2.8 workers per retiree) in 2010 to 50% in 2022 (2:1) and 78% (1.3:1) in 2060.[4] This does not bode well for Japan's long-term government debt, which was estimated at ¥1,062 trillion at the end of fiscal 2016.

There are efforts to make seniors pay a greater proportion of their health care and nursing costs and to introduce means testing for pension and health care benefits. But making these changes is politically difficult, as the elderly are more likely to vote than younger people.

Non-regular jobs

Many dankaisedai benefited from the lifetime-employment system, which has become increasingly rare. Non-regular jobs—such as part-time, contract and temporary positions—now comprise over one-third of the labor market and employ more than 20 million people. These positions pay less, include fewer benefits and offer poorer career prospects and less security than regular jobs.

Previously, these jobs were mainly held by women. Today, young men represent a large and growing proportion of the people holding non-regular positions. Without a conventional job, and the money and benefits that accompany it, these men are more likely to live with their parents into their 20s and 30s. Holding a non-regular job also makes young men less marriageable in Japan's "male-breadwinner–female-housekeeper" society, contributing to the nation's demographic woes and decreasing demand for housing. In a 2015 survey, 16% of working men and 46% of working women held non-regular jobs.[5]

Unlike Japan's youth, many seniors are wealthy. In 2007, 903,000 households had net financial assets of ¥100 million or more.[6] In 2015, people aged over 65 were estimated to own 60% of the ¥1.7 quadrillion in individually held financial assets in Japan.[7] Real estate makes up a large proportion of seniors' assets: in 2007, more than 89%[8] owned homes, which are mainly freestanding houses. However, this wealth is illiquid as the market for used homes remains small.

Younger people will inherit this wealth, but they will have to be patient. In 1970, the eldest child was typically aged 41–45 when his father died and 51–55 when his mother died, which is when children inherit the bulk of their parents' estate. In 2004, the eldest child was about 66 when his mother died.[9] This is significant because the incidence of home ownership increases with age and—by the time people reach their 50s—about 86% are homeowners, further increasing the likelihood that children will not live in the house or apartment they inherit. This adds to Japan's growing inventory of unoccupied dwellings, which reached a record 8.2 million in 2013.

A trend toward smaller families is concentrating Japan's wealth. A person born in 1947, for example, will inherit 20%–25% of her parents' assets. Someone born in 1957 will inherit about half, while a child born in 2005 will receive virtually all of her parents' estate. Again, this increases the likelihood that inherited property will be surplus and sold or rented out. It also divides Japan's elderly into two groups: the wealthy, who can afford a comfortable retirement, and those who depend on state assistance to survive. In March 2016, for the first time, seniors represented more than half of the people collecting welfare. The relative poverty rate of elderly women in single-person households is over 50%.[10]

The growing number of elderly poor is linked to a spike in the number of gray-haired prison inmates. Unable to survive on a modest government pension, they turn to crime. In Japan's orderly, safe society, even minor theft can result in a prison sentence, where the inmate will receive food, shelter and medical care. One-third of the people convicted of shoplifting are over 60.[11]

Changing households

The nature of Japanese households is changing. The number of households increased from 46.8 million in 2000 to 53.4 million in 2015[12] and is expected to continue growing until 2019. As the number of households has risen, their average size shrank from 2.67 people in 2000 to 2.38 in 2015. One-person households, meanwhile, rose from 27.6% of the total in 2000 to 32.7% in 2015.

Changing household composition

Millions of households

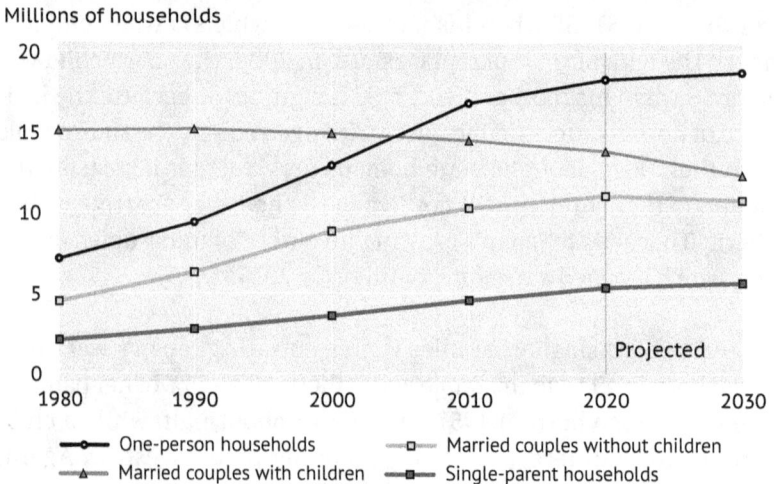

Legend:
- ——○—— One-person households
- ——□—— Married couples without children
- ——△—— Married couples with children
- ——■—— Single-parent households

Source: Household Projections for Japan 2010-2035, Government of Japan.

Fewer marriages and stable divorce rates contribute to the growing number of households and demand for smaller dwellings. In the early 1970s, there were over 1 million marriages per year. For three decades, that number ranged from 700,000 to 800,000, before falling below 700,000 in 2011. In 2015, just 635,000 couples were married.

Divorces rose from 142,000 couples in 1980 to a peak of 290,000 in 2002. Since 1996, there have been more than 200,000 divorces per year, with 226,000 couples splitting in 2015. More seniors are divorcing: In 1980, 0.08% of the female and 0.26% of the male population over 60 were divorced. By 2010, these numbers had grown to 0.37% and 0.81%, respectively.

Parents and children living apart add to the number of households. In 1980, more than half of the people over age 65 lived with their children. By 2010, fewer than one in five did.[13]

Dependent children

There has also been an increase in the number of households headed by single mothers, which topped 1 million for the first time in December 2008, and reached 1.23 million in 2011. More than half of these families live in poverty.[14]

"Parasite singles" are another defining feature of Japan's demography. The phrase, which was coined in 1999 by sociologist Masahiro Yamada, describes young, unmarried people who live with their parents, either by choice or circumstance, often into middle age.

This phenomenon is also common in Italy and Germany. What sets Japan apart is its prevalence. In 2016, 4.5 million Japanese between 35 and 54 were living with their parents. Many parasite singles have no savings or pension, and work irregularly.

For parasite singles, living with mom and dad means paying little or no rent, avoiding domestic chores and enjoying home-cooked meals. If they have a job, it lets the children spend their salaries on discretionary items, such as international travel. This arrangement is not necessarily lopsided. Many parents appreciate the company of their adult children and look forward to being cared for into their old age.

Parasite singles depress Japan's housing market. One estimate suggests that if just 10% moved out, they would boost housing demand by 1 million units.[15] In addition, parasite singles are unlikely to complicate their living arrangements by getting married or having children, events that cause people to start households.

As they age, some parasite singles become "pension parasites." This can go to extremes: In 2015, a woman in Gifu Prefecture was arrested for collecting ¥50 million in pension payments for 50 years after her parents' deaths,[16] while a man in Ehime Prefecture buried his mother's body in the garden of a home they shared so he could continue to collect her pension.[17]

Also related to the parasite single phenomenon is *hikikomori*, a form of acute social withdrawal that mainly affects young men. People with this condition lock themselves in their bedrooms for months, years or even decades, and half have another psychiatric condition. Some 260,000 families in Japan include someone with hikikomori, which leaves them totally dependent on their parents.[18]

A smaller population

Whether you hold it for a year, a decade or a century, you—or your heirs—will sell your Japanese real estate into a market that is smaller than it is today. From a peak of 128.1 million in 2008, Japan's population is expected to fall to 119.2 million–114.2 million in 2030 and to 94.6 million–80.0 million by 2060. In 2016, for the first time since the government began collecting data in 1899, Japan had fewer than 1 million births.

Japanese women are postponing marriage and having children later in life.

There are several reasons for the decline. With improved educational and career opportunities, more Japanese women are choosing to
remain single. The lifetime non-married rate* for women rose from
1.9% in 1960 to 10.6% in 2010.[19] And those who stay single are less
likely to be stigmatized for their decision than women a generation
earlier. In a 2015 survey of people aged 18–34, nearly 70% of unmarried men and 60% of unmarried women were not in a relationship,
and more than 42% were virgins. Both figures were up from the last
survey, which was conducted in 2010.[20]

Shrinking population

Millions of people

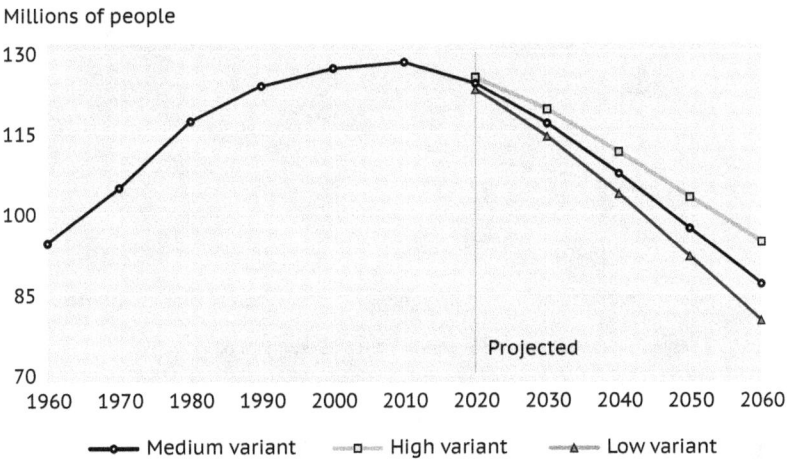

Source: Population Projections for Japan: 2011-2060, Government of Japan.

Women who marry are doing so later, at an average age of 29.4 in 2016
versus 24.2 in 1970. Contraceptive pills, which were legalized in 1999,
and accessible, socially acceptable abortions give women greater control over when they have children. Consequently, they are choosing
to have their first child later, at an average age of 30.7 in 2016 versus
25.6 in 1970.[21] This increases the likelihood that a woman's first child
will also be her last.

---

* The lifetime non-married rate is the mean value of the proportion remaining
single at ages 45–49 and the proportion remaining single at ages 50–54.

Japan's work culture is not family-friendly. Pregnancy often spells the end of a woman's career, and only 2.7% of eligible men working for private sector companies took paternity leave in fiscal 2015. That was double the 2008 figure, but far short of the government's target of 13% for 2020.

Older first-time mothers

Years

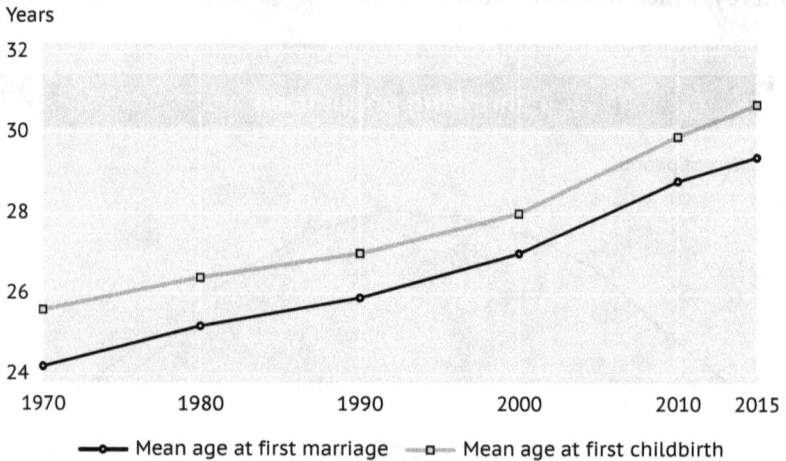

── Mean age at first marriage   ──□── Mean age at first childbirth

Source: Statistical Handbook of Japan 2017, Government of Japan.

Childbirth costs approximately ¥500,000 for a normal delivery, with Tokyo being more expensive than other parts of the country. Childbirth is not covered by national health insurance, but part of the cost is refunded as an allowance. In 2015, there was a shortage of more than 23,000 daycare places.

Japan's declining population became a public issue in 1990 after the "1.57 shock," when the total fertility rate for the previous year reached a record low 1.57 children per woman. In 2015, Prime Minister Shinzo Abe created a new cabinet post charged with stopping the decline in Japan's population. Abe also announced plans to increase the fertility rate to 1.8 by 2025, up from 1.46 in 2015, but well below the replacement figure for developed countries of 2.1.

Abe is backing his plans with money. The fiscal 2016 budget included an additional ¥164 billion for children and childcare. The government plans to spend ¥5.6 trillion on children in 2025, up from ¥4.8 trillion in 2012.

Immigration

Immigration is an obvious solution to a shrinking population, but Japan accepts few outsiders. At the end of 2014, there were 2.12 million registered foreign nationals in Japan, representing 1.67% of the population. That was down from a peak of 2.14 million, or 1.68% of the population, at the end of 2008.[22] The government estimates there are 60,000 illegal immigrants in Japan as of January 1, 2015, down from 92,000 five years earlier.

At the end of 2014, over 677,000 foreigners had permanent resident status and 358,000 individuals—mainly people of Korean and Taiwanese descent who were either born in Japan or moved there during Japan's colonial era—were special permanent residents.[23]

The Koreans and Taiwanese are classified as special permanent residents because Japan operates on the principle of *jus sanguinis* (citizenship by descent) rather than *jus soli*, which grants citizenship based on where a person was born. When a child is born to a mother or father who is a Japanese national, the child automatically has Japanese citizenship. Dual citizenship is technically prohibited (but often ignored), and the law states that "a Japanese national having foreign nationality shall choose either of the nationalities before he or she reaches 22 years of age." Dual citizenship received considerable news coverage in late 2016 when Renho—the Democratic Party leader who uses a single name—was found to have both Taiwanese and Japanese citizenship.

Recruiting talent

Japan has several programs to recruit foreign talent on a temporary basis. These include trainees who provide manual labor in factories; nurses who work in hospitals and homes for the elderly; and, more recently, top international talent through the Highly Skilled Foreign Professional (HSFP) scheme.

Each of these initiatives has had significant problems. More than 300 trainees have died since 1992, and the foreign trainee program was cited in the U.S. State Department's 2014 Trafficking in Persons Report. Only 10%–15% of the foreign nurses pass a written, Japanese-language examination. And interviews with five Japanese-speaking foreign university professors applying for HSFP visas revealed an application process that was opaque, confusing and inconsistent.[24]

The situation is equally bleak when it comes to attracting foreigners to settle permanently. Between 2006 and 2015, an average of 11,800 foreigners became naturalized Japanese citizens each year.[25] By comparison, the United States granted legal permanent residency to 1 million people and made 653,000 people naturalized American citizens in the year ended September 30, 2014.

There is widespread public awareness of Japan's demographic problems, but there is limited research into attitudes toward immigration. A 2013 paper by David Green and Yoshihiko Kadoya sought to test the widely held assumption that Japanese people opposed immigration. Green and Kadoya found that while perceptions of immigrants remained "generally negative," Japanese people with higher English conversational skills had more favorable attitudes toward immigrants. With the exception of Kobe and Osaka, individuals who lived in cities of more than 200,000 residents had more positive views about immigration, as did younger people.[26] These conclusions are worth considering if you are a foreigner thinking of living outside Japan's big cities.

Concentrating

Japanese people are moving to big cities. Between 2010 and 2015, the population of Tokyo's 23 wards rose 3.7%, while Yokohama added 1.0%, Osaka gained 1.0% and Nagoya increased 1.4%.

Forty of Japan's 47 prefectures experienced out-migration in 2016, with Hokkaido, Kumamoto and Hyogo each losing more than 6,700 people. Only Tokyo, Kanagawa, Chiba and Saitama (which comprise Greater Tokyo), Aichi, Osaka and Fukuoka gained residents.[27]

Regional variations

The process of concentration will influence the number, composi-
tion and size of households. For instance, between 2010 and 2035,
the number of households nationwide is expected to shrink 4.4%, to
49.6 million. But Akita will drop 21.4%, while Tokyo rises 3.6% and
Okinawa jumps 13.1%.

Over the same period, the number of households comprising a single person aged over 65 will increase 53.1%, to 7.6 million. But these
households will rise 12.8% in Koichi, 61.0% in Tokyo and 92.3% in
Okinawa.

Net migration from nonmetropolitan areas to Tokyo, Nagoya and Osaka

Thousands of people

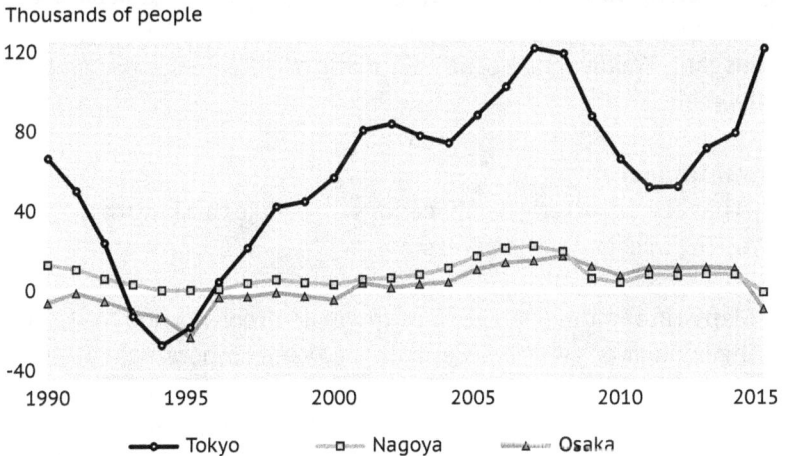

Note: Tokyo includes Saitama, Chiba, Tokyo and Kanagawa prefectures.
Nagoya includes Gifu, Aichi and Mie. Osaka includes Kyoto, Osaka, Hyogo and Nara.

Source: Population Statistics of Japan 2017, Government of Japan.

Between 2010 and 2035, Japan's mean household size will fall from
2.42 to 2.20 persons, with an average of 1.87 people in Tokyo and 2.59
in Yamagata.[28]

Greater Tokyo is the main beneficiary of Japan's migration patterns. Tokyo is a transport, commercial and cultural hub and home to the national government and many leading universities. Tokyo is a magnet for young people, who are attracted to its cosmopolitan lifestyle and career opportunities.

This migration pattern has two major effects. First, when women move to big cities, they have fewer children. In 2014, for example, the fertility rate for Tokyo was 1.15, versus 1.86 for Okinawa.[29] This exacerbates Japan's overall demographic decline.

Second, it accelerates the depopulation of rural areas. One study forecasts that if migration trends continued at their present rate, by 2040 the female population aged 20–39 would fall 50% or more in half of Japan's municipalities. Some 523 municipalities—or 29.1% of the total—were in danger of falling below 10,000 people and faced the "possibility of disappearance."[30] Communities in Hokkaido, Aomori, Yamagata, Wakayama, Tottori, Shimane and Kochi are particularly vulnerable.

Rural impact
This has several practical implications for people thinking of living or investing in depopulating areas.

▲ Many rural municipalities face financial problems due to shrinking populations—with fewer individual and corporate taxpayers—and aging residents, who require more social security spending. That forces cities to cut budgets, including maintenance for roads, bridges and tunnels. Much of Japan's infrastructure was built during the 1960s and 1970s and is approaching the end of its useful life. Without repairs, people could be hurt or killed as critical infrastructure fails. Cities could also be isolated from neighboring communities.

▲ A 2014 survey found there was a severe shortage of obstetricians in Fukushima, Chiba, Gifu, Wakayama, Hiroshima, Yamaguchi, Kagawa, Kumamto and Oita.[31] Rural areas also face a shortage of pediatricians because young doctors are not replacing older practitioners when they retire.

⏶ Some products and services are becoming harder to find. For instance, between 2005 and 2015, an average of 20 gas stations closed each week in Japan, many of them in rural areas.[32] It's common for these businesses, which often sell kerosene for heating, to have old, underground storage tanks that need to be replaced and elderly owners who are ready to retire.

⏶ The institutions that hold neighborhoods together are disappearing. Japan currently closes 500 schools each year, which hurts local businesses and removes disaster evacuation centers from the community.[33] Meanwhile, a quarter of Japan's 77,000 Buddhist temples don't have a priest, and 40% are expected to be closed by 2040.[34]

⏶ As the population density falls, it costs more on a per-person basis to provide services such as drinking water and garbage removal. This adds to the municipality's financial woes, prompting more people to leave, fueling a vicious circle of fewer taxpayers funding fewer services.

Yubari

Located in Hokkaido, just 100 kilometers from Niseko's ski slopes, Yubari illustrates the challenges confronting Japan's small towns. In 2006, the former coal mining hub was the first municipality in Japan to declare bankruptcy with debts of ¥32 billion. From a peak of 120,000 in the 1960s, the population slid to about 9,000, nearly half of whom are over 65.[35] Through death and migration, Yubari continues to lose about 500 people each year.

Yubari took drastic measures to survive. The number of city employees was slashed from 260 to under 100,[36] bus and snow removal services were cut, the local hospital was downgraded to a clinic and 275 families were relocated from public housing on the outskirts of Yubari to a new, central location. Today, Yubari's residents pay some of the highest taxes and receive the lowest level of public services in Japan. Debts of about ¥25 billion must be repaid by 2027.

YOUR NEW HOME

THE BUYING PROCESS

A logical place to start the buying process is to set a budget, which will help you determine what kind of home you can afford. As a reference point, in 2016 the average price of a new condominium in the Tokyo Metropolitan Area (Tokyo plus Chiba, Kanagawa and Saitama prefectures) was ¥54.9 million.[1]

Pre-owned condominium prices in Greater Tokyo

Million ¥

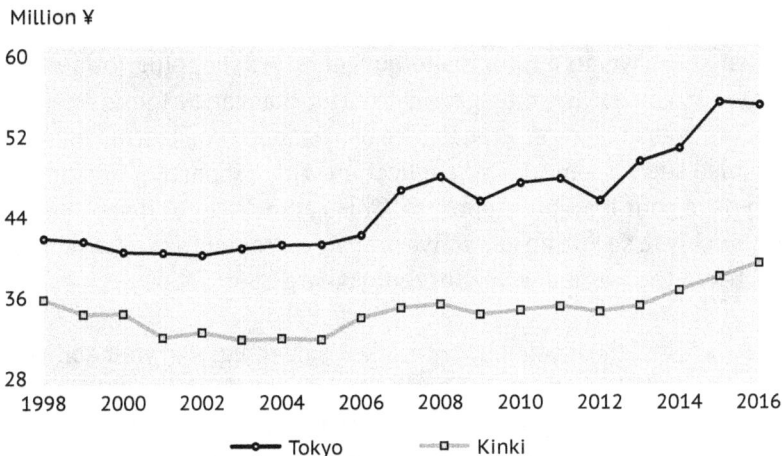

Note: Tokyo includes Saitama, Chiba, Tokyo and Kanagawa prefectures.
Kinki includes Osaka, Hyogo, Kyoto, Nara, Shiga and Wakayama.

Source: Real Estate in Japan 2017 and the Real Estate Economic Institute

Then visit one of the internet listing sites to see what is available at that price. With different combinations of building age, floor space, neighborhood, distance from the nearest train station and commuting time, you should locate a few homes that meet your requirements and preferences. Find two or three examples to eliminate outliers, such as condominiums that have been deeply discounted because of a recent death.

When you find a property that fits your needs and budget, add 7%–8% to the asking price for closing costs. These include taxes and registration fees, brokerage charges, mortgage origination and appraisal fees, insurance and moving costs. You may want to add 1%–2% for new furniture, appliances or decorations and unexpected delays and other contingencies. If you are buying a condominium, your budget should include the monthly condominium management (*kanri-hi*) and building repair (*shuzen tsumitate kin*) fees as well as land rental, parking, rooftop usage, cable TV and internet fees, if applicable. You may also need to pay monthly or annual dues to the local neighborhood association. For sample budgets, see "Choosing a Location" and "Investment Property."

When you have an approximate budget, start shopping for a mortgage. You can use the mortgage calculator that can be found on many lenders' websites to get a rough idea of how much you can borrow. You can also submit a mortgage application with supporting documents and have your loan pre-approved. This can be helpful if you need to act quickly to secure an attractive property. Pre-approval also demonstrates to the agent and vendor that you are a serious buyer.

Knowledge of the local housing market, sale prices and your ability to borrow will help you decide whether buying a home is a viable option. If it isn't and you would still like exposure to the real estate market, you can buy an investment property, stocks, mutual funds or real estate investment trusts (J-REITs).

Price information

Japan's real estate markets are notoriously opaque. A 2004 study concluded that imperfect information added ¥1 million in search activities to the cost of buying a used condominium in Tokyo.[2] Several companies are using the internet and artificial intelligence to improve the collection and dissemination of information, but Japan continues to lag behind markets such as the United States.

Transaction prices and valuations from real estate appraisers (who use the cost, income and comparable appraisal methods) are usually kept secret. If you are applying for a mortgage, the lender will have the property appraised. You will pay for the appraisal, but the lender will not share the results with you.

To further confuse matters, transaction prices and appraised values differ from the values used to calculate property taxes. As a result, one property can have many valid prices.

Despite the market's inefficiency, local investors have both money and expertise. There is usually a good reason for a property to sell at a discount. Problem properties can present an opportunity for a knowledgeable buyer, but for the unsuspecting they can be a costly, time-consuming nightmare.

Many buyers rely on free magazines such as *Suumo* for listings and market information. If you have chosen a neighborhood, real estate agents' window displays offer current, locally relevant listings.

The Ministry of Land, Infrastructure, Transport and Tourism (MLIT) has a bilingual website with sales data and monthly reports. Similar information is available from the Land Institute of Japan and the Japan Real Estate Institute.

Japan has a service called REINS (real estate information network system) that is similar to the listing website used by real estate agents in Canada and the United States. But unlike the North American site, REINS is only available to licensed real estate firms.

The MLIT has extensive plans to modernize Japan's real estate industry. This includes more emphasis on technology and encouraging the use of home inspectors to stimulate sales of pre-owned homes.

Buying a pre-owned home

1. The buyer sets a budget and determines his requirements, including size and location.

2. If financing is required, the buyer researches lending rates and terms, and shortlists lenders.

3. The buyer submits a mortgage application with supporting personal documents to the lender and receives pre-approval (optional).

4. The buyer finds a suitable neighborhood, building or home.

5. The buyer signs a contract appointing the real estate agent to negotiate on his behalf.

6. The real estate agent negotiates the price, closing date and other terms with the vendor.

7. The real estate agent makes a purchase offer to the vendor.

8. The vendor accepts the purchase offer.

9. The real estate agent reads the explanation of important matters (*juyou jikou setsumeisho*).

10. The buyer, the vendor and their real estate agents execute a sale and purchase (S&P) agreement. The buyer pays a deposit to the vendor, who issues a receipt. The property is removed from the market until the sale closes or is canceled.

11. The buyer submits a mortgage application (with supporting personal and property documents, and copies of the S&P agreement and explanation of important matters) to the lender for formal approval.

12. The lender reviews the mortgage application, appraises the home and approves the mortgage. A guarantor is arranged, if needed.

13. If required by the lender, the buyer joins a group life insurance plan.

14. The sale closes. Taxes and other costs are prorated to the closing date. The balance of the purchase price is transferred to the vendor, who surrenders the keys and title. The buyer pays the real estate agent's commission and judicial scrivener's fee, arranges fire insurance and takes possession of the property.

15. The judicial scrivener registers the property in the buyer's name at the Legal Affairs Bureau and pays the registration and license tax on behalf of the buyer.

16. The buyer inspects the property to ensure everything is as recorded in the fixture checklist.

17. The buyer pays the real estate acquisition tax, if applicable.

Shopping for a home

With the results of a mortgage calculator or a pre-approved mortgage, you can begin shopping for a home. Return to the internet listing sites and dig a little deeper: Compare trendy and less-desirable neighborhoods, old and new buildings, prestigious and second-tier builders, and houses and condominiums. These websites will also help you gauge the premium for living on a prestigious train or subway line, near a train or subway station, or close to the city center.

This information will help you narrow your search to one or two neighborhoods. Wander around the area and consult friends, relatives and co-workers who live nearby. When you are confident that you would like to live in the district, arrange to view prospective homes.

If the agent is finding properties for you, give him a clear written explanation of what you want. This will avoid confusion and make it easier to brief a second agent, if necessary.

When you have found a suitable property, you will sign an agreement appointing the agent to act on your behalf. This is a significant commitment for the agent, who is unlikely to sign a contract unless he believes you are serious, likely to complete the purchase and able to qualify for financing.

Real estate agents

At the end of fiscal 2015, more than 123,000 firms were licensed under the Building Lots and Buildings Transaction Business Law. More than 85% of the licenses were held by individuals.[3]

Smaller real estate firms (*takuchi tatemono torihiki gyousha*) focus on specific neighborhoods and congregate around train and subway stations. Their local knowledge can help you avoid problems like large redevelopment and infrastructure projects. In addition, agents often know about attractive properties that never appear on the internet.

Real estate agents charge a standard sales commission of 3%, plus ¥60,000. Both of these amounts are subject to consumption tax, which is currently 8%. A person buying a ¥10 million apartment would pay commission of ¥324,000 + ¥68,400 = ¥392,400. This commission structure gives agents little incentive to market old, rundown homes—some of which sell for as little as ¥2 million—or to provide much customer service. That includes answering buyers' questions about asbestos or seismic damage.

Traditional real estate agencies face growing competition from internet-based services.

Discounts can sometimes be negotiated, and agents may simultaneously represent and receive commissions from both the buyer and seller. If you buy a new home (whether completed or off-the-plan) from a developer or from a tied agent, you don't pay sales commission. But remember that the agent is working for the developer, not you.

Agents are prohibited from disclosing pricing information they have learned from dealings with a third party. A broker has a duty of care to the buyer or seller under the Real Estate Transactions Business Law, including the duty to disclose important information about the subject property.

Agents are licensed by the government and must renew their license every five years. Licenses use this format: Hyogo (4) 12345. Hyogo is the prefecture where the license was issued, (4) indicates the license has been renewed four times and 12345 is the license number.

Because it is difficult to pass the real estate agent's exam, the person handling your purchase may not be a licensed agent. The company owner may not hold a license, either. But the person who reads the explanation of important matters must be a licensed agent.

Three types of brokerage agreements apply to property sales. In an exclusive agreement, only the appointed agency may sell the property, and the vendor cannot sell the property to a buyer she has found independently. In a semi-exclusive agreement, only the appointed agency may sell the property, but the vendor can sell the property to a buyer she has found. A general agreement lets the vendor sell the property through multiple agencies and to buyers she has found. Agents like exclusive agreements because they can collect a commission from the buyer and vendor. For this reason, some agents only show properties for which they have an exclusive contract.

In Japan, it is illegal for an agent to offer a property that he knows is unavailable. However, unscrupulous agents use bait-and-switch techniques: advertising a home at a bargain price, then telling prospective buyers it has been sold and trying to sell them another more expensive dwelling.

Agents can be skilled in manipulating buyers' perceptions. Beware what Professor Robert B. Cialdini calls "setup properties" in his book *Influence: The Psychology of Persuasion*. Agents will show you ugly, overpriced homes to set your expectations before showing you nicer, better priced ones. The second group will seem far more appealing after you've seen the first batch, even if the second group isn't particularly attractive.

Duke University Professor Dan Ariely describes another technique for focusing a buyer's attention. The agent shows a customer three desirable, similarly priced homes: two colonial and a contemporary. One of the colonial homes, which Ariely calls the "decoy," needs repairs and is offered at a discount. The decoy serves as a point of comparison and makes the customer more likely to ignore the contemporary and buy the un-discounted colonial home.[4]

The agent will prepare a nonbinding offer (*kaitsuke shomei*, also known as a *fudosan kounyu moushikomisho*). If the property is desirable and competitively priced, the agent may include background on you, such as your health and employment history, how long you have been searching and your ratio of cash to borrowed funds. This information differentiates you from competing bidders and demonstrates that you are a serious buyer who is likely to obtain financing.

If you are shown a desirable, attractively priced property, you may have to decide to buy it on the spot. The more you know about prices for comparable properties, the neighborhood and the market in general, the better prepared you will be to assess the risk in such a decision. It also helps to know that your bank is willing to lend you money and how much they will lend.

Price is the key negotiating point with pre-owned properties, followed by the size of the deposit (also known as earnest money) and the buyer's ability to arrange financing. If the property has been on the market for some time, a cash offer can make it easier for the agent to negotiate a discount. Because Japanese buyers prefer new homes and fewer new homes are being built, many developers refuse to negotiate on price. However, it may be possible to negotiate other concessions.

Buying from the elderly

Seniors own much of Japan's residential property. In 2003, about 80% of elderly people lived in freestanding homes.[5] Over 89% of the elderly own their homes, with the land under these dwellings representing a large proportion of the households' wealth.[6]

In the United States, Britain and other countries, as couples age and their children become adults, many people sell their house, move into a smaller home and use the sale proceeds to fund their retirement. Retirees often downsize from a detached home to a condominium or a retirement community, where someone else can handle the maintenance and repairs.

Because of Japan's small market for pre-owned homes, elderly people frequently live in houses that no longer meet their needs. These homes are often too big, are expensive to heat and cool and are difficult for an elderly person to clean and maintain. In addition, many four- and five-story buildings in 1960s-era new towns lack elevators, making accessibility a problem as residents age.

Despite these drawbacks, one survey of new town residents found 70% of respondents aged 45 and above wanted to stay in their present homes.[7] The combination of family, friends and familiar surroundings means elderly people may be less motivated to sell than you might expect. Being a patient, pleasant buyer can sometimes make a difference, if the owner is not in a hurry to sell.

The explanation of important matters

After the real estate agent has negotiated the price, closing date and other conditions, he prepares the explanation of important matters (*juyou jikou setsumeisho*). Several days before the sale and purchase agreement (*baibai keiyakusho*) is executed, you should receive a copy of the explanation of important matters. You can retain a local lawyer (*bengoshi*) to review the explanation of important matters for you.

However, it is not unusual to make an offer, negotiate a price and sign a sale and purchase (S&P) agreement for a desirable, attractively priced property in one day. If you have a lawyer review the explanation of important matters, you will probably lose the property to a less cautious buyer.

The explanation of important matters is read aloud by a licensed real estate agent, who is liable for its accuracy, before the S&P agreement is executed. For a simple transaction, this process can take as little as 30 minutes and can be accomplished over a videoconferencing service such as Skype. The buyer, vendor and their real estate agents apply their registered seals (*jitsu-in*) to the explanation of important matters, and a copy is sent to the lender if the borrower applies for a mortgage.

While the S&P agreement is short and simple, the explanation of important matters is long and complex. It is broadly analogous to the terms and conditions of a sales contract in a common law country, and outlines the payment schedule, warranty terms, title registration and conditions under which the sale may be canceled.

In preparing the explanation of important matters, the real estate agent researches and completes a 46-item checklist covering a range of issues (see "Risk Factors") that could interfere with a buyer's ability to use, enjoy and obtain full value from the property. This includes:

▲ The presence of buried antiquities in the area.

▲ Whether the building has been tested for asbestos and the results of these tests.

▲ The presence of termites in the structure.

▲ Whether there has been a recent death, suicide, murder, rape or other violent crime on the premises.

▲ Whether the area has a history of floods, subsidence or landslides.

▲ The presence of soil contamination, which will cause the contract to be canceled if a house cannot be safely built on the land.

▲ Fire, damage or other structural problems affecting the building.

▲ Leftover items, such as pipes, wells, septic tanks or building foundations, that the buyer would have to remove if he is erecting a new structure.

In cases of soil contamination, the legal concept of strict liability may apply. Under strict liability, the current owner is liable for cleaning up polluted land, even if she was not negligent in causing the contamination. Strict liability may apply when asbestos is found in an old building.

Land, structure and fixture checklists

Before the sale and purchase agreement for a pre-owned home is executed, the vendor completes two checklists. Like the S&P agreement, these forms include spaces for comments, and copies are available for the vendor, buyer and their real estate agents. The vendor explains the contents of the checklists to the buyer, and the buyer and vendor attach their registered seals to the document.

Real estate agents are required to disclose defects, such as a history of subsidence, in the explanation of important matters.

The Association of Real Estate Agents of Japan produces four color coded checklists that are commonly used in the industry.

- ▲ **Blue,** for the equipment, fittings and appliances in a pre-owned house.

- ▲ **Pink,** for the land and structure of a pre-owned house.

▲ **Purple,** for the equipment, fittings and appliances in a pre-owned condominium.

▲ **Orange,** for the structure of a pre-owned condominium.

Fixtures checklist

On the blue and purple forms, the vendor lists the number and condition of the fixtures, appliances and other items that are included in the sale. When the buyer takes possession of the property, he uses the checklist to ensure nothing has changed since the S&P agreement was executed. These lists cover:

▲ **Water heater.** Gas-, electric- or solar-powered heaters; boiler.

▲ **Kitchen.** Sinks, water filter, stove, oven, grill, extractor fan, dishwasher.

▲ **Bathroom.** Shower stall, bathtub, basin, toilet and accessories, bathwater heater, dehumidifier, mirrors, mirror defogger, washing machine pan, taps, drains.

▲ **Heating and cooling.** Reverse-cycle air-conditioners/heaters; split-type or window-mounted air-conditioners; heaters; floor-heating systems; ventilator fans; central heating, ventilating and air-conditioning systems.

▲ **Electrical.** Indoor and outdoor lighting fixtures and associated switches, circuit breaker panel, electrical outlets, doorbell, conventional or video intercom, security system, TV antenna.

▲ **Storage.** Kitchen cabinets, underfloor storage, shoe cabinet, built-in shelving.

▲ **Doors and windows.** Interior and exterior doors, screen doors, shutters, Japanese sliding doors (*shoji*), windows.

▲ **Other.** Curtains and curtain rods, balcony or deck, garage or carport, garden shed, trees and stones in garden, fences and gates.

Land and structure checklist

On the pink and orange forms, the vendor states, to the best of her knowledge, the condition of the building and land. If vacant land is being sold, building-related information may be omitted. If a condominium is being sold, the land-related details may be omitted. See "Risk Factors" for additional information on the issues listed below.

Property condition

▲ **Water leaks.** Previous or current leaks, dates and locations, and remedial actions taken.

▲ **Termites.** Previous or current infestations, dates and locations, and remedial actions taken.

▲ **Corrosion.** Locations, remedial actions taken and possible causes.

▲ **Drainpipes.** Blockage or damage to drainpipes.

▲ **Inclination.** Parts of the building that are not level and the direction in which they tilt.

▲ **Remodeling.** Any renovation work done and the name of the contractor.

▲ **Fire or other structural damage.** Date, extent and location.

▲ **Boundary or boundary marker violations.** Location and nature of the violation.

▲ **Pipes.** Water, drain or gas pipes on the property that are owned by third parties.

▲ **Subsidence.** Parts of the property where subsidence has been observed and work undertaken to reinforce the building foundations.

▲ **Residual structures.** Septic tanks, pipes or foundations from a demolished building.

▲ **Soil contamination.** Pollution affecting the property, including problems caused by previous owners or neighbors.

▲ **Flooding.** Causes, dates and parts of the property that were affected.

▲ **Neighborhood building plans.** Construction plans of which the vendor is aware.

▲ **Noise, vibrations, odors, etc.** Anything that could interfere with the buyer's enjoyment of the property, such as noise from a nearby school, karaoke lounge or train tracks.

▲ **Radio frequency interference.** Radio or television channels affected.

▲ **Neighborhood association.** The name and contact information for the local neighborhood association.

▲ **Other information.**

Documents
In this section, the vendor states whether she has commissioned any of the work listed below and if she is willing to transfer plans, test results, certificates or related documents to the buyer.

▲ Architectural drawings for the original building.

▲ Remodeling or repairs.

▲ Asbestos surveys.

▲ Seismic evaluations.

▲ House performance assessments.

▲ Materials from previous owner.

▲ Name of real estate agent through which the vendor purchased property.

▲ Notes. This includes contact details for vendors, such as propane suppliers, and other information, such as the fact that the company that built the house went bankrupt, for example. This section usually states that the vendor will dispose of any garbage before the buyer takes possession.

The sale and purchase agreement

Most straightforward transactions use a standard S&P agreement, which has variations for vacant land, detached houses and condominiums. These forms are printed by real estate agencies and industry bodies such as the Association of Real Estate Agents of Japan. Detailed contracts are used for large or complex transactions, such as commercial deals.

The sale is legally binding when there is offer and acceptance, which usually occurs on execution of the S&P agreement. In Japan, it is possible to enter a binding oral contract, so buyers and vendors should be careful when negotiating.

Executing the S&P agreement

It is possible to execute an S&P agreement with a signature, but local buyers and vendors use a registered seal. It takes a day to have a seal made at a stamp (*hanko*) shop. The seal is then registered at the local ward office, which issues a card bearing the seal's registration number. The ward office also issues a document (*inkan toroku shomeisho*) that certifies that the seal has been registered.

Buyers usually pay a deposit of 10% of the purchase price or ¥10,000,000, whichever is less. The deposit is paid in cash or by banker's draft when the S&P agreement is executed. It is sometimes possible to make a smaller deposit or desirable to pay more than 10% if you are bidding on a property that is in demand.

S&P agreements often include a clause stating that the sale is contingent on the buyer obtaining financing. Vendors seeking a quick sale may exclude this clause from the S&P agreement. A buyer's negotiating position is stronger if he knows he can arrange financing or pay cash.

If a translation of the S&P agreement—or any other document used in the transaction—is provided, it should be considered a reference.

Only the original Japanese document is legally enforceable, and few Japanese companies will execute an English-language document.

S&P agreement contents

A typical S&P agreement includes the following information:

▲ **Land.** The location, lot number, category and size of the plot.

▲ **Building.** The building's location; structural details, including size, construction material, number of floors, size of each floor and type of roof; and any special provisions relating to the land or building. For condominiums, the S&P agreement will include the monthly management and building repair fees, information about the building's long-term maintenance plan and the deed of mutual covenant, which specifies the rights and obligations of the homeowners and the building owners' committee (also known as the union of owners or *kanri kumiai*). It will also indicate whether the building is on leased land and the monthly rent, if applicable.

▲ **Money.** The total sum payable, showing the amounts for the land, building and consumption tax; the deposit paid when the S&P agreement was executed; and the due dates and amounts of any partial payments. Consumption tax only applies to the building, not the land, and is only payable if the vendor is a company.

▲ **Logistics.** The date the property will be delivered to the buyer; the date the buyer will assume responsibility for taxes, utility bills and other expenses; the deadline before which the sale can be canceled by either party with only the forfeit of the deposit; whether the sale is contingent on the buyer obtaining financing and, if so, the name of the lender, amount of the mortgage and financing deadline.

▲ **Special provisions.** Any special terms agreed between the vendor and buyer, such as an organized crime exclusion clause (*boryoku-dan furonto kigyou sono jitsunou to taisaku*), which protects both parties if the yakuza are found to be involved.

▲ **Description of the transaction.** The names of the vendor and buyer and acknowledgment that they have entered into an S&P agreement for the property described on the date specified.

▲ **Identification.** The names, addresses and seals of the vendor, buyer and both real estate agents. The agents must provide their registration number and the name of their company president.

▲ **Stamp tax.** The S&P agreement will have a space to attach the stamps used to pay stamp tax on the transaction.

▲ **Terms and conditions.**

    ▲ The property is sold on an as-is basis, unless otherwise agreed.

    ▲ The buyer will pay the deposit when the S&P agreement is executed.

    ▲ Both parties waive any claim for compensation if the surveyed size of the property differs from the size indicated on the S&P agreement by less than one square meter (optional).

    ▲ The property and its title will be transferred to the buyer when the vendor has received full payment.

    ▲ The vendor will confirm the property's boundaries when the vendor delivers the property to the buyer.

    ▲ The vendor will transfer the property's title to the buyer free of all liens and encumbrances.

    ▲ The vendor is responsible for any damage to the property before it is delivered to the buyer.

    ▲ The buyer will forfeit his deposit if he cancels the sale before the agreed deadline. The vendor will pay the buyer double the amount of his deposit if she cancels the sale before the deadline.

    ▲ If either party fails to complete the transaction, they will pay the other party a penalty equal to 20% of the purchase price, regardless of the actual damages incurred. If the buyer fails to complete the transaction, the vendor will repay the money received from the buyer less the 20% penalty. If the vendor fails to complete the transaction, the vendor will repay the money received from the buyer plus the 20% penalty.

▲ If the S&P agreement states that the buyer requires financing to complete the purchase and he is unable to obtain financing, the buyer may cancel the sale until the date specified on the S&P agreement without paying a penalty. The vendor must return the buyer's deposit, but no interest is payable.

▲ Issues not addressed above will be handled in accordance with the Japanese Civil Code, other laws and trade practices for the real estate industry. Both parties will try to resolve any disputes through good-faith consultations. If consultations fail, the dispute will be subject to the jurisdiction of the court where the property is located, or another court that is agreed to by both parties.

Closing

If you are paying cash and have made the necessary arrangements, the transaction can be completed the same day the S&P agreement is signed. Otherwise, closing will occur when the lender approves your mortgage.

After the mortgage has been approved, the buyer, vendor, their real estate agents and the judicial scrivener (*shiho-shoshi*) meet at the office of the lender or vendor's agent. The fixed assets tax and urban planning tax are prorated to the date of the closing, and any other adjustments to the sale price, such as tenants' security deposits, are made.

The buyer completes the registration documents, the buyer and vendor execute the remaining sale documents and the lender transfers the balance of the purchase price to the vendor, sometimes in cash. The vendor surrenders the title deed and keys to the property. The buyer arranges fire insurance, takes possession of the property, reviews the items on the blue or purple checklist and reports any defects or shortfalls to his real estate agent.

The judicial scrivener immediately files an application with the Legal Affairs Bureau (*houmukyoku*) to record the change in ownership, and pays the registration and license tax. The buyer and vendor pay their own costs, such as judicial scrivener and real estate agent's fees.

Several weeks after the closing, the buyer receives an invoice for the real estate acquisition tax. If the home is new, an inspector from the Tax Department will conduct an appraisal. Depending on the results of the appraisal and the applicable exemptions, this tax may be waived.

Nonresidents buying an investment property are required to file a "Report Concerning or Rights Related Thereto" with the Bank of Japan within 20 days of the purchase. Buyers are not required to file the report if the property is used as a residence for the buyer, his relatives or employees; to house a business or non-profit business; or if the property is purchased from another non-resident.[8]

Title transfer

In Japan, the seller is required to deliver title free and clear of liens and encumbrances. Title transfer is handled by a judicial scrivener, a specialist lawyer who confirms the documents needed for title registration and submits the application to the real estate registry (*tokibo*) at the Legal Affairs Bureau on behalf of the buyer. The judicial scrivener's fee is negotiable and is typically ¥150,000 to ¥180,000. Fees increase if there are joint owners or multiple liens. Judicial scriveners can also register mortgages as well as land and building leases.

Land and buildings are registered separately. Under the Law of Real Estate Registration (Law No.123 of 2004), all buildings are required to be registered. However some buildings remain unregistered until they are sold.

The real estate registry is open for public inspection. Each entry contains the following information: a description of the property; the name of the current owner and date of acquisition; the names of previous owners; injunctions or attachments issued against the property; and encumbrances such as mortgages, easements and leases. Some records are incomplete because of damage sustained in natural disasters and World War II.

In Japan, it is difficult to obtain conclusive proof of good title. An entry in the real estate registry is evidence of registered rights, but it is not absolute proof of those rights. As a result, a buyer must rely on the judicial scrivener and real estate agent's representations and warranties about the quality of the title. There is no state guarantee of title, and title-guarantee or escrow companies do not operate in Japan. Furthermore, Japanese banks will only lend if they have first lien on the property.

Home inspections

If you buy an existing home, the explanation of important matters will list common problems, such as earthquake damage, termites and whether the home has been tested for asbestos. But you will receive this information after you have made an offer to purchase, so it is worthwhile to learn how to spot issues that would be difficult, expensive or impossible to fix.

When you visit a property, bring a camera or smartphone, a measuring tape, a notebook and a pen. With a spirit level you can check whether building components are plumb. A marble or ball bearing will help you identify sloping floors. See "Property Buyer's Checklists" at the back of this book for more information.

Commercial home inspection services are not as common in Japan as they are elsewhere. Until recently, most Japanese homes were demolished and rebuilt rather than being resold, so there wasn't much demand for inspection services. When you buy an income property or a foreclosed home, you will not be able to inspect the interior if the home has a tenant.

Warranty periods

The warranty period depends on the vendor and the nature of the defect. When pre-owned homes are sold, the warranty period can be shortened or lengthened and the S&P agreement and explanation of important matters amended accordingly.

If problems are discovered during the warranty period, they are resolved through a three-step process that starts with the real estate agents mediating the dispute. If the real estate agents are unable to arrive at a satisfactory solution, lawyers are brought in. If the lawyers cannot solve the problem, the two parties find themselves in court.

Pre-owned homes

For the fixtures, equipment and appliances listed on the blue and purple forms, the warranty is seven days from the date of the closing. Buyers should check everything thoroughly, including seasonal items such as heaters and air-conditioners, that may not be used for several months after the closing.

For pre-owned homes and condominiums, the warranty for major structural defects is three months if the vendor is an individual. If the vendor is a company, the warranty period is one year. If the vendor is a licensed real estate company, the warranty period is two years.

Under the Act for Execution of Defect Warranty Liability, the foundations of new homes are covered by a 10-year warranty.

The balance of a new home warranty can sometimes be transferred to a second owner.

New homes

Under the Act for Execution of Defect Warranty Liability (AEDWL), the warranty period for major structural defects in new homes is 10 years. For detached houses, the warranty applies to the foundations, walls, columns, roof trusses, sills, diagonal members, floor slabs, roof slabs and horizontal framing members, while roofs, exterior walls and openings for doors and windows are guaranteed against rainwater leakage. For condominiums, the foundations, pilings, walls and floor and roof slabs are guaranteed, while roofs, exterior walls, openings for doors and windows and drainage pipes are guaranteed against leaks. Buyers can extend the warranty to 20 years and include parts other than the basic structural elements.

Other parts of a new home, such as kitchens, bathrooms and individual appliances, are covered by separate warranties. These manufacturers' warranties range from a few months to several years. Many builders offer free after-sale maintenance and repair services as a way of enhancing their brand image and maintaining contact with clients.

WHAT TO BUY

In addition to picking an urban, suburban or rural location, home buyers must decide whether they want a new or pre-owned home and choose between a detached house or a condominium. These decisions are complicated in Japan, where people have a strong preference for new things. This includes homes, which are often viewed as consumer goods.

Japan's housing stock

Every five years, the Ministry of Internal Affairs and Communications conducts a housing survey. The following figures are from the 2013 survey, with 2008 numbers in parentheses.

Number—Total dwellings: 60.6 million (57.6 million); vacancy rate: 13.5% (13.1%).[1]

Floor area—National average: 94.4 square meters (94.1); privately owned: 122.3 (122.6); company supplied: 52.6 (53.2); publicly rented: 51.4 (50.9); privately rented: 44.4 (43.5).

Tenure—Owner-occupied: 61.7% (61.1%); privately rented: 28.0% (26.9%); publicly rented: 5.4% (6.1%); company supplied: 2.2% (2.8%).*

Type—Detached house: 54.1% (54.4%); apartment: 43.3% (42.8%); terraced: 2.5% (2.7%); other: 0.1% (0.1%).

Construction—Non-wooden: 42.5% (41.5%); wooden [fireproof]: 32.2% (31.7%); wooden [non-fireproof]: 25.2% (26.9%).[2]

---

* Totals do not equal 100% because some respondents did not indicate the type of housing they occupied.

New and improved

Historically, Japanese homes have had a short life span. Housing is typically demolished after 32 years, versus an average of 67 years in the United States and 81 years in the United Kingdom. Shorter life spans lead to a smaller market for pre-owned homes: In 2013–14, used homes represented just 15% of total sales, compared with 83% in the United States and 87% in Britain.[3]

Several factors support the preference for new homes. Houses have often been damaged or destroyed by earthquakes, discouraging owners from investing in durable construction. Buildings and land are separate legal entities. Buildings depreciate rapidly, while land does not depreciate at all. Until 2005, tax incentives were offered for new homes but not pre-owned dwellings. Many people continue to subscribe to the idea of "one generation, one home" and demolish houses that are still habitable. Finally, homes where people have died are seen as tainted and are usually razed and rebuilt.

In 2008, the government promulgated "The Act Concerning the Promotion of Long-Life Quality Housing," which included new construction standards that accommodate renovations and upgrades as well as programs to promote environmentally friendly designs. Long-life homes also qualify for housing loan tax reductions, exemptions from registration taxes and reductions in real estate acquisition taxes and fixed asset taxes.

The environmental benefits of these houses are significant. One study estimated that an ultra-long-life house would produce 21% less CO_2 and 46% less waste than an equivalent series of traditional houses.[4]

As part of the ultra-long-life house program, the government is encouraging home renovations, maintenance and associated record keeping. This is important because the perception of homes as consumable items, coupled with Japan's long working hours and the lack of a do-it-yourself culture, means basic maintenance is often neglected, unnecessarily shortening a building's life span.

Despite these initiatives, there is still a strong bias toward new homes, which are easier to finance and generally offer better energy efficiency than older units. New homes are also covered by a 10-year warranty (see "The Buying Process") and offer superior earthquake resistance. New condominiums are more likely to use vibration dampers and base-isolation devices between the building and its foundation. Base-isolation devices reduce the amount of energy reaching upper floors and limit the damage caused by a tremor. Base-isolation systems can be expensive, and tall buildings using them often sway in high winds and stay in motion longer after a tremor.

Pre-owned homes

It is possible to find attractively priced used homes, but you must buy carefully. Dates play an important part in the screening process:

▲ Avoid homes built before national construction standards were tightened in June 1981.

▲ Dwellings built from 1990 to 1993 can be interesting, because some developers continued to add expensive extras, believing that the market would rebound.

▲ In April 2000, the Housing Quality Assurance Act (HQAA) took effect. The HQAA includes standards for measuring housing performance, including earthquake resistance, and a compulsory 10-year warranty for new homes. The HQAA also includes a dispute-resolution system for home buyers, which operates through the Center for Housing Renovation and Dispute Settlement Support (CHORD).

▲ In October 2009, the Act for Execution of Housing Defect Warranty Liability came into force. Under the act, housing suppliers must buy insurance or participate in a deposit program so that warranties are honored even if the supplier becomes insolvent. The act also strengthened the dispute-resolution system introduced under the HQAA.

One of the biggest advantages to pre-owned homes is that they are often heavily or fully depreciated. A lot with an old building can be worth less than a nearby vacant lot, because the buyer must pay to have the old structure demolished and the debris hauled away. Home builder Sekisui Heim estimates the demolition of a detached home produces over 36 tonnes of rubble.

Earthquakes

To minimize the likelihood of earthquake-related problems, look for:

▲ Homes constructed by reputable companies, such as members of Japan's large corporate groupings (*keiretsu*).

▲ Buildings that have been regularly and properly maintained. Visible damage and water stains suggest that maintenance may be an issue.

▲ Base-isolation systems, which reduce earthquake damage and the intensity of tremors.

▲ Symmetrical buildings, where the load-bearing walls are evenly distributed.

▲ Buildings in which walls on upper floors are directly above and supported by walls on lower floors.

▲ Homes with reinforced concrete, continuous, mat or pile foundations.

▲ Newer buildings, which are generally more earthquake-resistant than older ones.

You should avoid:

▲ Neighborhoods near active fault lines.

▲ Reclaimed land, which is at risk of liquefaction during an earthquake.

▲ Homes situated on soft sedimentary rock, which amplifies seismic waves during an earthquake. Reclamations and sedimentary rock are common in the Tokyo area.

▲ Buildings that have undergone major structural alterations, especially if there was more than one modification, there are no plans or blueprints for the changes, or the building permit(s) for the alterations is missing.

▲ Buildings that have survived a major earthquake, landslide or fire. These homes may have suffered structural damage that will not be apparent in a visual inspection.

▲ Homes with large internal staircases that can distort the building's structure in an earthquake.

▲ Homes with non-rectangular floor plans, such as those shaped like an L or a T.

▲ Buildings with a deformed roof ridge or eaves, or with tilted walls or sloping floors.

▲ Wooden homes that have been weakened by termites or rot.

▲ Condominiums built, inspected or sold by Kimura Construction, Huser Management and E-Homes, all of which were associated with disgraced architect Hidetsugu Aneha. For more information, see "Risk Factors."

Unlike in other countries, home inspectors are rare in Japan. As a result, it can be difficult to identify problems in a pre-owned home. Older buildings may also use nonstandard fittings, such as odd-sized doors, which can complicate renovation projects. The electrical systems in these buildings may also need to be upgraded to meet modern requirements.

Condominiums

At the end of 2015, there were 6.23 million condominium units in Japan. About 103,000 condominiums, which are known as *manshon* in Japanese, were completed in 2015.[5] Condominiums are usually defined as steel-reinforced concrete, steel-framed reinforced concrete or steel-framed buildings that are three stories or taller.

Steel-reinforced concrete is a popular building material in modern condominiums.

In condominiums, top-floor units, corner units and units with southern exposure command higher prices. This is because:

▲ South-facing units receive more sunlight in the winter and less in the summer. This makes them warm during the winter and cool during the summer and thus less expensive to heat and cool. This advantage is less evident on lower floors and in densely built complexes that receive less sunshine throughout the year.

▲ Corner units have fewer adjoining homes, reducing the possibility that noise will be an issue for you and your neighbors. Corner units also enjoy better air circulation and receive more sunlight.

▲ Top-floor units are farther from street noise and have no upstairs neighbors. However, top-floor units can be more expensive to heat and cool if they are poorly insulated. This problem is more common in older buildings.

▲ The popularity of these units makes them easier to resell.

In November 2016, the government announced plans to increase the tax rate on condominium units on high floors. The overall tax rate would not change, but residents on upper floors would pay a higher proportion than people living closer to the ground.[6]

Off the plan purchases

New condominiums in Japan are commonly sold off the plan, allowing buyers to specify a floor plan, color scheme and interior fittings. Buyers make a deposit of 10%–20% of the purchase price when they sign a sale and purchase agreement and pay the balance on delivery of the finished dwelling.

If a buyer cancels a purchase before completion, she forfeits her deposit. If the developer cancels the sale, it refunds the buyer's deposit, plus an amount equal to her deposit as a penalty.

Developers are covered by insurance, protecting the buyer's down payment should the company fail. If the developer is late delivering the project, the buyer can terminate the contract, and the developer refunds the buyer's deposit, plus an amount equal to her deposit as a penalty.

In general, Japanese condominiums are designed and built to a high standard. But there have been several high-profile scandals, including two complexes in Yokohama and two buildings in Hokkaido that were built between 2003 and 2009 and subsequently found to have defective pilings. More than 1,000 condominiums were affected. For more information, see "Risk Factors."

Pre-owned condominiums

If you are buying a pre-owned condominium, ask to see the annual report prepared by the owners' committee, which will include financial projections for the building and the amount of money in the building's repair fund, as well as information about major problems and long-term rehabilitation plans. You should also ask if the committee intends to raise the monthly building repair fees (*shuzen tsumitate kin*) or retrofit the building to improve its energy efficiency or earthquake resistance.

Some condominiums—particularly buildings in desirable locations where property taxes are higher and those with extensive facilities— have high condominium management fees (*kanri-hi*). Many buyers overlook these buildings, because they prefer to spend their money on mortgage payments. If you don't mind higher fees, these buildings can sometimes offer an attractive combination of price, amenities and construction and maintenance quality.

Measuring up

Japanese dwellings are described by their size, which can be indicated in square meters; in *jo*, each of which is 180 centimeters by 90 centimeters or about the size of one standard tatami mat; or in *tsubo*, which are about 3.3 square meters. When measuring the area of a room, half the thickness of the wall is included.

Homes are also described using the LDK system, where L is the living room, D is the dining room and K is the kitchen. A 1K apartment has one room plus a small kitchen (often comprising a hotplate, a bar fridge and a sink). If the letters LDK appear together, the living room, dining room and kitchen are combined into one room. Therefore, a 3LDK apartment has three rooms, plus a combined living room, dining room and kitchen. A 2DK apartment has two rooms, plus a combined dining room and kitchen.

Older condominiums

More than 1.5 million Japanese condominiums are now over 30 years old. That figure is expected to reach about 3 million by 2025 and 5 million by 2035.

Older buildings have several issues. Condominiums typically need large-scale repairs 10 years after completion and again around the 20-year mark.[7] At around 30 years, most need to be redeveloped.[8] Furthermore, just 6% of mid-rise condominiums erected before 1970 have elevators, and 36% have less than 50 square meters of floor space. Many pre-1970 condominiums are built from reinforced concrete, in which the pipes are embedded. Unlike pipes on the outside of a building, embedded plumbing is difficult and expensive to replace.

Reconstruction of these buildings is difficult. A 2012 report by the Ministry of Land, Infrastructure Transport and Tourism showed that only 200 of Japan's 6 million condominiums have been reconstructed.[9]

Older houses and condominiums often include traditional features, such as rooms with tatami floors.

The rehabilitation process is complicated by the advanced age of large numbers of owner-occupiers, many of whom can't afford the expense, don't see the benefit of upgrading the building and aren't interested in relocating during the renovations. Tenants renting units in the condominium also need to be compensated if they are forced to move.

Height restrictions, sunshine laws and plot ratios, which specify a building's total permissible floor space in relation to the size of the plot on which it stands, are also barriers to redevelopment. Buildings that were in compliance with regulations when they were erected in the 1960s and 1970s are exempted from regulations that were enacted after they were completed. But if these buildings are redeveloped, their replacements must comply with new codes that could reduce the building's height or floor space. This is a common problem for condominiums erected before 1981 in major cities.

You can also buy units in government-built condominium complexes, called *kodan*, from Higashinihon Jutaku. Many of these buildings were constructed to a high standard during the 1960s and 1970s and properly maintained in the meantime.

Leasehold versus freehold

In Japan, land and buildings are separate legal entities and are listed individually in the registry (*tokibo*) at the Legal Affairs Bureau (*houmukyoku*). It is not unusual for a building owned by one person to be erected on land leased from a second person. Buildings on leased land are called leasehold properties, while those on owned land are freehold.

Leasehold condominiums can be purchased at a discount from comparable freehold units. Leasehold detached homes are also available. If you buy a leasehold condominium, you pay a monthly land rental fee in addition to condominium and building repair fees. Monthly rents of ¥10,000–¥30,000 are common, depending on the location, number of units in the building and other factors.

There are significant drawbacks to buying leasehold property:

▲ Buildings depreciate and have short life spans. Your home may have negative value at the end of the lease, if you have to pay the demolition and disposal costs.

▲ If a fire or earthquake destroys your home, you are left with nothing except the proceeds from any insurance policies you have purchased.

▲ Lenders may be reluctant to provide a mortgage for leasehold property.

▲ Owners of leasehold homes spend about 30% less on maintenance than freehold owners, and their homes are less likely to be in sound condition.[10]

▲ There is no guarantee the landowner will renew your lease, which typically has a 50-year term. Japanese homes typically last 30–60 years, however, so this is not usually a problem.

Detached homes

In the fiscal year ended March 31, 2016, 418,302 detached houses (*ik-kodate*) were built in Japan. Of these, 75.1% were wooden post-and-beam construction; 11.1% were wooden 2×4; 2.6% were wooden prefabricated; 9.4% were non-wooden prefabricated; and 1.8% were steel or reinforced concrete.[11]

Detached houses are built by companies ranging from small independent firms, which may only complete a handful of projects each year, to multinational corporations that operate across Japan and sell tens of thousands annually. Smaller builders focus on less expensive post-and-beam and some 2×4 construction. Mitsubishi Estate Home and Mitsui Home are examples of companies building homes with 2×4 frames.

Builders such as Daiwa House, Misawa Homes, PanaHome, Sekisui Heim, Sekisui House and SxL prefabricate house subassemblies using computerized manufacturing techniques. Subassemblies are built in factories, where they are protected from the weather during the manufacturing process. This helps the builders minimize defects, reduce waste and increase efficiency. The completed subassemblies are then delivered to a building site, where a roof is added and the interior work is completed.

Prices for small, basic single-family homes start at under ¥9 million, excluding land. Homes range from under 60 square meters to over 300 square meters and are usually customized to meet the buyer's requirements. Many large builders will also custom-design homes. The time from contract signing to handover is usually between two and four months.

Builders advertise through exhibitions, show homes, websites and catalogs, while their homes are sold through dealer networks. In general, builders do not offer financing, but dealers maintain relationships with lenders and help buyers arrange financing. Large builders will often acquire a plot of residential land, which they will subdivide into individual lots. The lots are sold to customers, who agree to buy a home from the builder immediately or at a later date. Customers can also buy a plot of land independently and then ask a builder to erect a

house for them (*uri tate*). Builders will also erect houses on a specula-
tive basis and then sell them (*tate uri*).

In the past, Japanese houses had a 30-year life span, which encouraged architects to create unusual designs.

Large builders often work with quasi-governmental organizations
such as the Urban Renaissance Agency and local government housing corporations. These organizations sell residential land to builders, which subdivide the land and sell plots to end users as described
above. Some of these projects are integrated developments that include schools, shopping malls, condominiums and rental housing.

Japan's leading builders invest heavily in research and development.
New homes are engineered to withstand earthquakes, typhoons
and fires, and to maintain a healthy indoor environment, with good
ventilation, consistent temperatures throughout the home and low
emissions of volatile organic compounds. Large builders also work to
maximize their homes' energy efficiency and reduce carbon dioxide
emissions through the installation of photovoltaic cells. Many companies offer recycling programs that reuse components from demolished homes, and virtually all builders promote the long life spans of
their new homes.

Wooden kit homes, which are known in Japan as log houses, are available through importers such as Lindal Cedar Homes and Sweden House, which also offer assembly services.

A new development in Kanagawa

A wrong turn helped Jean-Guy Rioux, Jr., and his wife, Noriko, find their new home in a subdivision 90 minutes southwest of Tokyo.

After renting for a decade, in 2000 Jean-Guy and Noriko began searching for a home of their own. A native of Canada, Jean-Guy is an information and communications technology manager who speaks Japanese and has lived in the Tokyo area for nearly two decades. Noriko is a human resources specialist in the pharmaceutical industry.

Jean-Guy and Noriko began their search around Hiratsuka, Kanagawa Prefecture, because Noriko's family lives nearby. The couple looked at houses and vacant lots in the area, but didn't see anything they liked and felt custom-building would be too difficult.

"Some real estate agents we spoke to didn't know foreigners could buy property in Japan," says Jean-Guy. "Several looked like yakuza and a few told us that, if we bought their lot, we would have to use a specific construction company to build our home. It wasn't encouraging."

Then, a wrong turn on a Sunday afternoon drive left them in front of a Tokyu Homes display house. Jean-Guy and Noriko got out of their van and struck up a conversation with a salesman.

"The salesman made it easy for us," notes Jean-Guy. "He understood the tax breaks and incentives that were available and helped us arrange a mortgage."

Two months later, Jean-Guy and Noriko moved into their newly completed home. Situated on a 180-square-meter lot in an 800-home development, the 130-square-meter, two-story detached house has five bedrooms, two of which were converted into a home office. Construction of the development, which comprises five phases, began in 1992.

Jean-Guy describes the home as a Japanese interpretation of a suburban home you'd find in Canada or the United States, but with local touches like a tatami room, a high-technology toilet and an automatic bathtub. The home uses 2×4 construction and includes a garden.

Jean-Guy and Noriko made a 50% down payment when they bought the home, which cost approximately ¥56 million, including taxes, fees and incidental expenses. Tokyu Homes helped the couple arrange a 3.5%, 15-year, fixed-rate mortgage from the Government Housing Loan Corporation* for the balance.

In 2005, Jean-Guy and Noriko replaced their mortgage with a 1.95%, five-year, fixed-rate mortgage from Shinsei Bank. A 1% tax credit from the national government on the outstanding balance of the mortgage meant the couple was effectively paying less than 1% per year to finance their home.

"We looked at six or seven banks, but Shinsei had the best rate," says Jean-Guy. "Shinsei's ATM [automated teller machine] cards work overseas, which was also a plus." While Jean-Guy had banked with Shinsei for more than a year before applying for the mortgage, he didn't think his existing relationship helped his mortgage application.

Jean-Guy and Noriko were happy with their home. The neighborhood is green and quiet, retaining the suburban feel that the couple wanted. Parks and a public swimming pool are nearby, and frequent bus and train services made it easy to commute to Tokyo or to the nearby cities of Hiratsuka and Odawara.

Jean-Guy and Noriko were also satisfied with the construction quality of their house. They experienced no significant problems, and Tokyu Homes made regular follow-up visits to fix minor issues, like adjusting door hinges and repairing scratches and dents. In fact, the only negatives the couple mentioned were the windows, which are double- and not triple-glazed, and that the utility cables are on poles and not buried like they are in newer developments.

---

* The Government Housing Loan Corporation was succeeded by the Japan Housing Finance Agency, which no longer originates home loans.

Jean-Guy recommends buying from a large developer to eliminate the need to deal with small local real estate agents, who he feels are not always trustworthy. Buying from a developer also meant the couple did not need to pay a large deposit to a construction company that might become insolvent halfway through the project.

In April 2010, Jean-Guy and Noriko made their final mortgage payment. On March 5, 2016, the couple—now retired—moved to Sarawak, Malaysia. Before leaving Japan, they sold the home for about half the original purchase price.

Jean-Guy believes the home was a good investment, because of the freedom that it provided. "We painted the house a color that Noriko liked, added a sun room and made many other modifications, without having to ask a landlord's permission," he says.

Jean-Guy also notes that over 16 years, the land appreciated about 8% while the value of the house fell to near zero. "The day you turn the key in the door, depreciation sets in," says Jean-Guy. "We knew this from the get-go, so we have no regrets."

MARKET DRIVERS

In addition to the changes outlined in the "Demographics" chapter, several other factors are having a long-term influence on Japan's property market.

Fukushima

The March 2011 Great East Japan Earthquake, the subsequent tsunami and the explosion, fire and ongoing release of radioactive material from the Fukushima Daiichi nuclear power plant killed nearly 16,000 people and demonstrated how vulnerable Japan—and the nation's nuclear industry—is to a major earthquake. It also caused considerable environmental damage.

節電のため、運転を見合わせて頂いております。
みなさまのご理解・ご協力をお願いいたします。

NOTICE
For saving the electricity.
Moving walkways are out of service.

恵比寿ガーデンプレイス Yebisu Garden Place

The Great East Japan Earthquake created electricity shortages and heightened interest in energy conservation.

Stabilizing, decommissioning and cleaning up the Fukushima plant will take decades. Cleanup costs reached ¥4.2 trillion by the end of March 2016, and in December of that year, the government raised the estimated total cost to ¥21.5 trillion, nearly double the 2013 estimate.[1] Those expenses are being borne by consumers, in the form of higher electricity bills, and taxpayers, exacerbating Japan's national debt.

In the meantime, electricity generated from nuclear sources fell from about one-quarter of the total before the earthquake to zero in 2014. Despite intense public opposition, by November 2016, five of Japan's 42 operable reactors had been restarted.

Most of the electricity from nuclear sources has been replaced by imported fossil fuels that increase Japan's carbon dioxide emissions by about 100 million tonnes and cost ¥3.8 trillion–¥4 trillion each year.[2] In fiscal 2011, Japan recorded its first trade deficit in 31 years.[3] In 2016, the country recorded its first trade surplus in six years.[4]

The Great East Japan Earthquake was a catastrophe, but it had some positive effects. Post-quake electricity shortages enhanced public awareness of energy conservation. Builders began focusing on the environmental performance of their houses and apartments, and solar water heaters as well as photovoltaic panels and battery-based storage systems became more common. Solar farms sprang up throughout the country, and the share of Japan's electricity supply coming from renewable sources increased from 0.3% in fiscal 2005 to 1.1% in 2015.

For additional information about earthquakes and Japan's nuclear industry, see the "Risk Factors" chapter.

Abenomics

Abenomics is a package of economic revitalization measures introduced by Prime Minister Shinzo Abe after his reelection in December 2012. Abenomics includes three "arrows": new fiscal stimulus, additional monetary easing and structural reforms. These measures were designed to replace the deflation that hobbled Japan's economy for two decades with a 2% annual inflation rate.

In September 2015, "Abenomics 2.0," which included proposals to raise the birth rate and improve women's participation in the workforce, was introduced. In January 2016, the Bank of Japan introduced negative interest rates in a bid to encourage lending and investment.

Assessments of Abenomics' success have been mixed. Abenomics has not delivered 2% inflation, wages are flat and Japan's economy remains weak. However, real estate prices in Tokyo have risen, particularly for offices and prime commercial and residential property. Where rental yields of 10% were not unusual for small Tokyo apartments in 2010, returns of 4%–6% are now more common.

Over the long term, Abenomics' greatest potential is its ability to reform Japan's bureaucracy. Relaxed regulations for agricultural land and the creation of National Strategic Special Zones could produce interesting opportunities for real estate investors. Moreover, infrastructure projects, such as the maglev train between Tokyo and Nagoya, will spur redevelopment.

Tourism

Japan has a long history of outbound tourism, but has only recently begun to market itself as a tourist destination. The introduction of tourist-friendly services—such as free Wi-Fi in Tokyo subway stations, multilingual signs and announcements in transport facilities and broad acceptance by retailers of China's UnionPay card—are also relatively recent.

In 2019, the Rugby World Cup will take place at locations throughout Japan.

Japan had hoped to attract 20 million tourists per year by 2020. But in 2016, this target was increased to 40 million by 2020 and 60 million by 2030. To put these figures into perspective, France—the world's top tourist destination—recorded 84.5 million tourist arrivals in 2015, while Turkey had 39.5 million and Japan had 19.7 million.[5]

The 2020 Olympics and Paralympics are expected to be a major tourist attraction. However, Japan has a shortage of hotel rooms. If Japan attracts just 25 million of the 40 million tourists targeted in 2020, it will be short between 10,000 and 24,000 hotel rooms.[6] These estimates include hotels that are now under development.

Airbnb-style arrangements, which are known in Japan as *minpaku*, have benefited from strong growth in tourist arrivals. In April 2016, the national government relaxed the Inns and Hotels Law to make it easier for homeowners to offer their dwellings as short-term rentals. However, local governments have divergent attitudes toward these services. For example, Osaka Prefecture and Tokyo's Ota-ku are broadly supportive of minpaku. Kyoto, on the other hand, is hostile toward the idea.

Furthermore, the current regulatory environment makes it all but impossible for hosts to operate legally. The Urban Land Institute estimates that 99% of minpaku hosts are technically breaking the law.[7]

Minpaku's opponents offer a familiar list of concerns. Hotel companies object to competition from homeowners who don't pay taxes or abide by health and safety regulations. Neighbors complain about having strangers in their midst, security and foreigners not following Japan's garbage-sorting rules. Some owners' corporations have banned residents from listing homes on Airbnb and on local competitors, such as stayjapan.com.

In addition to the 2020 Olympics, Japan will host the Rugby World Cup in 2019. Casinos, known as "integrated resorts," are another potential tourist attraction. In December 2016, the government passed a bill that would legalize casinos in Japan. The bill had the support of many business groups, which see casinos as a way of revitalizing the economy, and cities including Tokyo, Yokohama, Osaka and Sapporo want to host casinos. International gaming operators, such as MGM Resorts International, Genting, Las Vegas Sands and Wynn, are reported to be interested in Japan. The cost of building an integrated resort could be up to ¥1 trillion,[8] and the first casinos are expected to open by 2023.

Chapter 23 of Japan's criminal code states that gambling and running gambling businesses are illegal. However, lotteries and betting on horse, bicycle, motorcycle and motorboat races are permitted, as is pachinko, Japan's answer to pinball. Pachinko parlors are forbidden from paying cash prizes, but prizes can be exchanged for money at nearby booths. Pachinko is a big but declining business. A 2014 report estimated there were 11,000 pachinko parlors throughout Japan, where annual bets totaled ¥19 trillion.[9]

Industry sources expect that pachinko parlors will be able to offer cash prizes. But where the integrated resorts will be large, new projects that include hotels, retail and conference space, pachinko parlors are small, existing operations that could well be driven out of business by the casinos.

RISK FACTORS

Here are some of the more common risks you may encounter when buying or building a home in Japan. See the "Resources" section for information and tools for managing these risks.

Abandoned houses

In 2013, there was a record 8.2 million empty homes in Japan, representing more than 13% of the housing stock. Some 3.2 million of these homes, which are known as *akiya,* are not listed for sale or rent.[1] While many empty dwellings are located in towns, villages or rural areas, they can also be found in big cities. In Osaka Prefecture, for example, 15% of homes were reported to be empty, while the figure for Kyoto was 13% and Tokyo was 11%.[2]

Homes are abandoned for many reasons. Often, parents bequeath a rural or suburban house to a child who already owns a dwelling in the city, leaving the child with the cost of maintaining the home as well as property and inheritance taxes. When the home has little value, and the child has no interest in leaving the city, the inheritance goes unclaimed.

The poor construction quality of houses built during the "one generation, one home" era and consumers' preference for new homes also contribute to this trend, which is set to get worse as the population shrinks. If current construction and demographic trends continue, a third of the homes in Japan are projected to be empty by 2033.[3]

From a practical standpoint, abandoned houses are a potential fire hazard that provides refuge for vermin and vagrants. Aesthetically, they are eyesores that are often in disrepair, overgrown with weeds and filled with garbage. Finally, abandoned houses are a sign of a neighborhood—or a municipality—in decline. That, in turn, means a shrinking tax base and the prospect of cutbacks in essential services, such as schools and hospitals. Ultimately, nearby abandoned houses reduce the value of your home and make it harder to sell.

Demolishing a house, called *kaitai*, can cost ¥1 million or more, depending on the size and location of the home, as well as complicating factors, such as the presence of septic tanks and buried pipes. Some municipalities provide demolition subsidies. After the demolition is finished, the home must be removed from the real estate registry at the Legal Affairs Bureau. This process can be handled by a judicial scrivener.[4]

Authorities are taking steps to address the akiya problem. In 2015, the Diet adopted the Vacant Housing Law, which allows municipalities to inspect and order the repair or demolition of abandoned homes. Tax laws have been amended to encourage owners to demolish decrepit houses.[5] Some jurisdictions offer financial incentives to people who remodel old homes or convert them into commercial or community spaces. These incentives, which usually include covenants specifying how the funds may be spent and approved uses for the renovated building, are available in economically depressed areas throughout Japan.

Antiquities

Japan has 465,000 archaeological sites,[6] some of which date back 30,000 years to the Paleolithic era. As retired professor of archaeology and anthropology Charles T. Keally notes, nearly 70% of Japan is steep mountains, so the density of archaeological sites is very high on the remaining 30%.[7] Archaeological sites can produce unexpected finds: In 2016, 10 bronze and copper coins from the Roman Empire were discovered at an excavation in Okinawa.[8]

You are required to notify the Agency for Cultural Affairs before starting construction in an area known to have buried cultural properties. Unearthed relics must be given to the local chief of police. If a relic is believed to be significant, it is sent to the local board of education for evaluation. Where the artifact's owner is unknown, ownership generally reverts to the prefecture. Developers are expected to pay for the excavation and investigation of relics, although financial and technical assistance may be available from the government.

Maps of archaeological sites are available from your ward or city office. Real estate agents are required to disclose the existence of buried antiquities in the explanation of important matters.

Asbestos

Asbestos is a naturally occurring family of minerals known for its tensile strength and resistance to heat, electricity and chemicals. Inhaling asbestos fibers causes lung cancer, mesothelioma, asbestosis and other conditions, known as asbestos-related diseases (ARD), which can appear 10–40 years after exposure. The World Health Organization (WHO) notes, "No threshold has been identified for the carcinogenic risk of asbestos. Cigarette smoking increases the risk of lung cancer from asbestos exposure."

Asbestos in Japan

Japan was a major user of asbestos. From 1961 to 2000, Japan imported more than 100,000 tons of asbestos each year, with imports peaking at 350,000 tonnes in 1971. The import, manufacture and sale of asbestos-containing products was banned in 2006.[9]

The demolition of old buildings can release asbestos into the atmosphere.

Some 80% to 90% of the asbestos imported into Japan was used in building materials, such as flooring, shingles, ceiling tiles and wallboard. In 2003, the Japan Asbestos Association estimated that existing buildings contained over 5 million tonnes of asbestos.[10] These materials are generally safe unless they are cut, broken or drilled, at which point carcinogenic asbestos fibers can be released into the air. Building demolition and renovation projects are a risk because many contractors are small businesses that lack the skills and specialized equipment needed to safely handle asbestos. The 1995 Great Hanshin Earthquake released more than 26 kilograms of asbestos into the air,[11] and nearly two years after the March 2011 earthquake, levels of asbestos exceeding the WHO's limit of 10 fibers per liter of air were discovered at 17 sites in Miyagi, Fukushima, Ibaraki and Tochigi prefectures.[12]

Asbestos was commonly sprayed onto steel beams as a fire retardant. This poses a risk because, unless it is regularly and properly maintained, the asbestos coating degrades and releases fibers into the air. A 2009 survey by the Ministry of Land, Infrastructure, Transport and Tourism showed that 7% of the privately owned buildings in Japan with a floor area of 1,000 square meters or more had exposed surfaces with sprayed asbestos coatings.[13] The spray-on application of asbestos was banned in 1995.

Exposure risk

Most people who become ill from asbestos do so through occupational exposure. However, children in Japan have contracted ARD from their fathers' asbestos-contaminated work clothes. Nearly 200 people who lived near—but did not work at—Kubota Corporation's Kanzaki factory in Amagasaki, Hyogo Prefecture, developed mesothelioma. By 2007, 124 people working at this factory died from ARD.[14]

In addition to Amagasaki, residents living near facilities using or processing asbestos in Chichibu (Saitama Prefecture), Hashima (Gifu), Ikaruga (Nara), Oji (Nara), Ota-ku (Tokyo), Tsurumi-ku (Yokohama) and Tosu (Saga) have developed mesothelioma. Other hot spots include Sennan and Hannan (Osaka) and the City of Osaka, where many asbestos-based businesses were located; Kure (Hiroshima),[15] which was the site of Japanese naval shipyards; and U.S. military bases, such as those in Okinawa and Yokosuka, which have recorded ARD fatalities.[16]

To protect yourself against asbestos-related risks, research the neighborhood where you are planning to buy a home, paying particular attention to former industrial sites, such as shipyards and rail yards, which were heavy users of asbestos. Second, buying a home built after the 2006 asbestos ban reduces the likelihood of domestic exposure. If you are purchasing an older dwelling, choose one that is well maintained and check for spray-on asbestos. Finally, ensure that renovations involving an older home are conducted by a qualified contractor.

Real estate agents are required to disclose the existence of asbestos in the explanation of important matters.

Burakumin

Some 2 million to 3 million Japanese are descendants of the *burakumin*, people who performed "unclean" jobs in slaughterhouses, tanneries and morgues during the Tokugawa period (1600–1867).[17] These workers and their families were treated as outcasts and segregated in communities known as *buraku*, of which 3,000–6,000 remain.

Buraku are generally found in undesirable locations, such as swamps, flood-prone areas and slopes. Today, buraku are often indistinguishable from other districts. Clusters of businesses selling products manufactured from leather are often the only clue to a neighborhood's past. Buraku can be found in Naniwa-ku, Osaka; Asakusa, Tokyo; and Yanagihara, Kyoto.[18] Hokkaido and Okinawa are the only prefectures without these enclaves.

Property prices in buraku are generally lower, and public works projects often take longer than in other precincts, so Japanese buyers avoid these areas. Lists of buraku are also reported to be circulating on the internet.

Official discrimination against burakumin ended in the Meiji era (1868–1912), but burakumin routinely face prejudice today. Families will hire private investigators to check the family register (*koseki*) of prospective spouses to ensure they have no burakumin ancestors; landlords are unwilling to rent to burakumin; and major corporations will not hire them.[19]

Buraku are not shown on modern maps, although they can be found on old ones. In 2009, Google sparked a controversy in Japan when it added historical maps showing buraku to the Google Earth service. After complaints were received, Google removed the offending references.

Conservation

Japan has 4,775 structures that are officially designated as Important Cultural Properties, 282 of which are National Treasures. Half of these buildings are shrines and temples, but the list also includes hundreds of private residences and commercial buildings.

The Law for the Protection of Cultural Properties includes a system for creating Preservation Districts for Groups of Traditional Buildings. This program allows municipalities to conserve historic cities, towns and villages—including those built around castles, shrines and temples—by designating protected areas, creating preservation plans and carrying out renovation projects. Municipalities may apply to the national government to have their districts recognized as Important Preservation Districts for Groups of Traditional Buildings. In 2016, there were 110 nationally recognized districts in 43 prefectures, covering more than 3,700 hectares and 22,000 traditional buildings. Most of these districts are in rural areas.

Under the Law for the Protection of Cultural Properties, the Minister of Education, Culture, Sports, Science and Technology may register houses, public buildings and other structures (other than those recognized by national or local governments) that are in need of protection. Over 10,500 structures in all 47 prefectures have been registered.[20]

The owner of a designated cultural property is responsible for protecting it and for carrying out regular maintenance and repairs. These costs are partially subsidized by the government, and some property taxes are waived. Owners are required to advise the government if there is a transfer of ownership or damage to the property. Alterations to the property require permission from the Commissioner for Cultural Affairs.[21]

Death

In Japan, death doesn't mix well with real estate. Large discounts apply to properties where there has been a murder, suicide, natural death, rape or other violent crime. With Japan's aging population and the number of deaths reaching 1.3 million in 2015, this is going to be an ongoing problem.

Notification requirements

Real estate agents are required to disclose deaths and violent crimes in the explanation of important matters. After two title transfers, the death doesn't have to be disclosed to a prospective buyer.

If the death occurred inside a condominium unit, only the person buying or renting that unit must be told. But if the death occurred in a common area, like a lobby or parking lot, everyone in the building must be notified. Locations where fatal fires, bloody battles or wartime executions occurred are suspect. Properties near cemeteries and crematoria are also unpopular.

This can lead to elaborate charades, like corpses not being officially declared dead until they reach the hospital, to prevent a property from being tainted. It also poses a dilemma for real estate agents, who must choose between telling a prospective buyer about a death early in the process (and potentially scaring them off) or waiting until the explanation of important matters.

Agents selling property to non-Japanese buyers may feel that they can safely omit information about a death. And while it may not bother you to live in a home where someone died, it could unsettle family members and reduce your home's resale value. Talking to your prospective neighbors and asking the real estate agent directly may be a wise move, particularly if a property seems unusually inexpensive.

Dying alone

The aging of Japan's population and shrinking of household sizes have seen a rise in the number of people living and ultimately dying alone, which is known as *kodokushi.* An estimated 30,000 people die alone each year in Japan, with their bodies often undiscovered for days, months or years. Research by Dr. Yasuyuki Fukukawa at Tokyo's Waseda University shows that 60% of kodokushi victims were male with an average age at death of 61 for men and 71 for women. Many of the victims had little contact with friends, neighbors or family. Men are particularly vulnerable because they are more socially isolated than women.[22]

Companies specialize in cleaning homes where someone has died alone. This involves removing the deceased's personal effects as well as thoroughly cleaning the unit, a process that can cost ¥100,000 and up, depending on the size and condition of the dwelling.[23] Insurance companies offer policies that reimburse landlords for expenses and lost income when a tenant dies in their home.

Suicide

After hovering near 30,000 per year for more than two decades, Japan's suicide rate fell to 23,121 in 2015. That same year, suicide became the leading cause of death for people aged between 15 and 39.

When someone commits suicide in rented accommodations, landlords often charge the family a "purification" fee, plus renovation costs and lost rent. A support group called "Zenkoku Jishiizoku Renrakukai" helps families manage these claims, which can amount to millions of yen.[24] Rents in homes where a death has occurred are typically discounted 20% to 30%.

Defective design and construction

In November 2005, an architect (*kenchikushi*) named Hidetsugu Aneha was found to have falsified design data for 99 condominiums and hotels in 18 prefectures, mainly Tokyo, Kanagawa and Chiba. Many of the buildings—including condominiums sold under the Grand Stage brand—had a fraction of the earthquake resistance specified by the Building Standard Law and were rebuilt or demolished. Several companies, including developer Huser Ltd. and Kimura Construction Co., declared bankruptcy, leaving hundreds of buyers with uninhabitable homes and unpaid mortgages. The government provided some financial support to buyers and, in December 2006, Aneha was sentenced to five years in prison and a ¥1.8 million fine, and stripped of his architect's license.[25]

Post-Aneha amendments

After the Aneha scandal, the Building Standard Law was amended to require an expert review of structural calculations for reinforced concrete buildings over 20 meters in height. Interim inspections were mandated for apartment buildings that are three or more stories tall.[26] The government also increased penalties for architects found guilty of professional misconduct.

In 2007, the Housing Quality Assurance Act was amended to include the Act for Execution of Defect Warranty Liability. The amendment requires that developers buy insurance or participate in a deposit program, so that buyers will be covered by a 10-year warranty even if the developer becomes insolvent.

Piling scandals

In 2013, a condominium in Yokohama was found to be tilting because 19 of its pilings did not reach bedrock. The project was developed by Sumitomo Realty & Development and designed and built by Kumagai Gumi. Residents rejected a plan to rebuild the 262-unit complex in 2016.[27]

Another construction scandal erupted in 2015, when one of the four buildings in the 705-unit Park City Lala Yokohama residential complex was found to be tilting because eight of the condominium's 52 piles did not reach or barely reached bedrock. Residents subsequently voted to rebuild the entire complex, which was built in 2007 by Sumitomo Mitsui Construction for developer Mitsui Fudosan Residential. Mitsui Fudosan offered to repurchase condominiums from residents or cover their expenses if they moved out while the complex was being rebuilt.[28]

A subsequent investigation determined that an employee of Asahi Kasei Construction Materials falsified data on Park City's pilings. This, in turn, sparked a wider investigation that revealed Asahi Kasei had manipulated data on 360 projects throughout Japan between 2005 and 2015. As the scandal spread, six other piling companies, including Japan Pile, Mitani Sekisan and Nippon Concrete Industries, were found to have fabricated construction data on a total of 22 projects in 13 prefectures. The affected buildings included schools, hospitals, factories and a housing complex.[29]

As these examples show, design and construction problems affect companies throughout Japan's real estate industry, including large, well-known firms. These problems are compounded by widespread subcontracting, shortages of skilled labor that are exacerbated by Japan's aging population, and pressure on construction companies to finish projects on time and on budget.

Minimizing the risks

Buying from an established developer offers some protection against these problems, because these companies are usually more financially robust and have a reputation to protect. As a result, they are more likely go beyond the legal minimum if there is a problem.

If you are buying a pre-owned home, talk to people in the complex and around the neighborhood and conduct an internet search for the developer and building name. A little time spent on research can save a great deal of money and aggravation.

Earthquakes

Earthquakes present several threats to people and property, including embankments collapsing and liquefaction of reclaimed land, damage to buildings and other structures caused by earthquakes and subsequent fires, the release of hazardous materials such as asbestos into the environment and tsunami-related destruction. After a major earthquake, buildings may be uninhabitable; transportation, utilities and other key infrastructure may fail; and essential services may be interrupted.

Japan is a seismically active country, where earthquakes are a daily occurrence. Most are minor, but the 1923, M7.9 Great Kanto Earthquake, which left 105,000 people dead or missing; the 1995, M7.3 Great Hanshin Earthquake, which killed 6,434; and the 2011, M9.0 Great East Japan Earthquake (GEJE), which left 15,893 people dead and 2,556 missing, are notable exceptions.[30] See the "Market Drivers" chapter for more information about the GEJE.

Measuring earthquakes

The Japan Meteorological Agency Seismic Intensity Scale measures earthquakes by describing the degree of shaking in a specific area. The scale range is 0, 1, 2, 3, 4, 5 lower, 5 upper, 6 lower, 6 upper and 7, where 0 is only perceptible by seismometers. In a 7, it is impossible to remain standing, buildings collapse, cracks appear in the earth's surface and landslides occur.[31]

避難場所
피난소
避难场所　　避難場所
Safety Evacuation Area

隅田公園一帯
스미다 공원 일대
隅田公园一带　　隅田公園一帶
Sumida Park Area

Cities throughout Japan maintain evacuation areas for use in disasters.

The Japanese system, which is also known as the *shindo* scale, differs from the Richter scale, a logarithmic scale for measuring the magnitude of earthquakes, that was developed in 1935 in southern California. The Richter scale has been superseded by the more accurate moment magnitude scale. Earthquakes measured using the moment magnitude scale are described as a "magnitude 7.0" or "M7.0."

The Nankai Trough earthquake plan

The Japanese government used the lessons learned in the GEJE to model scenarios for an earthquake along the Nankai Trough, which runs parallel to the Tokai, Kinki, Shikoku and Kyushu regions. The trough comprises the Nankai (south), Tonankai (central) and Tokai (north) sections.

Since 1600, earthquakes over M7.9 struck all three sections in 1605, 1707 and 1854. The sections then diverged, with Tonankai recording a major quake in 1944 and Nankai in 1946. The Tokai section has not had a major earthquake since 1854, suggesting a major seismic event is overdue.

If a major earthquake struck along the Nankai Trough, the government estimates each region would have 32,000–323,000 fatalities and 940,000–2.4 million structures would be destroyed, with damages of ¥169.5 trillion. The entire country would experience losses of ¥50.8 trillion from transport disruptions and lower production and service levels.

Starting in 2013, the government introduced a series of legislative acts and amendments to strengthen the community's ability to respond to a major earthquake and tsunami along the Nankai Trough. The government designated 707 municipalities in 29 prefectures as Nankai Trough Earthquake Measures Promotion Areas, where earthquake-specific disaster risk reduction measures will be implemented. In addition, 139 municipalities in 14 prefectures were designated Nankai Trough Earthquake and Tsunami Evacuation Special Reinforcement Areas, where tsunami evacuation measures will be strengthened.

A framework for the central, prefectural and local governments, as well as public organizations, businesses and individuals to work together in case of a major earthquake was created. This framework covers emergency transport; rescue, first aid and firefighting; medical care; goods procurement and fuel supplies. The government also set a target of reducing the estimated number of fatalities by about 80% and cutting the amount of structural damage by 50% by 2025.[32]

The Tokyo earthquake plan

The government is also planning for the "highly imminent scenario" of an M7 earthquake directly under southern Tokyo. This scenario is based on the fact that a massive earthquake along the plate boundaries of the Sagami Trough happens every 200–400 years, with the last major one in 1923, and a megaquake occurs every 2,000–3,000 years, most recently the Genroku Kanto Earthquake in 1703.

This scenario estimates that 23,000 people would die and 123,000 would be injured; 610,000 buildings would be destroyed; and total losses would be ¥95 trillion.

In 2013, legislation was introduced to ensure the continued functioning of the central government if a major quake hit Tokyo. Chiyoda-ku, Chuo-ku, Minato-ku and Shinjuku-ku were identified as being critically important, and each of these wards was required to take special measures to protect residents and ensure the continued functioning of the government.

The government created Tokyo Inland Earthquake Emergency Management Areas, which cover the Tokyo Metropolitan Area; nine prefectures, including Saitama, Chiba, Kanagawa and parts of Ibaraki; and 309 municipalities. These areas are expected to experience seismic activity equal to or greater than 6 lower on the shindo scale and see tsunamis of 3 meters or more.

Several earthquake-related plans were created, covering business continuity systems to keep Tokyo functioning; seismic reinforcement and fire prevention programs; measures to address traffic paralysis; and initiatives to ensure all segments of society work together after a major earthquake. The government also addressed the need to evacuate foreign tourists if a quake struck during the 2020 Olympics.

The Tokyo plan includes a target of reducing the estimated number of fatalities and destroyed building by half by 2025. To achieve this goal, the government plans to have 95% of the houses in Tokyo seismically reinforced by 2020. The government is also evaluating in-home seismometric circuit breakers that disconnect the electricity supply when an earthquake occurs, reducing the incidence of house fires.

Building standards

Japan's building standards are designed to achieve two goals. In a moderate earthquake, up to about 5 on the Japanese scale, the building should suffer little or no structural damage and still be safe for occupancy. In a stronger earthquake, the building should not collapse and there should be no casualties as a result of structural failure.[33] This is important because 80% of the fatalities in the Great Hanshin Earthquake (GHE) were due to collapsing buildings.

The GHE demonstrated the importance of revisions to national building standards that took effect on June 1, 1981. Of 923 buildings surveyed in central Kobe after the GHE, 35% of those built before 1971 collapsed or were seriously damaged, 40% had moderate or minor damage and 25% had slight or no damage. For buildings constructed between 1972 and 1981, the statistics were 12%, 31% and 57%, respectively. But only 8% built after 1982 were seriously damaged, with 17% incurring moderate damage and 75% sustaining slight or no damage.[34]

Similar data was reported after the Great East Japan Earthquake. A December 2011 article by the Building Research Institute (BRI) concluded "damage to building structures due to seismic movement was relatively little. However, the degree of damage to buildings designed according to the old (pre-1981) earthquake resistance standards was greater."[35] The BRI article observed that buildings erected on swampland and former rice paddies suffered more damage than those built elsewhere. The BRI also noted that nonstructural elements, such as curtain walls, were often damaged in buildings that did not suffer structural damage, and this was particularly true in buildings erected using old construction methods.

Seismic retrofitting is not mandatory in Japan. In 2013, about 9 million of Japan's 52 million dwellings did not meet modern earthquake resistance standards.[36]

Feng shui and Chinese beliefs

Many people from Mainland China, Hong Kong, Singapore and Taiwan subscribe to traditional Chinese spiritual beliefs, including *feng shui*, which addresses the orientation of buildings, doors and windows, among other considerations.

In Cantonese, the number four is a homonym for death. Hong Kong apartment buildings, offices, hotels and hospitals often omit any floor with a four in it, effectively making the 4th, 14th and 24th floors disappear. Addresses and phone numbers containing the number eight, which sounds like success, are prized.

Chinese people avoid buying and renting homes near cemeteries.

Chinese buyers avoid homes near funeral parlors, cemeteries and crematoria. Research by Yeung Yuen-ting found that Hong Kong homes with a cemetery view were subject to a "significant" price penalty. Yeung noted that the discount was greater when the property market was buoyant and in wealthy neighborhoods. She also found that there was little difference in the size of the penalty between homes with a full cemetery view and those with a partial view.[37]

Even if you are unconcerned about ghosts, a home with bad feng shui or an inauspicious address can be difficult to sell or rent to Chinese people, who play an increasingly large role in Japan's property market.

Fire

Japanese homes are often made of wood and built close together, making fire a serious threat. In 2014, Japan had 11,855 house fires resulting in 1,006 deaths.[38]

Electrical sparks and broken gas mains after an earthquake pose a particular hazard, as do Japan's growing number of abandoned houses, many of which are filled with flammable materials. Buildings that exceed the 31-meter reach of the fire department's ladder units require special firefighting techniques. Between 2000 and 2009, the number of 100-plus-meter buildings in Tokyo more than doubled, to 333.

Residential fire regulations are covered by the Building Standard Law, which requires the use of noncombustible roofs and fire-resistive exterior walls, as well as fire-resistant designs.[39] The Fire Service Law covers the installation of sprinklers, alarms and fire-management systems. In dense urban areas, fire-resistant construction is required for buildings facing arterial roads. These fire protection zones are designed to stop the spread of flames and ensure the road can serve as an escape route. Quasi-fire protection zones—which have less stringent fire-resistance requirements—prevent the spread of flames within urban areas.

In general, when building codes are revised, existing structures do not need to be modified to bring them into compliance with the new regulations. These are known as "non-conformed existing buildings" and are different from illegal structures. When a non-conformed existing building is expanded, renovated or repaired, it must comply with the current codes.[40]

However, changes to fire regulations can require modifications to existing buildings. This happened in 2004, when the Fire Service Law was amended to require the installation of fire alarms incorporating heat sensors or smoke detectors in the bedrooms and stairwells of all dwellings. By June 2014, fire alarms were installed in approximately 80% of Japanese homes.[41]

Fire insurance is a standard condition for a mortgage.

Foreign exchange risk

If you operate in yen and a second currency, you'll need to manage your foreign exchange (forex) risk to ensure that a change in the value of the yen doesn't increase your costs or decrease your income. For example, some investors bought ski chalets in Niseko with the intention of renting them to Australian holidaymakers. But the exchange rate ranged from A$1=¥107 in July 2007 to A$1=¥56 in February 2009. As a result, the cost of renting a ¥30,000-per-night chalet nearly doubled, from a low of A$280 to A$526, making Japanese ski holidays prohibitively expensive for Australian tourists.

Changes in forex rates can also work in your favor. If the yen strengthens, for example, you could sell a property whose yen value has remained constant and take a profit on the currency appreciation without incurring capital gains tax in Japan.

It is possible to hedge your forex exposure using forward contracts and other instruments, although the cost of the hedge may outweigh the benefits for smaller transactions.

Hay fever

Each year from mid-February until the end of April, one-quarter of Japan's population suffers from hay fever, an allergic reaction to the pollen released by *Cryptomeria japonica* (*sugi* in Japanese and Japanese cedar in English).[42] Pollinosis, as hay fever is known in the medical community, is called *kafunshō* in Japanese.

The annual outbreak is caused by government policies that were designed to increase domestic lumber production by replacing slower-growing species with straight, fast-growing sugi. Billions of trees were planted between 1950 and 1970, but when cheaper imported lumber became available, the sugi were not harvested. That left large stands of mature sugi that produce massive quantities of pollen each year.

Researchers believe that air pollution worsens the effects of the pollen on sufferers, who spend billions of yen each year on face masks, air filters and antihistamines.

Higher interest rates

Japan has had a low interest rate policy since 1995, a zero interest rate policy since 1999 and quantitative easing since 2001. In 2016, the Bank of Japan introduced negative interest rates. These policies have made home loans extremely inexpensive. In September 2017, online banks were offering variable-rate loans for as little as 0.444% per annum. Rates at Japan's biggest banks were not much higher.

Japanese home buyers have become accustomed to what is effectively "free" money, and higher interest rates could hurt market sentiment.

Furthermore, interest payments on Japan's national debt represented 10.2%—or ¥9.9 trillion—of the expenditures in the central government's fiscal 2016 budget.[43] Higher interest rates would increase the cost of servicing this debt, diverting money away from public works, education, social security and other essential spending.

There are no indications that the Japanese government plans to increase interest rates. However, in December 2015 the United States Federal Reserve raised the funds target rate from zero–0.25% to 0.25%–0.5% in what many observers believe is the beginning of a series of increases. Higher American interest rates could encourage other countries—including Japan—to raise rates to defend their currencies.

Landslides

Heavy rains, mountainous terrain and frequent earthquakes make Japan susceptible to landslides. In 1792, for example, 15,000 people in Shimabara City were killed by falling debris and the resulting tsunami in what remains history's deadliest landslide. In 2014, 77 people in Hiroshima died after torrential rains caused mudslides that damaged or destroyed 400 homes.[44]

A 35-year study showed that landslides occurred in Japan every year between 1967 and 2002, resulting in almost 3,300 deaths—more fatalities than earthquakes in most years. Landslides in Japan cause an estimated $4 billion–$6 billion in damage annually.[45]

Contributing factors

Landslides are difficult to predict and are another reason why it is helpful to understand the history and geology of a neighborhood before buying a home. Erosion and deforestation are contributing factors, and some scientists believe that increased rainfall associated with climate change will increase the number of landslides.

Flat ground for housing developments is often created by removing the tops of hills and using the resulting soil to fill in nearby depressions. In some cases, 10–15 meters is cut from hilltops and used to fill valleys 15–20 meters deep. Some 13,000 developments throughout Japan use this technique, many of them built in suburban neighborhoods from the 1960s to the 1980s.

Landslides and earthquakes

After the 2011 Great East Japan Earthquake, 950 artificial fills in residential developments in nine prefectures failed. Houses built on the boundary between cuts and the fills were most heavily damaged. Hundreds of slope failures were observed in Miyagi Prefecture's Midorigaoka, Oritate, Sakuragaoka and Taiyo New Town.[46]

Real estate agents are required to disclose landslide risks in the explanation of important matters. However, not all residential land has been surveyed, so real estate agents may not know a house was built on a filled-in valley. Many local governments produce hazard maps that can provide useful information.

Megaprojects

Megaprojects are a mixed blessing for property owners. In the short term, the noise, dirt and disruption that accompany their construction can be stressful and diminish the value of nearby homes. Cracked foundations and other damage are not unusual. Over the longer term, megaprojects can revitalize stagnant economies, spur the development of new technologies and create jobs and investment opportunities.

For example, a ¥5.5 trillion magnetic levitation (maglev) train line is now under construction between Tokyo's Shinagawa Station and Nagoya Station in Aichi Prefecture. Known as the Linear Chuo Shinkansen, the train will link Tokyo and Nagoya in 40 minutes when it begins operation in 2027. An extension from Nagoya to Osaka is scheduled to enter service by 2045 and bring the project's total budget to ¥9 trillion.[47]

Megaprojects, such as new Shinkansen lines, can create risks and opportunities for investors.

The maglev project has been opposed by a group of 700 homeowners who launched a lawsuit in May 2016, citing concerns about passenger safety and groundwater contamination. The plaintiffs are also worried about the project's economic viability. That's a valid concern given that the Joetsu Shinkansen line experienced a 100% cost overrun. And as Oxford University Professor Bent Flyvbjerg observes, the cost of megaprojects is typically underestimated, while the benefits are overstated. Flyvbjerg's research shows that rail projects have an average cost overrun of 44.7% and an average demand shortfall of 51.4%.[48] Ultimately, taxpayers foot the bill, with property taxes being a favorite revenue collection vehicle.

Politicians love megaprojects, because they create photo opportunities. Evidence of these publicity campaigns can be found in your local newspaper's archives and your city hall or ward office.

National debt

At the end of fiscal 2016, Japan's gross public debt was estimated to be 205% of gross domestic product (GDP)—more that twice the size of Japan's economy—the highest level in the industrialized world.

At ¥1,062 trillion, Japan's debts are massive. However, much of the debt is held by Japanese banks and individuals, which gives the government some breathing room. On a net basis (debt less government-owned assets) the debt level is over 130% of GDP.

According to the Ministry of Finance, "Japan's unprecedentedly high level of public debt is a key risk. In the absence of a detailed and concrete strategy to achieve its fiscal targets, Japan could face a loss of confidence in its fiscal sustainability, which in turn could destabilize the financial sector and the real economy with large spillovers to the world economy."[49]

North Korea

Since assuming power at the end of 2011, North Korean leader Kim Jong Un has adopted an increasingly belligerent stance toward the West. On August 29 and September 15, 2017, North Korea fired missiles over Japan. Both passed over Hokkaido's Cape Erimo, which is about 100 kilometers from Niseko, before falling into the ocean.[50] On September 3, 2017, North Korea tested what is believed to have been a hydrogen bomb. It was the most powerful weapon the country had tested to-date.

Kim Jong Un is secretive and unpredictable. North Korea's nuclear weapons program is a cause of grave concern in Japan.

Nuclear power

The March 2011 explosion at the Fukushima Daiichi power plant (see the "Market Drivers" chapter) turned the Japanese public against nuclear power.

In fiscal 2010, nearly one-quarter of Japan's electricity was generated from nuclear sources. This was expected to reach 41% in 2017 and 50% in 2030.[51] By May 2012, however, all of Japan's 50+ reactors had been shut down. Despite several large protests and court cases, a handful of plants have since been restarted.

Japan has had several serious nuclear accidents, including a 1995 fire and nonradioactive sodium leak at the Monju fast-breeder reactor in Tsuruga, Fukui; a 1997 fire at a waste bitumenization facility in Tokaimura; a 1999 criticality (uncontrolled nuclear chain reaction) accident at a fuel plant in Tokaimura; a 2004 nonradioactive steam leak in Mihama, Fukui; and a radioactive leak and fire at a power station in Kashiwazaki, Niigata, after a 2007 earthquake. Several of these accidents resulted in fatalities, and there have been many less serious incidents.[52]

Japan's nuclear industry has a history of hiding problems. For instance, a 1999 criticality accident at the Shika Nuclear Power Station in Ishikawa was not reported to the Nuclear and Industrial Safety Agency until 2007.[53] The president and chairman of Tokyo Electric Power Company were forced to resign in 2002 after cases of data falsification spanning more than a decade became public.[54] In 2012, it emerged that Monju's operator had failed to conduct mandatory safety checks on 10,000 of the reactor's components.[55] Two years later, 50 security cameras at Monju were found to be inoperative. When the government decided to decommission Monju in 2016, the ¥1 trillion reactor had been operational for just 250 days since achieving criticality in 1994.[56]

Pandemics

Global influenza outbreaks in 1918, 1957/8 and 1968/9 killed more than 50 million people, and some scientists believe that we are overdue for a new pandemic. Influenza is spread by coughing and sneezing and is usually most lethal for the young and old. The Spanish Flu outbreak of 1918, which killed many young adults, was a notable exception to this pattern.

Japan's crowded commuter trains, growing number of elderly people and overstretched medical system mean an influenza pandemic could have devastating consequences.

Radon

Radon is a colorless, odorless, tasteless, radioactive gas that occurs from the natural decay of uranium in soil and rocks, particularly granite. When the radon breaks down, it produces decay products that cause lung cancer. Like asbestos, radon poses a greater hazard to smokers than nonsmokers.

Radon risk is usually associated with basements because radon rises from the earth and enters buildings through cracks and holes in their foundations. A survey of 700 locations conducted between 1997 and 1999 found outdoor radon concentrations were highest in the Chugoku region of southwestern Japan, where granitic soil is common. The Kanto region had the lowest concentrations among populated areas.[57] Investigations conducted in 2014 found elevated indoor radon levels at U.S. military bases in Kanagawa and Okinawa. One building had radon levels six times those recommended by the U.S. Environmental Protection Agency.[58]

Maintaining adequate airflow, either through open windows or a mechanical ventilation system, reduces indoor radon risk.

Sick house syndrome

Sick house syndrome (SHS, or *shikkuhausu* as it is known in Japanese) is a group of nonspecific symptoms that include headaches; coughing; irritation of the eyes, nose, throat or skin; dizziness; nausea; difficulty concentrating; and fatigue. It is similar to sick building syndrome, but occurs inside dwellings instead of offices and other public facilities. There is no standard clinical definition of sick building syndrome or SHS, but people suffering from either condition usually feel better soon after leaving the building.

A definitive cause for SHS has not been identified, but it is associated with indoor air pollution, particularly from the volatile organic compounds (VOCs) that are found in adhesives, furniture, wall coverings, paint, flooring, wood products, solvents and cleaning solutions, pesticides and many other products. SHS has also been linked to biological contaminants, such as mold, bacteria, viruses and pollen, and is exacerbated by inadequate ventilation and poor building maintenance.[59] Nearby factories, garbage dumps, farms, golf courses, gas stations and other facilities where VOCs are used or emitted can exacerbate SHS.[60]

Developmental factors mean that children are potentially more susceptible to SHS and other forms of environmental chemical exposure than adults. Homemakers and other people who spend a great deal of time at home are at risk, as are the elderly and people with compromised health.[61] Stress and anxiety can play a role in SHS, and some researchers believe SHS symptoms may be triggered by exposure to "chemical" smells.[62]

Adhesives, dyes and flame-retardants found in household items can contribute to sick house syndrome.

Laws and guidelines

The Ministry of Health, Labour and Welfare has guidelines for indoor air levels of 13 VOCs, including toluene, xylene and formaldehyde, and limits total VOC levels to 400 micrograms per cubic meter of indoor air.[63]

The Building Standard Law divides construction materials, including plywood, medium-density fiberboard (MDF), particleboard, laminates, wallpaper, adhesives and thermal insulation, into four groups, based on the amount of formaldehyde they emit. Products in group 1 are banned; those in groups 2 and 3 may be used in limited areas; products in group 4 can be used without restriction. Mechanical ventilation systems must be installed in all buildings, except traditional wooden houses, which are not airtight. Ventilation and formaldehyde-emission specifications apply to attics, crawlspaces, storerooms and similar areas.

Indoor air quality is one of 10 items covered by the Housing Performance Indication System (HPIS), a voluntary program that helps buyers compare homes erected by different builders. The HPIS covers performance levels exceeding the minimum levels stipulated in the Building Standard Law.[64]

Sick houses in Japan
Because VOCs are used in construction materials, SHS is common in new and recently renovated homes, especially dwellings that have been sealed to increase their energy efficiency.

In a 2004 survey of 1,479 people living in 425 detached houses located throughout Japan, about 14% of respondents were found to suffer from SBS. The homes in the survey had an average age of 3.3 years, and the authors note that—based on international experience—if multifamily homes were included in the study, the symptom prevalence might be higher.[65]

SHS is widely recognized in Japan and covered by Japanese health insurance.[66] In the first ruling of its kind, in October 2009 the Tokyo District Court ordered developer Dia Kensetsu Co. to pay ¥36.6 million in damages to a woman who developed SHS. Teiko Okaya suffered from ill health after moving into a Yokohama condominium that she bought from Dia Kensetsu in 2000.[67]

Solutions to SHS typically involve a combination of the following:

▲ Increasing the ventilation rate and ensuring proper air circulation throughout the home

▲ Using a filtration system to remove airborne particles

▲ Removing the source of the air pollution. This can including cleaning ventilating ducts and air filters; removing materials, such as pesticides or adhesives, that are releasing pollutants; replacing water-stained carpets and ceiling tiles that can harbor mold; and allowing paints and adhesives in a newly remodeled dwelling to fully off-gas before moving in.

Soil and water pollution

With the arrival of U.S. Commodore Matthew Perry in 1853, Japan began a period of rapid industrialization. Factories, mines, chemical plants, refineries and other facilities opened throughout the country, especially from the 1950s to the 1970s.

Industrialization

Unfortunately, industrialization resulted in serious soil and water pollution. Minamata disease, for example, poisoned 2,252 people—1,043 of whom died—through exposure to methylmercury in Kumamoto and Niigata prefectures in the 1950s and 1960s.[68] In 1968, the national government officially recognized *Itai-Itai* disease, which was caused by cadmium in Toyama Prefecture's Jinzu River. The first case of Itai-Itai disease, which ultimately poisoned 196 people, is believed to have been recorded in 1911.[69]

Heavily contaminated groundwater delayed the relocation of the Tsukiji fish market to its new home in Toyosu.

Soil and water pollution also affects Japan's big cities. In Tokyo, for instance, a chromate manufacturing plant operated in Komatsugawa, Edogawa-ku, from 1940 to 1972. The plant generated over 300,000 tonnes of chromium slag, which was buried nearby. In January 2013, meltwater samples in a public park near the site contained levels of the carcinogen hexavalent chromium that were more than 700 times the permitted quantity.[70]

The new site for Tokyo's Tsukiji fish market in Toyosu, Koto-ku, experienced similar problems. Levels of carcinogenic benzene 79 times the allowable limit were found at Toyosu in late 2016, after the site was supposed to have been remediated. There are concerns that earlier test data may have been falsified.[71]

Other Japanese cities have similar issues. For example, the Universal Studios theme park in Osaka was built on reclaimed land where 700,000 tonnes of industrial waste had been dumped. Before being remediated, the site had high levels of lead, chrome, arsenic and selenium.[72] Extremely high levels of hexavalent chromium were discovered in Namimatsu Park in Sakai City, Osaka Prefecture, in September 2016.[73]

Deindustrialization

The economic slowdown that began in the late 1980s, combined with the decline of Japan's heavy industries and the departure of manufacturers to countries like China, saw many factories close. Often, the land under the plants was not cleaned up.

According to *Environmental Finance* magazine, over one-third of former manufacturing sites in Japan have contaminated soil.[74] The Ministry of the Environment estimates 113,000 hectares of land valued at over ¥43 trillion are contaminated.[75] Some 928,000 sites need to be investigated for possible soil contamination.

Metal and semiconductor manufacturers, laundries and dry cleaners, and chemical and electrical equipment factories were among the worst polluters. Contaminants typically include volatile organic compounds, heavy metals or a combination of the two. Heavy metals—including lead, mercury and cadmium—and persistent organic pollutants, such as dioxin and polychlorinated biphenyls (PCBs) accumulate in the environment and pose a long-term threat to humans and animals.

In addition to being carried in dust, soil pollution can leach into groundwater, which is often a source of drinking water. The carcinogen trichloroethylene has been found in the groundwater of cities and towns in Chiba, Fukui, Kanagawa, Shiga, Tochigi and Yamagata prefectures.[76] In Taishi City, Hyogo Prefecture, trichloroethylene concentrations of 8,000 parts per billion were recorded in 1984. The current maximum is 10 parts per billion.[77]

Chemical legacies

About 59,000 tonnes of PCBs were manufactured in Japan between 1954 and 1972, mainly for use in electrical equipment. Importing and manufacturing PCBs, which are suspected carcinogens, have been outlawed since 1974, but large quantities remain in storage throughout Japan because of public opposition to the construction of treatment facilities.

According to the Japan Environmental Storage & Safety Corporation (JESCO), a government-owned company responsible for PCB waste treatment, "... most of the banned PCB products are still stored at their holder's sites, and fear of damage to the environment caused by leakage, misplacement or dumping of the wastes is still a crucial issue." JESCO operates PCB treatment facilities in Aichi, Fukuoka, Hokkaido, Osaka and Tokyo.

PCBs are one of the toxic chemicals that were used at U.S. military bases in Okinawa. Others include DDT, dioxin (a component in Agent Orange, a defoliant used during the Vietnam War) and "insecticides, rodenticides, herbicides, inorganic and organic acids, alkalies, inorganic salts, organic solvents and vapor degreasers." Media reports state that these chemicals were improperly stored and discarded at the bases, killing wildlife and making people sick.

Soil contamination in Okinawa is controversial because the United States is returning its bases to Japan and because there have been allegations that the U.S. military has hidden the true extent of the problem. Anyone thinking of buying or renting property near current or former bases in Okinawa should read the work of investigative reporter Jon Mitchell, who has covered this story for several years.[78]

Japan also has illegal chemical dumps, like the one in the Ohyachi-Heizu district of Yokkaichi City, Mie Prefecture. Nearly 3 million tonnes of waste was dumped at the site between 1981 and 1994, including large amounts of benzene, dioxin, arsenic, lead, boron and fluoride.[79]

Barriers to cleanup

Property owned by small companies is frequently affected because their lots are compact, the contamination affects a large proportion of the land, and the owners often lack the money to pay for remediation, which can cost ¥50,000 per cubic meter of soil.

Landowners typically don't want to test for soil contamination because of high remediation costs, the local preference for excavation and removal of contaminated soil (instead of less expensive containment measures) and the stigma associated with owning contaminated land. In a 2003 survey by the Japan Real Estate Institute and Meikai University Graduate School of Real Estate Sciences of residential buyers' attitudes toward contaminated land, only 9% of respondents said they would be willing to buy land or an apartment on a site that had been remediated. Nearly two-thirds would not purchase a property if there was a history of soil contamination.[80]

Reporting requirements

According to the Soil Contamination Countermeasures Act, when a facility using hazardous substances is abandoned, the owner must commission an authorized company to investigate whether the soil is contaminated. The government can initiate an investigation if a site is believed to constitute a public health hazard. Prefectural governments maintain lists of contaminated sites, which remain on the list until the authorities are satisfied that the site no longer poses a threat.

Real estate agents are required to disclose soil contamination in the explanation of important matters. Given the risk posed by some chemicals, researching a neighborhood's history is a sensible precaution, particularly if the area was converted from industrial to residential use in the 1960s and 1970s, before there was much awareness of, or testing for, soil contamination. Local libraries, universities and government offices can be useful sources of information.

Subsidence

Subsidence is a drop or depression in the earth's surface that can create large bills for homeowners, who must repair and reinforce foundations. In extreme cases, subsidence can leave a building uninhabitable. It can also damage sewers, as well as water, gas and electricity supplies.

The Great East Japan Earthquake left sewers exposed in subsidence-prone Urayasu, Chiba.

In Japan, subsidence has many causes. For example, parts of the Kanto Plain—which includes Tokyo and parts of Chiba Prefecture—fell as much as 4 meters below sea level as a result of groundwater depletion caused by urbanization and industrialization. But through regulation and monitoring, the depletion was reversed, creating a new problem. Groundwater levels were low in the 1960s, when the underground sections of Tokyo and Ueno train stations were built. As the situation improved and groundwater levels rose, both stations began to "float" and had to be restrained with a system of anchors and weights.[81]

The Great East Japan Earthquake caused subsidence in two ways. In volcanic regions 150–200 kilometers from the rupture zone, the GEJE produced a depression ranging from 5 to 15 centimeters over a 300-square-kilometer area.[82] The earthquake also caused liquefaction-related subsidence in a 42-square-kilometer area around Tokyo Bay. Reclaimed land in Urayasu was especially prone to subsidence.[83]

In November 2016, a 12,000-cubic-meter sinkhole opened in downtown Fukuoka, swallowing a five-lane road. The cave-in was believed to be related to excavation for a subway line extension and underground water flows. A similar incident occurred two years earlier.

To avoid subsidence problems, investigate the neighborhood to determine if it is located on reclaimed land, is near underground construction projects or has a history of groundwater-related subsidence.

Termites

Termites are an important part of the global ecosystem, helping to break down plant matter and aerate soil. There are more than 2,800 species of termites, about 10% of which are considered pests. In the United States, termites cause an estimated $3 billion in damage each year.

In Japan, two of the most common urban species are the Japanese termite (*Reticulitermes speratus* [Kolbe]) and the Formosan subterranean termite (*Coptotermes formosanus*),[84] although dry-wood termites (*Incisitermes minor*) have been found in 24 of Japan's 47 prefectures, including Tokyo. Dry-wood termites, which can destroy a wooden house, are believed to have arrived in building materials and furniture imported from the United States.

Dry-wood termites are more mobile, harder to exterminate and immune to the chemicals used to kill the subterranean Japanese and Formosan termites, which prefer damp environments. Dry-wood termites often inhabit roofing materials, which should be treated with termiticidal chemicals before construction.

Termite damage can be difficult to detect until it has reached an advanced stage, so a professional inspection is wise if you suspect your home is infested. The presence of shelter tubes, which termites use as protection from the elements and predators, frass (termite excrement) and shed wings are indications of a problem. Infested homes are usually treated by killing the colony with chemicals and then introducing barriers to prevent the termites from returning.

Typhoons and floods

Japan is a wet country. The average annual rainfall ranges from 1,107 millimeters in Sapporo to 1,529 in Tokyo and 2,266 in Kagoshima.

In an average year, 25.6 cyclones of tropical storm strength or greater form in the seas around Japan, with 2.7 making landfall. Typhoons usually arrive between July and October, with August being the peak month. Okinawa is particularly prone to typhoons with an average of 7.4 per year.

Subway systems in Tokyo and other cities are vulnerable to floods and storm surges.

Typhoons and floods have a high human and economic cost. For example:

▲ Typhoon Isewan, which struck the Tokai region in September 1959, was the worst storm in Japanese history. With peak winds of nearly 200 kilometers per hour, Isewan left more than 5,000 people dead or missing and washed away over 4,600 homes.[85]

▲ In September 2000, 535 millimeters of rain fell on the Tokai region in a 24-hour period, an event that happens once every 350 years. The rain overwhelmed flood defenses and isolated Nagoya from the outside world.[86]

▲ In July 2004, torrential rains in Niigata Prefecture killed 16 people, flooded 2,500 hectares of land and damaged or destroyed nearly 20,000 buildings. The flood was blamed on the failure of local levees.[87]

▲ In July 2012, storms battered Kyushu for four days, causing 32 deaths. Some 400,000 people were evacuated and 108 millimeters of rain fell in a single hour.[88]

▲ In September 2015, Typhoon Etau destroyed nearly 20,000 buildings and flooded one-third of the city of Joso, north of Tokyo. The rains also increased radiation levels due to the resuspension of radioactively contaminated river sediments from the Fukushima disaster.[89]

Experts say that Tokyo will eventually be hit by a powerful storm like 1947's Typhoon Kathleen, which killed 1,100 people and flooded the eastern parts of the city. Tokyo is vulnerable because 20% of the population lives in low-lying, flood-prone wards, such as Arakawa-ku, Katsushika-ku, Adachi-ku, Edogawa-ku, Sumida-ku and Koto-ku.[90] Nakano-ku, Nerima-ku and Suginami-ku, plus Mitaka and Musashino cities tend to receive heavy rains.[91] Furthermore, nearly 10 million people live in the Arakawa River basin, which runs through Tokyo. The Central Disaster Management Council estimates that if the Arakawa River burst its banks, the resulting flood would kill 2,000 people, flood 97 subway stations and cause ¥33 trillion in damage.

Governments have built flood-control structures including pumping stations, concrete river embankments and dams that have greatly reduced the intensity and frequency of floods and enabled development in previously unusable areas. But by concentrating the runoff and shortening the period between the rainfall and peak water discharge, these structures can create new risks, particularly when embankments fail or rainfall exceeds a waterway's design specifications.

Low-lying areas and land near rivers, canals and other waterways are at particular risk from floods. In the absence of physical clues, names that include words like basin (*bonchi*), marsh (*numi*), ditch (*mizo*), channel (*suido*) or valley (*tani*) may suggest that a neighborhood is vulnerable to flooding.

Volcanoes

A volcano is a rupture in the crust of the Earth that allows lava, ash and gases to escape from a magma chamber below the Earth's surface. Volcanoes are often found where tectonic plates meet. The North American, Pacific, Eurasian and Philippine plates meet under Japan, giving the nation its many hot springs and 110 active volcanoes.[92] "Active" is a subjective term that means scientists believe the volcano has the potential to erupt.

Risks

Erupting volcanoes produce pyroclastic flows (fast-moving currents of hot gas and volcanic matter); lahars (destructive, fast-moving mixtures of pyroclastic material, rocky debris and water); carbon dioxide; and other gases, including sulfur dioxide, which contribute to acid rain.

Volcanoes create serious hazards including earthquakes; explosions that send debris into the air; lava, lahars, mud-flows and pyroclastic flows that bury or burn anything in their path; landslides and tsunamis; and clouds of ash that damage jet engines and cause respiratory problems for nearby residents.

Volcanoes in Japan

Japan is home to about 7% of the volcanoes that have erupted in the past 10,000 years.[93] Fifty of Japan's active volcanoes are monitored around the clock with seismographs and video cameras.

In September 2014, Mount Ontake, which is located between Nagano and Gifu prefectures, erupted killing 57 people and leaving six missing. As a result of the Ontake fatalities, in June 2015 the government passed a law requiring the 142 cities, towns and villages around the 50 monitored volcanoes to create hazard maps or evacuation plans. In March 2015, only 20 of those municipalities had evacuation plans.[94]

Other recent eruptions include Mount Aso (Kumamoto, 2016); Mount Shindake (Kagoshima, 2015); and Mount Hakone (Kanagawa, 2015). Kagoshima's Mount Sakurajima last erupted in 2016, but has been erupting regularly for the last century.[95] Japan also has undersea volcanoes, like the one that formed an islet adjoining Nishinoshima Island in the Ogasawara Islands, 1,000 kilometers south of Tokyo in 2013.[96] Mount Fuji, which last erupted in 1707, is one of the 50 monitored volcanoes.[97]

In 2014, two professors from Kobe University released a report warning that, over the next century, Japan had a 1% chance of experiencing a colossal volcanic eruption that could endanger the entire country.[98]

Warning system
Real time warnings about volcanic activity in Japan are available from the Japan Meteorological Agency, which has a five-stage warning system—Level 1: Potential for increased activity; Level 2: Do not approach the crater; Level 3: Do not approach the volcano; Level 4: Prepare to evacuate; Level 5: Evacuate.

Predicting volcanic activity is difficult. Media reports from 2014 noted that the Japan Meteorological Agency's forecasts were wrong 80% of the time.

Practical implications
Research your property to determine if is near one of the volcanoes that are under constant surveillance. While this advice is particularly applicable to rural properties and ski chalets, it also applies to urban areas—the Sakurajima volcano is only 10 kilometers from Kagoshima City.

If you are near a volcano, obtain a copy of your municipal government's hazard map and evacuation plan. You may want to create an emergency plan for your family, including a "bug-out bag," and places to meet and methods for communicating if you get separated.

The yakuza

Unlike the triads, mafia and other criminal groups that are organized as secret societies, the yakuza (also known as *boryokudan*) are both visible and legal in Japan. At the end of 2016, the National Police Agency estimated boryokudan groups had 39,100 full- and part-time members. It was the 12th year that the number of mobsters declined, due in part to demographics and new laws.[99]

Yakuza gangs have longstanding connections with political and business leaders. These relationships facilitated their involvement in public-works projects, where protection, bid rigging, trucking and managing labor relations on building sites became important sources of yakuza revenues.

Police boxes, or *koban*, are a common sight throughout Japan.

In the 1980s, the boryokudan became active in Japan's booming stock and real estate markets often buying property with loans they were confident would never be repaid. The yakuza also expanded beyond their traditional, vice-based businesses into debt collection, corporate extortion (*sokaiya*) and bankruptcy management services.

The enactment of the Law Concerning Prevention of Unjust Acts by Boryokudan in 1991 made it illegal for designated boryokudan gangs to engage in extortion and intimidation and gave the authorities a greater range of powers with which to prosecute them. Between 2009 and 2011, the law was supplemented by prefectural yakuza-exclusion ordinances, which penalize people who pay-off, do business or cooperate with the yakuza.

The 2020 Tokyo Olympics and legalization of gambling in Japan involve large building projects as well as long-term opportunities for gang-related businesses, such as extortion, loan-sharking and prostitution.

Property-related businesses

The yakuza offer property-related services such as mediating real estate disputes and land-sharking (*jiage*), a process in which small landowners are intimidated into selling their property so that it can be incorporated into a larger development. They will also use information gathered from prostitutes and other trusted sources to buy key parcels of land in areas that are being redeveloped. The developer will then be forced to pay a premium to the yakuza for the missing blocks of property.[100]

Using the tenant-protection provisions in Japanese law, the yakuza employ professional squatters (*senyuya*) to occupy property. Through senyuya, the yakuza enjoy rent-free use of commercial and residential property; purchase real estate at below-market prices after they scare off other prospective buyers and then resell it at a profit; and collect payoffs for vacating occupied property.[101] Companies will also hire yakuza gangs to evict tenants from office buildings that they wish to redevelop.

Demolition work—including debris removal, asbestos abatement and waste disposal—is a lucrative field for the yakuza. These services are subject to safety and training regulations, which the yakuza ignore. They will hire foreign migrant workers, who remove asbestos without protection or illegally dump toxic waste in rural areas, allowing the yakuza-run company to turn a profit while offering cut-rate prices.[102]

Avoiding problems

Having gang members as neighbors can reduce a property's rental and resale values and cause stress for you and your family, so checking for yakuza involvement should be part of your due diligence process.

Start by walking around the neighborhood and looking for the telltale signs: black Mercedes-Benz and Lexus sedans driven by hard-looking men with punch-permed hair, tattoos and missing digits. As yakuza-owned businesses have moved up-market, so has gang members' image. Fewer now look like the stereotypical gangsters described above.

Consulting local merchants, prospective neighbors, and officers in the local police box (*koban*) and nearest police station may also provide useful information, although these inquiries will need to be made in Japanese. The National Center for Removal of Criminal Organizations may also be helpful.

You should also check the credentials of your real estate agent, advises Jake Adelstein, the author of *Tokyo Vice: An American Reporter on the Police Beat in Japan*. Adelstein says that in 2005 the Tokyo Metropolitan Police Department identified over 1,000 yakuza-run companies in Greater Tokyo, 170 of which were real estate firms.

If you're working with a smaller real estate firm, Adelstein recommends you check with the local government to ensure the company is licensed to conduct real estate transactions. In addition, Adelstein says, "You should also see if the firm has a home page and have someone fluent in Japanese check it out." Agents display their license number on their business cards and websites, and the absence of a license number should be considered a red flag.

Contracts in Japan often include an organized crime exclusionary clause, which nullifies the agreement if either party is connected to organized crime.

Zoning

In Japan, existing buildings generally do not have to be rebuilt to comply with new zoning regulations. However, new rules can make it difficult to redevelop a property or build a new home. Changes to the shadow restrictions (*nichiei kisei*), which prevent a new structure from blocking sunlight from reaching an existing building, make it uneconomical to redevelop some condominiums, because the new building will have to be smaller than the one it replaces.

Similar problems can be encountered with setbacks, which specify the minimum distance between a building and the roadway, especially if the road was widened since the building was erected. Height restrictions (*zettai takasa no seigen*), the building coverage ratio (*kenpei ritsu*) and the floor-area ratio (*youseki ritsu*) can also cause problems.[103]

LOCATIONS

CHOOSING A LOCATION

If you plan to live in the property you are buying, your needs and preferences, rather than just economic factors, will shape your choice of location. Proximity to railway and subway stations, employment, schools, family, shopping and recreational facilities will influence your decision.

For a given budget, city dwellers usually choose between a smaller, centrally located home and a larger one farther from the city center. Urban living offers convenience and access to more shopping and entertainment choices. Drawbacks include more noise, traffic and air pollution. Large cities also charge higher urban planning taxes.

Pre-owned condominium prices in Greater Tokyo

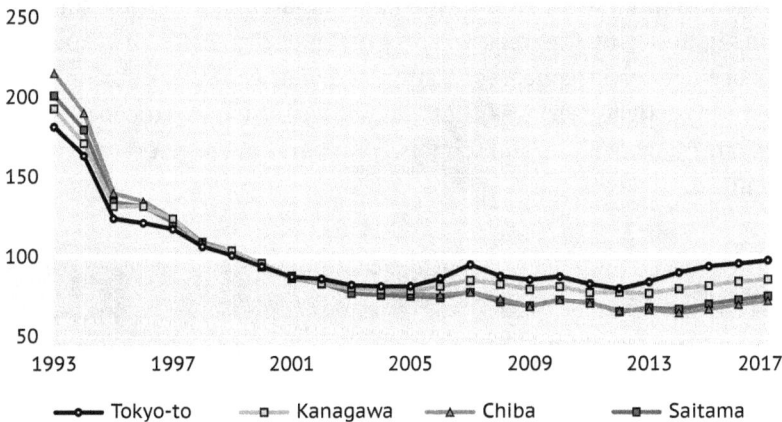

Source: Japan Real Estate Institute. January 2000 = 100.

Regardless of the location, southern exposure is popular because it provides more sunlight. This is both an aesthetic benefit and useful for photovoltaic installations, which are increasingly common in Japanese homes. Hilltop dwellings are prestigious and perceived as safer in earthquakes and floods.

Research

Buying or building a home is a big commitment, so you will want to ensure you like the neighborhood before you sign a sale and purchase agreement. Universities, public libraries and local government offices can be useful sources of information when you are researching a neighborhood's past and future. Older, long-term residents are often happy to share their recollections.

Some people take this a step further by renting an apartment before they buy. Renting can be a good idea if you are moving to an area that is significantly more or less expensive than your old neighborhood. Research by Professor Dan Ariely shows that buyers use the price of their old home as an "anchor" when they buy a new home. This often results in people buying a smaller dwelling when they move into a more expensive area and buying a larger home when they move into a less expensive neighborhood.[1]

At a minimum, walk around the new neighborhood during the day and night, during the week and on weekends. Try the train or subway service between the nearest station and your workplace during rush hour. Investigate services that you will use, such as grocery stores, restaurants, hospitals and schools. Visit parks and other recreational facilities.

Bad neighbors

When shopping for a home, avoid:

▲ Flood zones

▲ Reclaimed land, which is at risk of liquefaction during an earthquake

▲ Neighborhoods with abandoned homes, known in Japanese as *akiya*

▲ Cemeteries and crematoria

▲ Red-light districts, such as Tokyo's Kabukicho, Fukuoka's Nakasu and Sapporo's Susukino

▲ Neighborhoods with a *burakumin* or wartime history. In Tokyo, one such location is the site of the former Sugamo Prison (now Sunshine City) in Ikebukuro, where war criminals were executed after World War II.

▲ Yakuza offices

▲ Flag lots, which are square or rectangular parcels of land that are only accessible by a narrow strip of land. The access path resembles a flagpole.

▲ Current and former industrial zones. The area around the Port of Tokyo, for example, is home to garbage incinerators as well as treatment facilities for sewage and polychlorinated biphenyls (PCBs).

Red-light districts are a common feature of Japanese cities.

For more information, see the "Risk Factors" chapter, the city and region chapters that follow and the checklists at the back of this book.

Finally, find out whether large infrastructure or urban renewal projects are planned for the area. The noise, dust and traffic disruptions that accompany projects like the Linear Chuo Shinkansen can degrade your quality of life over the short term. However, these projects often revitalize fading neighborhoods and drive property prices higher.

Transportation

Homes near train or subway stations command higher prices and rents. They also offer better access to shops, restaurants and services, which cluster around transport hubs. Stations also attract vehicular and pedestrian traffic and the sound trucks used by campaigning politicians and other groups.

Real estate listings include the walking time to the nearest station, which assumes a speed of 80 meters per minute. There are two ways to calculate walking time. The first measures the actual, street-level distance to the nearest station entrance, but ignores time spent waiting at traffic lights. The second measures the distance "as the crow flies" over the tops of buildings and other obstacles. With the second method, a walk that is advertised as 10 minutes can easily take twice as long.

Train and subway stations attract political groups and candidates, and their sound trucks.

A 2010 paper by the Center for Spatial Information Science (CSIS) at the University of Tokyo observed that the price of used condominiums in the Tokyo area fell when the walking time to the nearest railway station exceeded 10 minutes. Prices fell again at the 17-minute mark, the point at which most people are believed to take a bus, bicycle or car to the station.[2]

As people age and a 10-minute walk becomes more difficult, the premium for homes near train and subway stations should increase. The national government's "compact city" initiative—which encourages the construction of hospitals, nurseries, government offices and other essential facilities near railway stations—also supports this trend. The compact city program will drive urban renewal in city centers and help local governments serve shrinking populations more cost effectively.[3]

An earlier version of the same CSIS paper examined the effect of station-to-station commuting time on condominium prices. The authors noted that prices fell when daytime travel between the station nearest the condominium and seven target stations—Ikebukuro, Shibuya, Shinagawa, Shinjuku, Tokyo and Ueno on the Yamanote Line, which circles downtown Tokyo, and Otemachi subway station— took more than 15 minutes.[4]

Education

As in other countries, homes near good schools and universities command a premium price. If you have young children or are planning to start a family, investigate the availability of daycare in your target neighborhood. Daycare admissions are managed at the municipal level, and cities have different eligibility criteria, depending on the age of the child and the parents' occupation and marital status.

The shortage of daycare has become a national issue, as families move away from the "male-breadwinner–female housekeeper" model and more women join and remain in the workforce. In April 2015, there was a shortfall of 23,000 spaces, and many parents simply gave up on finding a place for their children.[5] Prime Minister Abe pledged to create places for 400,000 children between fiscal 2013 and 2017, but it takes time to build faculties and train staff. In the meantime, desperate parents send their children to unlicensed facilities.[6]

Cities vs. suburbs

One of the first choices facing a home buyer is whether to live in the city or the suburbs.

Here are two sample listings taken from the internet in March 2017. The examples illustrate the costs involved in buying a condominium and the relationship between a property's price and its size, age and distance from central Tokyo. In short, if you are willing to commute for at least an hour each way and live in an older unit and a less-prestigious neighborhood, you can buy 12% more space for less than half the price.

Note that fire and earthquake insurance are not included. Example No. 1 uses a fixed-rate mortgage, while example No. 2 uses a variable-rate mortgage. Both examples use mortgage rates that were current in March 2017.

Example No. 1: Downtown Tokyo

This 51-square-meter condominium is in Nishi Azabu in central Tokyo's Minato-ku. It is a seven- and nine-minute walk, respectively, from the Hibiya and Chiyoda subway lines, for a best-case commuting time of 16 minutes to Tokyo Station. The 11-story building is three years old and is constructed from reinforced concrete on owned land. The apartment is a 10th floor corner unit, facing southwest and has a balcony.

Purchase	
Price	¥78,000,000
Plus 10% closing costs	7,800,000
Subtotal	85,800,000
Less 10% down payment	(8,580,000)
Mortgage amount	**¥77,220,000**

Monthly costs	
Mortgage payment (30-year fixed mortgage @ 1.08%)	¥251,218
Condominium fee	14,700
Repair fee	3,100
Taxes (estimated annual tax divided by 12)	34,125
Total	**¥303,143**

Example No. 2: The suburbs

This 57-square-meter condominium is in Tachikawa, in Tokyo's western suburbs. It is a 7-minute walk to the nearest train station, for a best-case commuting time of 55 minutes to Tokyo Station. The 11-story building is 17 years old and is constructed using reinforced concrete on owned land. The unit is on the sixth floor with a balcony and northwestern exposure.

Purchase	
Price	¥34,800,000
Plus 10% closing costs	3,480,000
Subtotal	38,280,000
Less 10% down payment	(3,828,000)
Mortgage amount	**¥34,452,000**

Monthly costs	
Mortgage payment (30-year floating rate mortgage @ 0.5%)	¥103,077
Condominium fee	10,310
Repair fee	4,500
Taxes (estimated annual tax divided by 12)	15,225
Total	**¥133,112**

Rural living

Low prices, abundant fresh air and good quality of life have sparked a renewed interest in Japan's rural areas. If you do not need to commute to the city every day or want to immerse yourself in the Japanese experience, rural living can be attractive. But there are drawbacks.

A rural house with land can be purchased for a few million yen, a price that will seem absurdly low to anyone who experienced the property bubble of the 1980s and early 1990s. The fall in the price of rural property has been exacerbated by rural depopulation and a decline in the number of farmers. Without a reversal in Japan's immigration policy or a spike in the fertility rate, the rural population will continue to fall. As a result, you will almost certainly sell your property for less than you paid for it.

Falling prices and a shrinking, illiquid real estate market make banks hesitant to lend on rural property, and foreigner-friendly banks will only lend on urban property. This can make it difficult to finance your purchase and to sell your property when you are ready to move on. In addition, the isolation and quiet foreigners appreciate is often seen as a negative by local buyers.

Many rural areas depend on infrastructure spending by the national government to create jobs and to maintain essential services. Without this support, these communities are not economically viable.

Houses with land in rural areas can be purchased for a few million yen.

There are few international schools in rural areas. Families may have to choose between sending their children to a local school or home-schooling, an increasingly viable option with a high-speed internet connection.

Physical isolation and the inability to obtain services in English can be an issue if you don't speak Japanese. As in other countries, it takes time for an outsider to gain trust and acceptance in a rural community.

Finally, most rural houses offered at bargain prices are in need of re-pair, which can be costly and time consuming. Buyers thinking of changing the use of their land should research this carefully, because the process can be extremely difficult.

Japanese addresses

Japan is divided into 47 prefectures, 43 of which carry the suffix *ken*. The remainder use different suffixes. Hokkaido is a *do*, Osaka and Kyoto are *fu*, while Tokyo is metropolis (*to*).

Prefectures are subdivided into cities (*shi*) or counties (*gun* or *shicho*). *Gun* and *shicho* are further divided into towns (*machi* or *cho*) and vil-lages (*mura* or *son*), which may be split into large sections (*oaza*), sec-tions (*aza*) or small sections (*koaza*).

The 15 largest cities—Chiba, Fukuoka, Hiroshima, Kawasaki, Kitakyushu, Kobe, Kyoto, Nagoya, Osaka, Saitama, Sapporo, Sendai, Shizuoka, Tokyo and Yokohama—are subdivided into wards (*ku*). Ku are further divided into *machi* or *cho,* which are separated into city districts (*chome*), city blocks (*banchi*) and building numbers (*go*).

A typical Japanese address (in this example, the Minato Ward Office) is: 1-5-25, Shiba-koen, Minato-ku, Tokyo 105-8511, where "1" is the chome number; "5" is the city block number; "25" is the building number; "Shiba-koen" is the town; "Minato" is the ward; and "105-8511" is the postal code.

When written in Japanese, addresses begin with the large (prefecture) and end with the small (building number). When written in English, this order is reversed.

Major thoroughfares, like Tokyo's Yasukuni Dori, have names, but most streets do not. In old neighborhoods, building numbers often reflect the order in which the structures were erected. In newer areas, building numbers may be sequential. Kyoto and Sapporo use variations on the addressing scheme outlined above.

Japanese addresses are made even more confusing because place names are often reused. For example, the name Okinawa refers to a prefecture, an island and a city.

HOKKAIDO

Covering 83,424 square kilometers (including the Northern Territories, see below), Hokkaido is Japan's northernmost prefecture. Sapporo is Hokkaido's capital and there are 14 sub-prefectures.

Climate

Unlike other parts of Japan, Hokkaido does not have a rainy season, but it does receive heavy snowfall. In an average year, 1.8 typhoons come within 300 kilometers of Hokkaido, versus 3.1 in the Kanto Plain and 7.4 in Okinawa.

Houses in Hokkaido are built to withstand cold winters and heavy snowfalls.

History

The earliest traces of *Homo sapiens* in Hokkaido are more than 30,000 years old. Pottery from the incipient Jomon period, which is thought to have been brought to Hokkaido from Honshu 13,000 years ago, has been found in Obihiro. The Okhotsk culture, which arrived in Hokkaido from Sakhalin in the fifth century, is believed to have met the Satsumon culture, which arrived from Honshu in the seventh century, between the eighth and ninth centuries. The Ainu people inherited elements of the Okhotsk and Satsumon cultures, and Japanese people began living in southern Hokkaido around the 13th century.

Some 12,000 Paleolithic, Jomon and Ainu remains—including tools, graves, dwellings and villages—have been found in Hokkaido. The discovery of archaeological remains can complicate the construction of homes and other projects.

The Ainu

As settlers from the Japanese mainland arrived in Hokkaido, conflict with the Ainu increased. The Ainu waged and lost the battles of Kosyamain in 1457, Syaksyain (1669) and Kunasiri-Menasi (1789) and ultimately fell under Japanese control.[1] Ainu land was redistributed to Japanese farmers, Ainu people were forced to take Japanese names and the use of the Ainu language was banned. In 2008, the Japanese government officially recognized the Ainu as "an indigenous people with a distinct language, religion and culture."[2] A 2006 survey by the Hokkaido government concluded there were 23,782 Ainu living in the prefecture.[3]

World War II

About 3,000 people in Hokkaido were killed in Allied air raids and shelling on July 14 and 15, 1945. In Sapporo, most of the bombs fell near Shiroishi Station and Okadama Airfield (now Okadama Airport) and in what is now known as Teine-ku in the north of the city.[4]

Russia and the Northern Territories

Comprising the Habomai Islands plus the islands of Shikotan, Kunashiri and Etorofu, the Northern Territories cover 5,036 square kilometers northeast of Hokkaido's main island. The Northern Territories are rich in natural resources, including fish, timber, oil and gas, and metals such as gold and silver.

In 1875, Japan received the Kuril Islands in exchange for ceding Sakhalin Island to Russia. At the end of World War II, however, the Soviet Union annexed the southern Kuril Islands. These islands are at the center of an ongoing dispute between Russia and Japan, which maintains that the Northern Territories are illegally occupied by Russia.

Regional tensions

In August 2017, 1,500 troops from Japan's Self-Defense Force and 2,000 U.S. Marines took part in Operation Northern Viper, a 14-day, annual live-fire exercise in Hokkaido.

In August and September 2017, North Korea fired ballistic missiles that passed over Cape Erimo before landing in the sea east of Hokkaido.

Transport

Hokkaido is connected to Honshu by the 54-kilometer Seikan Tunnel, which runs from Hakodate to Aomori. Opened in 1988, the tunnel carries freight and passenger trains, including the Hokkaido Shinkansen.

The *Hokutosei* overnight train between Tokyo and Sapporo has been replaced by a high-speed Shinkansen service.

Flights between Sapporo and Tokyo began in 1937. In 2015, Sapporo–Tokyo Haneda was the world's second-busiest airport pair. Airports in Asahikawa and Hakodate offer scheduled flights to domestic destinations as well as cities in China, South Korea and Taiwan. Several smaller airports serve domestic routes.

Short- and long-distance ferry services are available from Hakodate, Otaru and Tomakomai to destinations in Honshu.

Demographics

In 2015, Hokkaido had a population of 5.4 million, down from a peak of 5.7 million in 1997. More than one-third of the prefecture's people live in Sapporo. With 343,000 people, Asahikawa is Hokkaido's second-largest city. Hakodate, with 270,000, is third.

Hokkaido's demographic prospects are grim. The population is expected to fall to 4.9 million by 2025 and 4.4 million by 2035.[5] Furthermore, by 2035, 37.4% of Hokkaido's population is projected to be over age 65, 3.7 percentage points higher than Japan as a whole.[6]

The number of households is expected to decline from 2.4 million in 2015 to 2.1 million in 2035. Elderly, one-person households will grow from 316,000 in 2015 to 380,000 in 2035.

Commerce and industry

With over one-fifth of Japan's land, Hokkaido is the nation's largest source of agricultural products, including seafood, beef, milk and cheese, rice and vegetables. Tourism, forestry and food-related industries play important roles in the economy.

Hokkaido has one nuclear power plant, which is located in Tomari, a seaside village about 30 kilometers from Niseko and 70 kilometers from Sapporo.

Forests and water conservation zones

Hokkaido has special reporting requirements for transferring forestland and land in water resource conservation zones (WRCZs). These requirements reflect Hokkaido's abundant natural resources, its location between Russia and Honshu and concerns about foreigners owning Japanese land.

Owners transferring land in a WRCZ must advise the government three months before the transfer document is signed. This regulation applies even if the owner does not know the identity of the person or company acquiring the land. Lists of WRCZs are available from the Hokkaido government and from sub-prefectural bureaus.

Anyone purchasing forestland—or acquiring it through inheritance, donation, corporate merger or other means—must notify the government within 90 days of the transaction. This requirement is waived if the vendor has filed a land trade notification with the government. Additional information is available from the Hokkaido government's Department of Fisheries and Forestry, the forest affairs division of the local sub-prefectural bureau or the forestry office of the local municipality.[7]

Sapporo

Until 1869, Sapporo was a trading post. In the years that followed, the Hokkaido Development Commission turned Sapporo into a planned city with a grid of streets and avenues modeled on Kyoto. Sapporo has 10 wards and an area of 1,121 square kilometers.

Demographics
In 1970, Sapporo's population surpassed 1 million for the first time. Today, Sapporo has 1.9 million people, making it Japan's fifth-largest city. The population is expected to be stable until 2035 when it will fall to 1.8 million. The city continues to benefit from migration from other parts of Hokkaido.

Transport
Sapporo is served by New Chitose Airport, which is Hokkaido's main international gateway, offering flights to cities in Japan and to Mainland China, Hong Kong, Malaysia, Russia, Singapore, South Korea, Taiwan, Thailand and the United States. In winter, there are flights to Australia.

Sapporo has seven train lines operated by JR Hokkaido, three subway lines and a streetcar line. By 2031, the Hokkaido Shinkansen will serve Sapporo Station.

Tourism
The city government actively promotes Sapporo as a destination for Asian tourists. Since 1950, it has organized the annual Sapporo Snow Festival. The city hosted the 1972 Winter Olympics and is reported to be considering a bid for the 2026 winter games. Sapporo is a host city for the 2019 Rugby World Cup.

Climate

August is Sapporo's hottest month, with an average maximum temperature of 26.4°C. January is the coldest month, with an average minimum of -7.0°C.[8] Sapporo uses heated underground malls, electrically heated sidewalks and central building heating systems to make the city livable during the winter months.

Family life

Sapporo has several family-friendly initiatives, including subsidized medical care and daycare programs for children. In 2017, the city began allowing same-sex couples to swear a civil-union oath. While it does not confer legal rights, the oath is expected to explain the couple's relationship to real estate agents, hospitals and other organizations.[9]

Niseko

Located in southwestern Hokkaido, about 90 kilometers from Sapporo, the Niseko resort area centers on the 1,308-meter Mount Niseko Annupuri. Closer to the town of Kutchan than to Niseko, the resort comprises the Annupuri, Higashiyama, Hirafu and Hanazono areas, all of which have gondola or ski lift access to Niseko Annupuri.

An emerging destination

Niseko is famous for the quality and quantity of its snow. It is not unusual for snow to fall for 150 days each year and for 14 meters to accumulate over a season. Deep, dry "champagne" powder and a long ski season have made Niseko popular with Australians—who represented 32% of foreigners' room nights in 2014/15—and growing numbers of visitors from Hong Kong (18%), Singapore (9%), China (6%), Taiwan (6%) and South Korea (4%).[10] During the 2006/07 season, Niseko attracted about 14,000 foreign visitors, 70% of whom were from Australia. By 2014/15, the number of foreign tourists had reached 148,000.

The area's emergence as an international destination is relatively recent. In part, this is because Japan's tourism efforts have focused on serving domestic holidaymakers and outbound travelers rather than welcoming inbound vacationers. While Hokkaido is a popular destination for Japanese tourists, most visit during the summer.

The local tourism industry has been driven by a group of Australian pioneers who saw Niseko's potential and started businesses ranging from tour companies to real estate agencies. The area's popularity has attracted international investors: Park Hyatt and Ritz-Carlton hotels are scheduled to open in 2019 and 2020, respectively. There is growing interest from individual and institutional investors from Hong Kong and Mainland China.

The Niseko resort area has condominiums, houses and ski chalets.

Niseko has benefited from the national government's plan to attract 40 million foreign tourists by 2020 and 60 million by 2030. Infrastructure for tourists and foreign residents has also improved. In 2012, an international primary school opened, and the number of automated teller machines capable of accepting non-Japanese bank cards has grown from one in 2009 to 17 today.

Transport

Most visitors arrive by air via Sapporo's New Chitose Airport. It is 2.5 hours by bus and about 3 hours by train from New Chitose Airport to Niseko. Using a combination of Shinkansen, express and local trains, you can travel from Tokyo to Kutchan in as little as eight hours.

Real estate

Developers custom-build vacation homes in Niseko. Decorated to international standards, these condominiums and houses allow residents to walk out their front door and onto a ski lift.

These properties are marketed to people who want to use them for one or two weeks each season and have a professional manager rent them out on a short-term basis during the rest of the year. Most are equipped like a serviced apartment, with furniture, bed linens, satellite TV, a stereo and Wi-Fi. Appliances with English controls are common, and managers will prepare condensed English-language manuals to help guests operate equipment with Japanese labels.

Property management services are usually available from the company that built the house or condominium, or from a specialist property manager. Regardless of its affiliation, the manager should be licensed by the Ministry of Land, Infrastructure, Transport and Tourism.

Typically, managers offer a turnkey package covering everything from marketing and renting the units to maintenance and repairs. They can also pay bills and provide assistance with insurance, banking, local taxes and snow removal.

Custom-built homes

You can also custom-build your chalet. There are foreigner-friendly contractors and architects in the area, and raw land is available for sale.

Niseko has zoning laws that address building colors, heights, floor-area ratios, setbacks, landscaping and approved land uses. In addition, the town has reporting requirements for the purchase of lots larger than 10,000 square meters. Permission is required to fell trees on private land that is covered by a regional forest management plan, and there are restrictions on building on agricultural land.[11]

Several condominium hotel projects ran into difficulties because they were being built on quasi-national parkland. These projects were approved by the national Ministry of the Environment but not by the prefectural government.

Money matters

Property prices in the Niseko area have appreciated dramatically over the past decade. During the year ended January 1, 2016, residential land prices in Kutchan rose 19.7%.[12]

In the fall of 2017, apartments near the ski slopes ranged from ¥40 million to ¥400 million. A pre-owned, 66-square-meter cottage with 526 square meters of land located 5 kilometers from Annupuri Village was offered for ¥12 million. Houses and land that are a 20–30 minute drive from the ski hills are cheaper still.

According to Riccardo Tossani—an architect who has designed several high-end residential and commercial projects in Niseko—a single-family, two-story, wood-frame home can be built to a high specification for ¥1.2 million–¥1.4 million per *tsubo* (3.3 square meters), excluding land. Tossani notes that wealthy people are building luxury homes in the area with total budgets of ¥750 million or more. Construction costs for these houses are typically ¥2 million–¥3 million per tsubo.

Foreign nonresidents purchasing real estate in Niseko pay cash, because Japanese banks do not lend to nonresident foreigners buying recreational property. Vendor financing may be available for new properties or off the plan sales.

Consider the potential impact of exchange rates if you plan to rent your chalet to overseas skiers. For example, the Australian dollar fell from about ¥98 in January 2008 to ¥57 in October 2008, nearly doubling the cost of a Japanese ski vacation for Australian travelers.

Niseko is evolving from a winter resort to a year-round destination. As a result, rental revenues from your property during the off-season will range from low to zero. The local tourism community is working to attract more visitors during the summer—organizing bicycle tours, whitewater rafting and hot-air balloon rides—but Niseko remains best known for its skiing.

Infrastructure and development

Hokkaido Shinkansen—In 2016, the Hokkaido Shinkansen began offering service between Shin-Aomori—where it connects with the Tohoku Shinkansen from Tokyo—and Shin-Hakodate-Hokuto. By 2031, the Hokkaido Shinkansen service will extend to Sapporo Station, with four intermediate stops, including one in Kutchan. Travel time between Tokyo and Sapporo will be reduced to a little over five hours.

Infrastructure cutbacks—Hokkaido's ongoing depopulation has resulted in infrastructure cutbacks. In November 2016, for example, the president of JR Hokkaido said the railway was having trouble maintaining operations on 13 money-losing routes covering over 1,200 kilometers, or about half of its network. JR Hokkaido plans to replace trains on three of the routes, which currently serve fewer than 200 passengers per day, with buses.[13]

Sapporo integrated resort—Sapporo has been suggested as the site for an integrated resort, following the passage of legislation to legalize gambling at the end of 2016.

Sapporo Station improvements—The city is making improvements to the area around Sapporo Station in preparation for the debut of the Hokkaido Shinkansen.

Sapporo urban renewal—The City of Sapporo has launched several urban renewal projects, including the North 1-West 1, North 8-West 1, and South 2-West 3 Southwest developments.

GREATER TOKYO

Tokyo is situated in central Honshu at the head of Tokyo Bay, where the Sumida, Edo, Ara and Tama rivers form deltas and enter the Pacific Ocean. Occupying most of the Kanto Plain, Tokyo is the nation's capital, a hub for transport, commerce and culture, and home to many of Japan's leading universities.

Tokyo's skyscrapers are complemented by dozens of manicured parks, including Shinjuku Gyoen.

Tokyo is among Japan's most cosmopolitan cities. English-speaking service providers, such as lawyers and real estate agents, are relatively common, and information is available in English about topics ranging from government services to the city's superb restaurants. As a result, it is easier for non-Japanese people to live and invest in Tokyo than elsewhere in Japan.

From cleanliness and safety to parks and public transit, Tokyo is a model city. These attributes, combined with the city's broad economic base, a stable population and growing number of households, make Tokyo a popular investment destination.

Climate

Tokyo has four distinct seasons, with hot, humid summers and mild winters. The hottest month is August, with an average maximum temperature of 30.8°C. January is the coldest, with an average minimum of 0.9°C. The city receives an average of 1,529 millimeters of precipitation each year. September is the wettest month, and typhoons are common in the late summer and early fall.

History

There is archaeological evidence of hunting and gathering civilizations on the Kanto Plain dating back at least 4,000 years. In 1457, Ota Dokan built Edo Castle on the grounds of what is now the Imperial Palace. Tokugawa Ieyasu set up his headquarters in Edo in 1590 and established the Edo Shogunate 13 years later.

In 1853, U.S. commodore Matthew Perry and his Black Ships arrived in Edo Bay, marking the end of Japan's self-imposed international isolation. Edo was renamed Tokyo in 1868, and the emperor moved from Kyoto to Tokyo the following year.

Natural and man-made disasters have punctuated Tokyo's history. Massive fires, claiming hundreds of thousands of lives and destroying large sections of the city, occurred in 1657, 1682, 1721, 1772 and 1872. Daily life was disrupted by the eruption of nearby Mount Fuji in 1707 and Mount Asama in 1783. Major earthquakes devastated Tokyo in 1855 and 1923. On the night of March 9–10, 1945, the air raids of Operation Meetinghouse killed 100,000 people, left over a million homeless and incinerated 41 square kilometers of central Tokyo.

Tokyo rebounded after World War II, with the population topping 10 million for the first time in 1962. Two years later, the city hosted the Olympics, and Shinkansen service commenced between Tokyo and Osaka.

As the Japanese economy grew, land prices in Tokyo rose at an unprecedented rate. In 1990, the bubble collapsed. Two decades of economic stagnation followed.

Tokyo combines the history of Edo Castle with the conveniences of a modern metropolis.

Tokyo's economy has benefited from Abenomics (the economic revitalization measures introduced by Prime Minister Abe in 2012), from a boom in tourism and from infrastructure spending ahead of the 2020 Olympics.

Recent redevelopment projects in Tokyo include the Ark Hills complex, which was completed in 1986, Roppongi Hills (2003) and Tokyo Midtown (2007). The 634-meter Tokyo Skytree opened in 2012.

Transport

Tokyo is a national, regional and international transport hub. The city has two main civilian airports, Haneda in Ota-ku and Narita in Chiba Prefecture. Haneda is primarily a domestic airport, while Narita handles international traffic. Chofu Airport in western Tokyo has flights to the Izu islands.

Rail is the dominant mode of transport. The region is crisscrossed by a dense network of subways, commuter train lines, monorails, streetcars, cable cars and Shinkansen lines that make it easy to reach remote parts of the city and the rest of the country. The East Japan Railway Company (JR East) is Tokyo's largest railway company, and there are several smaller operators—including Keio, Keisei, Odakyu, Seibu, Tobu and Tokyu—many of which are active in real estate and retailing. Subway services in Tokyo are provided by Tokyo Metro, which is owned by the national government and the Tokyo Metropolitan Government (TMG), and by TMG-owned Toei Transportation. Unlike many cities, Tokyo's rail services stop around midnight.

Tokyo is surrounded by three ring roads—the Central Circular Route, the Tokyo Outer Ring Road and the Metropolitan Inter-City Expressway—sections of which are under construction. The Bayshore Route bypasses central Tokyo and links Kanagawa with Chiba, while the Tokyo Bay Aqua Line runs under Tokyo Bay between Kawasaki and Chiba. Tokyo is connected to the rest of Japan via the Tomei, Chuo, Kan-Etsu, Tohoku, Joban and Higashi-Kanto expressways. Central Tokyo is served by the Shuto Expressway, which is a network of toll roads.

The Port of Tokyo operates the Harumi Passenger Ship Terminal and the Takeshiba Terminal, which cater to cruise ships and ferries to the Izu islands, respectively. The Port of Yokohama operates Osanbashi Yokohama International Passenger Terminal, which serves cruise ships.

Greater Tokyo

There are many potentially confusing ways to define Tokyo. This chapter covers Greater Tokyo, which comprises the Tokyo Metropolis plus neighboring Saitama, Chiba and Kanagawa prefectures.

Greater Tokyo's population is 36.1 million, or more than 28% of the national total,[1] and its gross prefectural product is ¥163.8 trillion, or over 32% of Japan's total.[2] At current exchange rates, Greater Tokyo's economy is larger than South Korea's, while its population is larger than that of Saudi Arabia.

Tokyo is a magnet for talent, a trend that is reflected in national migration statistics. As other prefectures' populations have shrunk, Greater Tokyo has grown. The capital's population peaked in 2015, the same year that Japan's population began to decline. However, the number of single-person households is increasing, so the total number of households in Greater Tokyo is projected to grow until 2025.[3]

The Tokyo Metropolis

The Tokyo Metropolis has a population of 13.5 million and occupies 2,106 square kilometers. It comprises the 23 special wards in central Tokyo, and 26 cities, three towns and one village in the Tama area. The Izu, Ogasawara and Okinotorishima islands are included in the Tokyo Metropolis, despite being 1,000 kilometers south of Honshu. The sea surrounding these sparsely populated islands, which include two towns and seven villages, is rich in natural resources and plays an important role in demarcating Japan's territory.

At the end of 2014, there were 417,442 foreign residents in the Tokyo Metropolis, with 350,863 living in the 23 wards, 66,334 in the Tama area and 245 in the islands. The largest groups of foreigners were Chinese (172,769), Koreans (94,010) and Filipinos (28,681), however these numbers are influenced by Japan's citizenship policies, as explained in the "Demographics" chapter.[4]

The 23 special wards
Tokyo's 23 special wards occupy 627 square kilometers and have a population of 9.2 million. The wards range in size from 10 square kilometers (Taito-ku) to 61 square kilometers (Ota-ku) and in population from just over 53,000 (Chiyoda-ku) to nearly 900,000 (Setagaya-ku).

Demographics
Tokyo's three central wards—Chiyoda-ku, Chuo-ku and Minato-ku—have a combined nighttime population of about 375,000 and a daytime population of 2.3 million. Every day, nearly 2 million workers and students commute from other wards and Kanagawa, Saitama and Chiba to central Tokyo.

The city's wards have divergent population prospects. Using 2010 as a baseline of 100—only Chuo-ku, Koto-ku and Minato-ku will grow by 2040, with scores of 114, 109 and 105, respectively. Suginami-ku, Katsushika-ku and Adachi-ku will see their populations fall to 85, 81 and 79, respectively.

The wards also have different aging profiles. In 2040, Sumida-ku (28.1%), Arakawa-ku (28.4%) and Koto-ku (28.5%) will have the smallest percentage of people under age 65. The oldest wards will be Adachi-ku (35.7%), Nerima-ku (39.0%) and Suginami-ku (39.6%).

If you are buying an investment property, Koto-ku offers a young, growing population, while both Suginami-ku and Adachi-ku's populations are aging and shrinking.

At the end of 2014, Shinjuku-ku had 36,016 foreign residents, followed by Edogawa-ku (25,294) and Adachi-ku (23,679). Chiyoda-ku (2,484), Chuo-ku (5,153) and Meguro-ku (7,386) had the fewest foreigners.

While same-sex marriages are not recognized in Japan, Nakano-ku and Shibuya-ku[5] are known for being LGBT-friendly.*

Neighborhoods
Tokyo's wards are distinctive. Some, like Shibuya-ku and Minato-ku, feature affluent residential neighborhoods, manicured parks and leafy boulevards. Others, such as Ota-ku, Koto-ku and Shinagawa-ku, include garbage incinerators and chemical waste treatment facilities built on reclaimed land.

Tokyo has working-class neighborhoods like Nihonzutsumi—an area in Taito-ku better known as Sanya that has been airbrushed out of city maps—that are popular with day laborers. But unlike most cities, where "working class" is synonymous with crime, trash on the streets and a lack of public services, Tokyo's working-class areas are clean, safe and well served by public transit.

The Tama area
The Tama area is a suburban region west of Tokyo's 23 wards that covers 1,160 square kilometers and has a population of 4.2 million. Major cities include Hachioji (population 579,740), Machida (428,766) and Fuchu (259,082).

Tama has a large manufacturing base, including printing and related industries, metalworking and production machinery. The area also has numerous universities and research institutions.

---

*   Osaka's Yodogawa-ku also welcomes lesbian, gay, bisexual and transgender residents. Sapporo has begun recognizing same-sex civil unions.

Tama is a bedroom community for Tokyo, with commuter rail lines serving key stations such as Shinjuku, Shibuya and Tokyo. You can travel from Hachioji to Shinjuku in as little as 35 minutes, although trains are crowded during rush hour and before the last train of the day.

Value for money, low urban density and proximity to nature are Tama's main attractions.

Chiba Prefecture

Located east of Tokyo, Chiba Prefecture occupies 5,083 square kilometers and has a population of 6.2 million. Chiba City, with 973,183 residents, is the prefectural capital.

Chiba is among Japan's most important sources of agricultural products and seafood. Good rail connections and inexpensive homes make it a popular choice for people commuting to the capital. Chiba City is 40 minutes from Tokyo Station by train.

Located on the eastern shore of Tokyo Bay, the Keiyo Coastline Industrial Belt is a 40-kilometer strip of more than 200 steel plants, oil refineries, chemical plants, electrical generation facilities and other heavy industries. Chiba is also home to Narita International Airport, Tokyo Disneyland and Makuhari Messe, a large convention and exhibition center.

Kanagawa Prefecture

Located south of Tokyo, Kanagawa occupies 2,416 square kilometers and has a population of 9.1 million. Yokohama (see below) is the prefectural capital, while Kawasaki (population 1.5 million) is Kanagawa's second-largest city.

Kanagawa is home to heavy industry, as well as tourist attractions such as Kamakura, an ancient capital of Japan, and Hakone, a town famous for its hot springs.

Yokohama
With an area of 435 square kilometers and a population of 3.7 million, Yokohama is Japan's second-largest city.

Foreigners have lived in Yokohama since 1859, when the port was opened to international trade and the government established a residential area for non-Japanese inhabitants. On March 31, 2017, Yokohama had 87,563 foreign residents, including 35,885 Chinese nationals, 12,785 Koreans and 7,276 Filipinos.[6]

From a trading hub in the 1800s, Yokohama became a manufacturing and chemical center in the 1930s. The Great Kanto Earthquake in 1923 killed 20,000 residents and destroyed 60,000 homes. In 1945, American bombers reduced 42% of the city to ashes. Today, Yokohama is home to numerous information technology and biotechnology companies.

Yokohama offers a cosmopolitan lifestyle, with lower home prices than the 23 wards of Tokyo. Yokohama is a 25-minute train ride from both Tokyo Station and Haneda Airport. Shinkansen service from Shin-Yokohama Station connects the city to the rest of the country.

Saitama Prefecture

Located north of Tokyo, Saitama Prefecture occupies 3,768 square kilometers and has a population of 7.3 million, nearly 146,000 of whom are foreigners.[7] Saitama City is the prefectural capital and has 1.3 million residents.[8]

Saitama is a bedroom community for Tokyo. Omiya Station, Saitama City's main train station, offers Shinkansen service and is a 33-minute ride from Tokyo Station.

Saitama's industries include manufacturing, agriculture and sake brewing. Value for money, low urban density and proximity to nature are Saitama's main attractions.

Infrastructure and development

Many major projects are planned for Greater Tokyo. This list is not exhaustive and development plans change frequently, so consult your local ward or city office for up-to-date information.

Haneda Airport connections—The monorail connecting Haneda Airport to Hamamatsucho Station in Minato-ku will be extended to Tokyo Station, improving links between the airport and the national Shinkansen network.[9] JR East plans to build three new lines linking Haneda Airport to Tokyo, Shinjuku and Shin-Kiba stations, respectively. The new services are expected to begin in 2024–25.[10]

Hibiya Line station—A new subway station between Kamiyacho and Kasumigaseki on Tokyo's Hibiya Line is scheduled to open by 2020.[11] Tentatively named Toranomon New Station, the new facility will improve access to the Toranomon area, where Mori Building has a large redevelopment project. In 2014, a ¥270 billion, multilevel road opened between Toranomon and Shimbashi.

Olympic Stadium—Located in Kasumigaoka, Shinjuku-ku, Tokyo, the new National Olympic Stadium is being built on the site of the stadium used for the 1964 games.[12] Construction of the controversial facility started on December 1, 2016, after the original designer, Zaha Hadid, was replaced by local architect Kengo Kuma.

Olympic Village—Located in the Harumi district of Tokyo's Chuo-ku, this facility will house 17,000 competitors and be converted into 5,000 private dwellings after the Olympics.[13]

Ring roads—Two ring roads are being built around Tokyo to complement the Central Circular Route, which was completed in 2015. The Tokyo Outer Ring Road and the Metropolitan Inter-City Expressway are expected to be 90% complete by 2020, with new sections under construction in Tama, Chiba, Kanagawa and Saitama.

Shinagawa rail yard redevelopment—With a budget of ¥500 billion and an area of 13 hectares, Global Gateway Shinagawa will create 1 million square meters of floor space in southern Tokyo. Developed by JR East, this project includes hotels, condominiums and commercial space. Phase one is scheduled for completion by 2023–24.[14]

Tokyo–Osaka maglev train—The high-speed Linear Chuo Shinkansen, which uses superconducting magnetic levitation technology, is expected to begin service between Shinagawa Station and

Nagoya Station in 2027. The service will be extended to Osaka by 2045.[15]

The monorail serving Haneda Airport will be extended to Tokyo Station, improving access to the national Shinkansen network.

Tokyo Station redevelopment—In 2014–15, major developers including Mitsui Fudosan and Mitsubishi Estate announced plans to redevelop the Yaesu and Otemachi areas near Tokyo Station.[16] The projects, which will be completed between 2022 and 2029, will create about 800,000 square meters of commercial space.[17]

Tsukiji fish market—Tsukiji's relocation has been delayed after excessive levels of benzene, arsenic, mercury and other contaminants were discovered at the new site in Toyosu, which was the location of a gas plant.[18] The Toyosu facility is over-budget, and the company responsible for building it has been accused of cutting corners.

Yamanote Line redevelopment—Three busy stations on the Yamanote Line, each of which is an interchange for subways and suburban train lines, are being redeveloped. The projects at Shibuya Station and the west exits of Ikebukuro and Shinjuku stations are scheduled for completion between 2020 and 2028.[19] The Shibuya redevelopment is a huge project that includes new high rises and the realignment of train and subway lines in one of Tokyo's leading fashion, shopping and entertainment hubs.[20]

Yamanote Line station—A new station on the train line that circles downtown Tokyo is expected to open by 2020. The currently unnamed station will be between Shinagawa and Tamachi stations and is part of the Global Gateway Shinagawa project.[21]

Yokohama Station redevelopment—JR East is planning a development at the west exit of Yokohama Station that will include 70,000 square meters of commercial space and 28,000 square meters of offices. The project is expected to be finished in 2020.

NAGOYA

Nagoya is the capital and the largest city in Aichi Prefecture. Located near Japan's geographic center, Nagoya comprises 16 wards and occupies 326 square kilometers.

The Nagoya area is known by several names, including the Chubu region, which comprises Aichi, Gifu, Toyama and Ishikawa prefectures; Greater Nagoya, which is the area within a 100-kilometer radius of Nagoya's central business district; and the Chukyo major metropolitan area, which comprises Aichi, Mie and Gifu prefectures.

Climate

Nagoya has a relatively extreme climate. With an average minimum temperature of 0.8°C in January, Nagoya is colder than Osaka. It's also hotter than Tokyo, with an average maximum temperature of 32.8°C in August. In an average year, Nagoya enjoys 200 more hours of sunshine than Tokyo and nearly 100 more hours of sun than Osaka.

History

Nagoya is home to one of Shinto's most important shrines, Atsuta Jingu, which dates to the sixth century.

In 1607, Tokugawa Ieyasu—founder of the Tokugawa shogunate and one of Japan's three great unifiers—chose Nagoya as the site for his new castle town. Nagoya offered a strategic location between the Kanto Plain to the east and Osaka and Kyoto to the west, freshwater from the Shonai River and access to shipping via Ise Bay. Nagoya's iconic castle was completed in 1612.

Nagoya soon became a rest stop on the Tokaido Road between Edo (Tokyo) and Kyoto. By the 18th century, the city was a regional trading center. With an area of 13 square kilometers and a population of 157,000, Nagoya became a municipality in 1889.

By 1934, Nagoya had a population of more than 1 million. In the run up to World War II, Nagoya produced more than 60% of Japan's aircraft.

Nearly one-quarter of the city—including Nagoya Castle, which was rebuilt in 1959—was destroyed in the war. On November 1, 1945, the population reached a post-war low of 597,941.

Civic leaders saw reconstruction projects as an opportunity to improve Nagoya. Several 100-meter-wide boulevards were created and graveyards were consolidated in Heiwa Park. In addition, land readjustment projects—where irregular plots are converted into more usable shapes and public facilities such as roads and parks are built or improved—were completed in nearly two-thirds of the city. By 1955, Nagoya had absorbed 65 nearby towns and villages, giving the city its current size and a population of 1.9 million.

In 1959, Typhoon Isewan struck, killing 5,000 people.

Demographics

With a population of 2.3 million, Nagoya is Japan's fourth-largest city, after Tokyo, Yokohama and Osaka. As of April 1, 2017, 24.2% of Nagoya's population were aged 65 or older, 61.9% were 15–64, and 12.2% were 0–14. The average age of Nagoya's 1,136,789 men was 43.9 years, while the city's 1,166,281 women had an average age of 46.7.

Nagoya is Japan's fourth most populous city, after Tokyo, Yokohama and Osaka.

Nagoya's wards range in size from 8 square kilometers (Higashi-ku) to 46 square kilometers (Minato-ku). With 243,466 residents, Midori-ku had the largest population. Atsuta-ku, with 65,957 people, had the smallest. At the end of 2016, Nagoya had 72,683 foreign residents. Chinese (22,056), Koreans (17,192) and Filipinos (8,441) comprised the three largest groups.[2]

Transport

The city's transportation network is among the most developed in Japan, with excellent road, rail, sea and air services. Nagoya is about four hours from Tokyo on the Tomei Expressway, while Osaka is a two-hour drive on the Meishin Expressway. Chubu Centrair International Airport is a 30-minute train ride from Nagoya Station.

Nagoya has six subway lines, with a total length of 93 kilometers. Local and regional rail services are provided by JR Central, Kintetsu Railway, Nagoya Railroad (better known as Meitetsu) and several smaller operators. Tokyo Station is 99 minutes from Nagoya Station by Shinkansen. Shin-Osaka Station is 50 minutes from Nagoya Station.

Commerce and industry

The Nagoya area is an industrial powerhouse. According to the Chubu Bureau of Economy, Trade and Industry, Chubu represents just 8% of the country's land, but makes over 21% of Japan's manufactured products and 45% of its transportation machinery and equipment.[3]

The region has one of the world's largest clusters of automotive and automotive-related businesses. More than 3,000 domestic automotive companies, such as Toyota and Denso, and global firms, including Volkswagen and Magna International, employ nearly 300,000 people. The Port of Nagoya shipped 1.4 million vehicles in 2016 and is Japan's busiest port in terms of total cargo throughput.[4]

Nagoya is also a hub for Japan's aerospace industry. Mitsubishi Heavy Industries manufactures the Mitsubishi Regional Jet; makes rockets for JAXA, Japan's national aerospace agency; and produces major airframe components for the Boeing 777 and 787. Several hundred companies, including Kawasaki Heavy Industries and Fuji Heavy

Industries, build aerospace products in the area. Plans are in place to boost Chubu's aerospace exports from ¥351 billion in 2013 to ¥680 billion in 2020 and increase aerospace-related jobs from 18,600 to 25,000 over the same period.

In a 2014 survey, Nagoya's central business district offered inexpensive office rents, charging an average of ¥3,269 per square meter, versus Tokyo at ¥5,092 and Osaka at ¥3,369. Residential land costs were similar, at ¥164,900 per square meter in Nagoya, compared with ¥504,800 in Tokyo and ¥231,900 in Osaka.[5]

Green plans

In 2009–10, the city introduced the Water Circulation Restoration 2050 Nagoya Strategy, the Low Carbon City 2050 Nagoya Strategy and the Biodiversity 2050 Nagoya Strategy. Each of these programs shapes the Nagoya Green Master Plan and the Nagoya City Urban Master Plan, which were introduced in 2011, and the Nagoya Transportation Urban Development Plan, which was launched in 2014.

The city's water strategy protects biodiversity and prevents floods by improving water management through the construction of levees and drainage systems. The strategy includes a goal of making 50% of the city's sidewalks and 70% of its parking facilities water-permeable. Water strategy is particularly important because Nagoya experienced serious flooding in September 2000 and 2011. Furthermore, Sakae Station flooded in September 2013 and the subway portion of Nagoya Station flooded in September 2014.

The carbon strategy targets a 25% cut in CO_2 emissions from 1990 levels by 2020 and an 80% reduction from 1990 levels by 2050. It will achieve these goals by encouraging the use of passive design, pedestrianization, product innovation, alternative energy sources and green lifestyles.

The biodiversity strategy aims to increase the city's green cover—and thus the habitat for different species—from 25% to 40%.

The urban master plan focuses on building networked station areas, which combine commercial, residential and cultural functions in a walkable environment within 800 meters of the city's railway stations. The green master plan includes initiatives to promote civic engagement in environmental issues, the creation of green streets and blocks, and the preservation of existing green spaces. The transportation plan, meanwhile, focuses on developing low-carbon transport systems that are safe and easy to use, and creating a human-oriented street environment.[6]

Infrastructure and development

Expressway network—The Central Nippon Expressway Company is expanding the highways surrounding Nagoya. The Shin-Meishin Expressway and the Nagoya-Daini-Kanjo Expressway (Nagoya-Nishi Junction to Tobishima Junction) are scheduled for completion in fiscal 2018. The Shin-Tomei and Tokai-Kanjo expressways and the Tokyo-Gaikan Expressway (Chuo Junction to Tomei Junction) are expected to open in fiscal 2020.[7]

The Linear Chuo Shinkansen will link Tokyo's Shinagawa Station with a new terminal under Nagoya Station in just 40 minutes.

Linear Chuo Shinkansen—Scheduled to enter service in 2027, this high-speed train will link Tokyo's Shinagawa Station with a new terminal under Nagoya Station in just 40 minutes, making it possible to work in one city and live in the other. By 2045, it will run between Nagoya Station and Shin-Osaka Station.

Nagoya Station redevelopment—The Linear Chuo Shinkansen has been a catalyst for redeveloping the area surrounding Nagoya Station. Scheduled for completion in 2027, this project includes the construction of 14 large buildings, some of which are complete; redevelopment of the square in front of the station; construction of underground walkways; improved road and rail access and more.[8]

KANSAI

Located in the center of Honshu, the Kansai region comprises Hyogo, Kyoto, Mie, Nara, Osaka, Shiga and Wakayama prefectures. The region has a population of 22.5 million and occupies 32,860 square kilometers.

Kansai is second only to Tokyo in Japan's economic hierarchy. There is a longstanding rivalry between the two regions, and many Kansai people resent the concentration of economic and political power in Tokyo.

Kansai's economy is driven by the cities of Osaka, Kyoto and Kobe. Since 2000, these cities' suburbs have seen their populations shrink and age far faster than the urban core. Consequently, suburban land prices have fared poorly.[1]

Climate

Kansai has mild, damp winters and hot, dry summers. Osaka's average minimum temperature is 2.8°C in January, nearly 2 degrees warmer than Tokyo. But the average maximum in August reaches 33.4°C. Osaka's average relative humidity is 61% in January and 66% in August, versus 52% and 73%, respectively, for the same months in Tokyo.

Transport

Kansai International Airport (KIX) is the region's aviation hub, with flights to Japanese cities and to Africa, the Americas, Asia, Europe and the Middle East. Osaka International Airport (ITAMI) and Kobe Airport serve domestic destinations.

Osaka, Kyoto and Kobe have Shinkansen links to the rest of the country, as well as commuter trains run by the West Japan Railway Company (JR West) and other operators, including Hankyu, Hanshin Keihan, Kintetsu and Nankai.

Kansai has an extensive road system that includes the Hanshin Expressway surrounding Osaka and Kobe, and the Meishin, Chugoku,

Sanyo, Kinki, Nishi-Meihan and Hanwa expressways linking Kansai to surrounding communities.

Cruise ships call on the Port of Osaka, which offers ferry services to Shanghai and Busan as well as sightseeing cruises. Car ferries sail from Osaka Nanko to Kyushu and Shikoku.

Hyogo Prefecture

Hyogo occupies 8,401 square kilometers. Kobe (see below) is the prefectural capital. Hyogo has a population of 5.5 million, which is expected to drop to 5.2 million in 2025 and 4.8 million in 2035.[2]

Fujitsu, Kawasaki Heavy Industries, Kobe Steel, Mitsubishi Electric, Mitsubishi Heavy Industries and Toshiba have manufacturing or research and development facilities in Hyogo.

Kobe

An attractive, compact city, Kobe has an area of 557 square kilometers divided into nine wards. Much of the population lives on the strip of land between the waterfront and Mount Rokko, an area that includes Sannomiya Station, Kobe's main commuter hub.

Kobe's waterfront includes hotels, shopping and entertainment.

History

The Port of Kobe opened to foreign trade in 1868, and Kobe remains one of Japan's more cosmopolitan cities. There are numerous Western-style houses and buildings in Kitano-cho and Kyu-Kyoryuchi, many of which are more than a century old. Kobe is home to Japan's first mosque, which opened in 1935, as well as a synagogue and a Jain temple.[3]

The Great Hanshin Earthquake

In January 1995, Kobe was devastated by the Great Hanshin Earthquake, which killed 6,434 people and caused ¥10 trillion in damage. Fire consumed 82 hectares of urban land and more than 100,000 buildings were destroyed. By 2004, the City of Kobe had debts of ¥290 billion, forcing the government to cut staff and social welfare spending.

In reconstructing Kobe, the city established six land-readjustment areas—in Moriminami, Rokkomichi, Matsumoto, Misuga, Shin-Nagata and Takatori—where wider roads and parks were built. Two urban redevelopment projects totaling 26 hectares were completed in Shin-Nagata and Rokkomichi. A third project, called HAT Kobe, includes public housing, the Hyogo Prefectural Museum of Art and the Great Hanshin-Awaji Earthquake Memorial. These improvements strengthened the city's ability to respond to natural disasters.[4] Kobe is also one of the few cities in Japan with disaster plans that address the needs of non-Japanese residents.[5]

Demographics

Kobe has 1.5 million people, 45,221 of whom are foreigners. The Great Hanshin Earthquake caused a 100,000-person drop in the city's population. Kobe regained those losses by 2004, but the city government estimates the population will shrink to between 1.1 million and 1.3 million by 2060. An estimated 2,500 people, many of them fresh graduates, leave Kobe for Tokyo each year.[6]

Transport

Kobe has two subway lines—green and blue—and two automated people movers, the Rokko Liner and Port Liner. The Kobe-Kansai Airport Bay Shuttle connects KIX and Kobe Airport.

Commerce and industry

Kobe's steel and shipbuilding industries played an important role in Japan's industrialization. The Kobe area has Japan's largest cluster of life sciences companies, including basic research institutions, specialized hospitals and some 300 firms providing medical products and services.

There are 35 international educational institutions, ranging from preschools to high schools, and 20 universities in the Kobe area.

Kyoto Prefecture

Kyoto Prefecture has an area of 4,612 square kilometers. Kyoto City (see below) is the prefectural capital. The prefecture's population is 2.6 million, which is projected to fall to 2.5 million in 2025 and 2.3 million in 2035.[7]

Kyoto produces textiles, lacquerware, metals, ceramics as well as seafood and vegetables. Tourism is a large part of the prefectural economy.

Kyoto City

With an area of 828 square kilometers, Kyoto City has 11 wards.

Residents and tourists enjoy dining alongside Kyoto's Kamo River.

History

Kyoto was the imperial capital for more than 1,000 years and is known as Japan's cultural center, with 20% of Japan's national treasures. The city was largely spared the bombing that devastated other Japanese cities during World War II, preserving its exceptional selection of temples and shrines.

Demographics

In 2017, Kyoto had 1.5 million people, 11.2% of whom were 14 years of age or younger, 61.3% of whom were 15–64 and 27.5% of whom were 65 and above. Couples aged over 65 made up 12.2% of the city's 705,142 households, and elderly singles represented 9.9%.[8] In 2012, the city had 40,796 foreign residents.[9]

Transport

Kyoto has two subway lines, the Karasuma and Tozai lines, as well as nonstop train service to KIX. The Arashiyama and Kitano streetcar lines can trace their history to Japan's first electric streetcar service, which debuted in Kyoto in 1895.

Commerce and industry

The city's rich history underpins a vibrant tourism industry. Kyoto attracted 3.2 million overseas visitors in 2015, up from 1.1 million in 2013. Municipal government programs such as free Wi-Fi for tourists, multilingual telephone help lines and English-speaking taxi drivers make Kyoto a foreigner-friendly destination.

Urban planning

The municipal government and Mayor Daisaku Kadokawa play an active role in setting the city's direction and preserving Kyoto's visual appeal. The current master plan, known as the Miyako Plan, runs from 2011 to 2020 and encourages recycling and a low-carbon lifestyle. The plan also promotes the development of pedestrian-friendly zones and the city's public transport network.[10]

In 2007, Kyoto introduced the New Landscape Policy, which is intended to maintain the city's beauty and ensure an orderly urban design.[11] Under this policy, 27,800 commercial signs were removed or redesigned to prevent them from interfering with the city's views. Rooftop, flashing and oversize signs were banned. Kyoto also has strict regulations covering building heights, the choice of exterior wall and roof finishes, balconies and the preservation of scenic views. The city's attitude toward urban planning is summed up by this quote from a presentation entitled Kyoto City Landscape Policy: "Buildings may be private property, but landscape is public assets" (sic).

Anyone thinking of buying a home in Kyoto to rent through Airbnb should know that Mayor Kadokawa is staunchly opposed to *minpaku* services. In June 2016, the city announced plans to set up an email address and a telephone hotline where concerned citizens can report illegal minpaku operators.[12]

Machiya

If you are looking for a distinctive home, Kyoto's traditional town-houses (*machiya,* also known as *kyo-machiya*) might fit the bill. Machiya are long, narrow wooden houses with earthen walls and baked tile roofs that combine work and residential spaces. These elegant homes often feature an enclosed garden and are popular with people seeking a slower, relaxed lifestyle.

Only about 28,000 machiya remain in Kyoto, and hundreds are demolished each year. Owners cite the cost of maintenance and repairs as well as burdensome fire and earthquake regulations as key reasons for tearing down these homes.

You can buy machiya, with prices beginning at ¥25 million.[13] Renovation budgets start at ¥10 million, with the actual cost determined by the home's size, condition and location.

Machiya have been recognized as an important part of Kyoto's architectural heritage, and the World Monuments Fund has added them to its watch list. For details, contact the Machiya Information Center or the Kyoto Center for Community Collaboration, which provides financial support for renovating and preserving these homes.

Osaka Prefecture

Osaka Prefecture has an area of 1,905 square kilometers. Osaka City (see below) is the capital. The prefecture has a population of 8.8

million, which is projected to drop to 8.1 million in 2025 and 7.4 million in 2035.[14]

Osaka Prefecture is one of the few areas in Japan where minpaku rentals are permitted.[15]

Osaka City

Osaka City occupies 225 square kilometers at the mouths of the Yamato and Yodo rivers. In May 2015, voters narrowly rejected a proposal to merge the city's 24 wards into five semi-autonomous wards.[16]

Osaka is an important commercial and industrial center.

About 90% of Osaka is on flat lowlands, and the entire city is at risk of inland flooding, which occurs when rainfall exceeds the sewage system's drainage capacity. All wards except Minato-ku and Taisho-ku are at risk from flooding if one or more of the city's rivers burst their banks. Minato-ku, Taisho-ku, Nishiyodogawa-ku, Suminoe-ku and Nishinari-ku are most vulnerable to flooding from tsunamis.[17]

Transport

Osaka has eight subway lines, one tram and an extensive bus network. The municipal government plans to privatize the city's subway and bus services in 2018.[18]

By train, Osaka is about 60 minutes from KIX, 20 minutes from Kobe, 30 minutes from Kyoto and 50 minutes from Nara.

Demographics

In 2015, Osaka had 2.7 million people, 11.2% of whom were aged 14 years or younger, 63.6% of whom were 15–64 and 25.3% of whom were 65 and over. Among the city's 1.4 million households, 8.0% were couples over age 65 and 14.9% were single people over 65.

History

Osaka emerged as a political and economic center in the fifth century. The imperial capital was briefly located in Naniwa, as Osaka was then known, in the seventh century. Osaka began industrializing in the 1880s, when cotton-spinning factories were established south of the city. Metallurgy, shipbuilding and chemical industries soon followed. By World War I, Osaka was known as "the city of smoke."

Before World War II, when American bombers leveled some 5,000 hectares and destroyed 310,000 houses, Osaka was Japan's preeminent commercial and industrial city. In 1935, Osaka had more than 13% of Japan's factories. By 1945, that proportion had fallen to 4%.[19]

Osaka's economy rebounded during the high-growth, post-war years, benefiting from rising demand for the region's heavy engineering and chemical products. In the 1980s, however, Osaka's economy stagnated as Tokyo and Yokohama emerged as high-technology hubs. A strong yen, expensive land and cheap overseas competitors challenged Osaka's traditional industries. Tokyo's lead grew as it became an international finance center and companies from across Japan moved their headquarters to the capital.

To revitalize the economy, local and regional governments invested in KIX, the INTEX Osaka exhibition center, Osaka Technoport, Osaka Teleport, the Asia-Pacific Trade Center, the World Trade Center and similar developments. A 1994 survey by the Osaka Kansai Industrial Revitalization Center indicated there were 866 projects underway in the region, with construction costs for 612 of these projects estimated at ¥41.5 trillion.[20] Many of these projects were not economically viable, and by 2004 the City of Osaka had accumulated debts of ¥90 billion and was nearly bankrupt.[21] Osaka's financial situation has improved—Moody's assigned the city's domestic bonds an A1 rating, its fifth highest, in April 2017.

Commerce and industry

Today, Osaka is an important business hub. Many leading Japanese companies were founded or are headquartered in Osaka, including Daihatsu, Itochu, Kubota, Nippon Life, Nomura, Orix, Panasonic and Sumitomo. Several prefabricated home manufacturers, such as Daiwa House, PanaHome, Sekisui House and Yamada SXL Home, are located in the Osaka area.

One of Osaka's attractions is that, compared with Tokyo, property is inexpensive. According to the City of Osaka, the price of commercial land and residential land is about one-third and one-half, respectively, of the cost of similar space in Tokyo. Office and home rentals in Osaka are roughly two-thirds the cost of those in Tokyo.[22]

Neighborhoods

Nishinari-ku is home to three of Osaka's most distinctive neighborhoods. Thousands of day laborers and homeless people can be found in Kamagasaki, which is reputed to be Japan's largest slum. Like Sanya in Tokyo, this neighborhood has been erased from official maps.[23]

Shinsekai is also in Nishinari-ku. Half of this quirky, century-old district is modeled on Coney Island in New York and half on Paris. Finally, Tobita is Osaka's oldest red-light district. Prostitution is illegal in Japan, but takes place openly in Tobita.

Infrastructure and development

Several major infrastructure and redevelopment initiatives are planned for the Kansai area.

Hokuriku Shinkansen—By 2050, two extensions to the Hokuriku Shinkansen will shorten the trip from Shin-Osaka to Kanazawa from the current 2½ hours to 80 minutes.[24]

Kansai expressways—One of the Kansai Economic Federation's goals is to "Rectify the excess concentration of important functions to Tokyo and establish a Kansai model that leads the way toward regional revitalization." To achieve this goal, the federation is pushing to eliminate missing links in Japan's expressway network, particularly road links with Nagoya and the Chubu region.

Kobe redevelopment—Sannomiya Station, Kobe's main commuter hub, is being redeveloped to make it more pedestrian-friendly and to better integrate the six train and subway stations that serve the downtown core.

Kyoto priority areas—For the 2011 to 2020 planning period, Kyoto City named Kamigamo district, the historical urban district, Toji Temple historical urban district and Fushimi historical urban district as priority areas. These neighborhoods have been targeted for "intense and total maintenance and improvement of the historical scenic beauty" and will also see road improvements and the installation of underground electrical cables.[25]

Osaka Bay rail network—Extensions are planned for the Chuo subway, the Keihan Nakanoshima and the JR Sakurajima lines. The extensions have a total length of 20 kilometers and a budget of ¥574 billion.

Osaka–KIX rail line—The Naniwasuji Line will run from a new station on the north side of JR Osaka Station to Kansai International Airport.

Osaka Nakanoshima—Nakanoshima 4-chome, which is home to the Osaka Science Museum and the National Museum of Art, Osaka, is being redeveloped into an arts- and academia-themed district. Nakanoshima 5-chome, the location of Osaka International Convention Center, will focus on information and international exchange.

Osaka Umekita—Umekita is a large development built on a former rail yard immediately north of JR Osaka Station. The first phase of the project, which covers 3 hectares and includes a hotel, offices and retail space, opened in 2013. The second, 8-hectare phase is scheduled to open in 2022.

Osaka Yumeshima—Osaka bid for the 2025 World Exposition, which will be awarded in November 2018. If Osaka is successful, the expo will be held at a ¥125 billion facility on Yumeshima, an artificial island in Osaka Bay.[26] Yumeshima has 190 hectares available for development and has been proposed as the site for a casino, which the Japanese refer to as an integrated resort.

FUKUOKA

Fukuoka is the capital of Fukuoka Prefecture and the largest city in Kyushu. With an area of 343 square kilometers, Fukuoka has seven wards. The city was formed through a merger of Hakata and Fukuoka in 1889.

Climate

Fukuoka enjoys mild winters, with an average minimum temperature of 3.5°C in January, and hot summers, with an average maximum in August reaching 32.1°C. Relative humidity ranges from a low of 63% in January and February to a high of 75% in July. Fukuoka receives the most rain in July, with an average of 278 millimeters.

Fukuoka's open-air food stalls, called *yatai*, offer delicious, affordable meals.

History

Located on Hakata Bay—one of the nation's largest and most sheltered natural harbors—Fukuoka is the closest major Japanese city to China and South Korea. Hakata was Japan's sole official port of call for diplomats and traders from China and Korea for more than 300 years.

Archaeological evidence suggests that Fukuoka-area residents have been in contact with the Asian mainland for 1,800 years.[1]

World War II solidified Fukuoka's role as a hub, with organizations such as the Bank of Japan and Japan's postal service establishing regional headquarters in the city. But on June 19, 1945, American aircraft firebombed Fukuoka, killing 902 people, injuring 1,078 and leaving 244 missing. More than 60,000 people were made homeless and nearly 13,000 buildings, or about one-fifth of Fukuoka's total, were destroyed. Eighty percent of the city center, including Hakata Station, was razed.

During the post-war era, industrialization drove economic growth in regional Japan. Fukuoka had little heavy industry, with steel mills and coal mines concentrated elsewhere in Kyushu. Ultimately, this worked in Fukuoka's favor, as the city avoided much of the pollution that choked places such as Kitakyushu. Furthermore, the lack of heavy industry forced the city's businesses to focus on services. This benefited Fukuoka in the 1990s, when many Japanese manufacturers moved to China and other low-cost countries.

The post-war years saw the city government adopt the forward-looking policies that characterize Fukuoka today. In 1959, for instance, Fukuoka began producing a biweekly residents' newsletter. Two years later, Fukuoka became one of the first cities in Japan to create a master plan. And in 1968, the city surveyed 1,088 residents to determine their concerns about urban life. While these measures seem unremarkable now, they were a departure from the top-down style of municipal governance that was common in Japan.

During the 1970s and 1980s, Fukuoka's government continued to encourage civic participation and to focus on quality-of-life issues, such as pollution. A youth culture with a vibrant local music scene emerged.

As Japan's economic bubble was bursting, Fukuoka celebrated its centennial and hosted the 1989 Asia-Pacific Exposition at Seaside Momochi.[2] Originally part of a land-reclamation project in Hakata Bay that included 6,000 middle-class homes, Seaside Momochi became an affluent residential neighborhood.[3] Seaside Momochi is now home to Software Research Park Fukuoka, the 234-meter Fukuoka Tower and the 38,000-seat Fukuoka Yafuoku Dome, a multipurpose sports arena.

The success of Seaside Momochi inspired a similar reclamation project, Island City, which opened in 1995 on the east side of Hakata Bay. Completed late and over-budget, the 401-hectare artificial island in Higashi-ku remains underutilized and dependent on public funds. In 2015, Island City had a population of about 6,500 people.[4]

In February 2016, Moody's Investors Service assigned an A1 rating to Fukuoka City. Moody's based its rating on the city's strong and diversified economy; its financial performance, which is better than its national peers; and Fukuoka's good expense control.

Demographics

Fukuoka's population grew 4.1% between 2010 and 2015, to 1.5 million, making it the sixth-largest of Japan's 20 "Ordinance-designated cities." The population is expected to peak at 1.6 million in 2035.[5]

Fukuoka is a relatively young city. In 2010, residents had an average age of 41.3 years, second only to Kawasaki among Japan's ordinance-designated cities. In 2015, couples aged over 65 made up 10.5% of the city's 763,824 households, and elderly singles represented 7.4%.

Transport

Fukuoka has a well-developed transportation network. The Sanyo Shinkansen, which connects Hakata and Shin-Osaka stations, was completed in 1975, and the Kyushu Shinkansen, which links Fukuoka and Kagoshima, entered service in 2011. The Fukuoka City Outer Ring Road opened in 2012.

The Port of Hakata receives more international tourists than any other sea port in Japan. In terms of takeoffs and landings, Fukuoka Airport is Japan's third-busiest, after Haneda and Narita, and has flights to 24 international destinations.[6] Unlike Narita and Kansai International Airport, Fukuoka Airport is near the city center. Fukuoka Airport is served by one of the city's three subway lines. JR

Kyushu and Nishi-Nippon Railroad, better known as Nishitetsu, provide rail services in and around Fukuoka.

The Nanakuma Line is the newest of Fukuoka's three subway lines.

Earthquakes

On March 20, 2005, Fukuoka Prefecture was struck by a magnitude 6.6 earthquake that killed one person, injured 500 and destroyed 65 homes. The quake was noteworthy because Fukuoka had been considered relatively safe from natural disasters: The last major earthquake in the area was the M6.3 Kumamoto earthquake in 1889;[7] the General Insurance Rating Organization of Japan puts Kyushu in its lowest earthquake risk category; and Hakata Bay's narrow mouth shelters the interior of the harbor.

On April 14–15, 2016, seven earthquakes ranging from M5.4 to M7.3 rocked Kumamoto Prefecture. The quakes killed 49 people in Kumamoto and injured nearly 1,700 in Fukuoka, Kumamoto, Oita, Miyazaki and Saga prefectures. Eight thousand houses were destroyed and more than 120,000 were damaged. Direct economic losses were estimated at ¥2.6 trillion–¥4.6 trillion.[8]

After the Kumamoto earthquakes, the Kyodo news agency conducted surveys to determine how prepared Japanese municipalities were to deal with foreign residents in the event of a disaster. Kyodo found that only two cities in the Kyushu-Okinawa region—Oita and Miyazaki—had emergency guidelines for foreigners. Fukuoka had no such plans.[9]

Quality of life

Fukuoka's 1971 master plan articulated the hope that the city would continue to evolve into a "Human Metropolis" (*ningen toshi*).[10] Today, that goal has been achieved in several ways. Fukuoka is a human-scale city, with clean air, tree-lined streets, beautiful parks and excellent museums. Several international magazines have named Fukuoka one of the world's most livable cities.

City hall's green roof symbolizes Fukuoka's commitment to environmental protection.

Fukuoka retains its focus on services, rather than manufacturing, and has embraced environmentalism. Electric vehicle charging stations are common, as are environmentally friendly buildings such as city hall, which features a foliage-covered roof.

National strategic special zone

In 2014, Prime Minister Shinzo Abe designated Fukuoka City a national strategic special zone. In addition to providing tax breaks for start-ups, this classification relaxed visa requirements for foreign workers and labor conditions at start-up companies. The city government also offers incentives, such as employment, rent and land purchase subsidies, to companies establishing operations in Fukuoka. The subsidies are available to foreign and foreign-affiliated companies, and to firms in the software and content development, medicine, health care, environment and energy, logistics and light manufacturing sectors.[11]

Infrastructure and development

Fukuoka Airport—Fukuoka Airport is scheduled to be privatized by April 2019. In addition, a second runway is expected to enter service in 2025.[12] The new runway is expected to cost ¥164 billion and increase the airport's capacity to 188,000 flights per year.

Nanakuma Line extension—A 1.6-kilometer, ¥45 billion extension to the Nanakuma Subway Line is now underway and scheduled to open in fiscal 2020.[13] Construction of the extension, which will link Hakata and Tenjin-Minami stations, was disrupted by a giant sinkhole in November 2016.

Tenjin Big Bang—A decade-long project to revitalize the Tenjin district of Chuo-ku, Tenjin Big Bang takes advantage of the relaxed building regulations that accompanied Fukuoka's designation as a strategic special zone. By 2024, 30 old buildings will be redeveloped, boosting total floor area from 444,000 square meters to 757,000 square meters.[14]

Waterfront redevelopment—The Chuo and Hakata wharves are now being upgraded to make them more attractive to both tourists and residents.

OKINAWA

Comprising 160 islands and 2,281 square kilometers, Okinawa is Japan's southernmost prefecture.

The prefecture is divided into four island groups. The Okinawa Islands are closest to Kyushu and include Okinawa Island and the prefectural capital, Naha. The Sakashima Islands, which include Miyako, Yaeyama and Ishigaki, are closest to Taiwan. The Daito Islands are sparsely populated coral islands in the Philippine Sea. The uninhabited Senkaku Islands are controlled by Japan but claimed by China and Taiwan. Only 49 of Okinawa's islands are inhabited.[1]

Climate

Okinawa enjoys a warm climate. In January, the average minimum temperature in Naha is a comfortable 14.6°C. The average maximum in July, the hottest month, reaches 31.8°C, which is cooler than the hottest months in Nagoya, Osaka and Fukuoka. Relative humidity ranges from a low of 66% in December to a high of 83% in June.

Okinawa's warm waters and abundant marine life make it a popular destination for scuba divers.

May, June, August and September are the wettest months, with average monthly precipitation ranging from 232 to 261 millimeters. In an average year, 7.4 typhoons come within 300 kilometers of Okinawa.[2]

History

Okinawa has been inhabited since prehistoric times. During the Gusuku era, from the 12th to the 15th centuries, residents began trading with China and three principalities—Hokuzan, Chuzan and Nanzan—emerged. In 1429, Sho Hashi unified the islands and established the Ryukyu Kingdom, an independent country that traded with China and with other countries, including Japan, the Philippines and Thailand.

In 1609, the Satsuma clan from Kyushu invaded and brought the Ryukyu Kingdom under the control of Japan's Tokugawa shogunate. During this period, the kingdom was nominally independent so it could maintain commercial links with China. In 1879, Japan annexed the islands to form Okinawa Prefecture.

World War II and the U.S. military

The Battle of Okinawa was fought on Okinawa Island from April 1 to June 22, 1945. One of the largest operations ever staged by the U.S. military, the battle resulted in more than 250,000 deaths, including over 100,000 civilians.[3] Unexploded ordnance and the remains of war dead continue to be discovered in Okinawa. The battle has been featured in several films, including *Okinawa* (1952), *Gekido no showashi: Okinawa kessen* (1971), *Okinawa: The Afterburn* (2015) and *Hacksaw Ridge* (2016).

When the U.S. military government took control of the prefecture in 1945, the dollar replaced the yen and the administrative powers of the Japanese government and the nation's courts were suspended. But the occupiers allowed Japanese laws to stand, as long as they did not conflict with American regulations. Japan's City Planning Act and Urban Building Act remained in force, but were superseded by U.S. laws as the reconstruction process began.[4]

As a result of their strategic location, Okinawa's U.S. bases played key roles in the Korean and Vietnam wars. The bases stockpiled materiel—including chemical, biological and nuclear weapons—and B52s bombed targets in Southeast Asia from airfields in Okinawa.[5]

In 1972, Okinawa returned to Japanese control, but the United States retained a military presence in the prefecture. As of June 2015, there were about 25,000 American military personnel and a similar number of family members and civilian contractors spread over 32 installations in Okinawa, the majority of which are on Okinawa Island. Some 70% of the land occupied by the U.S. military in Japan is in Okinawa, which represents less than 1% of Japan's landmass.[6]

The Okinawan and national governments are now in a legal battle over a multibillion-dollar plan to move U.S. Marine Corps Air Station Futenma in Ginowan to reclaimed land in the Henoko area of Nago (see below). Okinawa Governor Takeshi Onaga and many local residents oppose the move, demanding instead that the Futenma facility leave Okinawa. Public discontent over issues such as the U.S. military bases has sparked demonstrations and encouraged Okinawa independence groups.[7]

In December 2016, the United States returned approximately 4,000 hectares of land in the Northern Training Area on Okinawa Island. Between 2024 and 2028, the United States plans to move 4,000 of the Marines stationed in Okinawa to Guam. Another 3,000 are expected to be transferred to Hawaii. Ultimately, the number of Marines in Okinawa is expected to drop to 10,000–11,000.[8]

Native conflicts
The Okinawan people have a distinct culture. Ryukyuan arts and crafts, dance, and popular and classical music incorporate centuries of influences from Okinawa's neighbors and trading partners. Okinawans are proud of their heritage, which stands apart from the rest of largely homogeneous Japan.

There are longstanding tensions between Okinawans and mainland Japanese. As Waseda University's Hideaki Tobe observes, "Many people in Japanese society expressed pejorative views and opinions of Okinawa as a backward society... an impoverished island region stranded from development, with an indolent subtropical lifestyle and the marked absence of modern hygienic concerns and practices."[9]

During World War II, Japanese troops reportedly executed Okinawans as spies for speaking their native language, and Okinawans were forced to commit suicide rather than surrender to American forces.[10] In a *Japan Times* interview, Masahide Ota—a student conscript who served as governor of Okinawa from 1990 to 1998—likened Okinawans' World War II experiences as being "attacked by tigers at the front gate and wolves at the back."[11]

Okinawan civilians, who had been warned of the savagery of the American soldiers, were surprised when they were treated well. But after World War II, the U.S. military confiscated farms to build bases. And over time, the rapes, murders and other crimes committed by American military personnel became a source of anger. In 1995, for example, three servicemen raped a 12-year-old Okinawan girl.[12]

Crime continues to be an issue. In 2016, Independence Day celebrations on U.S. bases were canceled following the arrest of a civilian worker and Marine veteran for the rape and murder of a 20-year-old Japanese woman. In June 2016, a 21-year-old American sailor whose blood alcohol content was six times the Japanese limit was arrested after she drove into two cars and injured two people.[13]

Other problems include noise pollution, forest fires from live-fire exercises and numerous aircraft crashes, one of which killed 17 people— including 11 elementary school students—in 1959.[14] Deployment of the crash-prone MV-22 Osprey tiltrotor aircraft sparked a protest by tens of thousands of Okinawans in 2012.

But the bases' biggest threat may be environmental. In 2015, research conducted by Jon Mitchell under the U.S. Freedom of Information Act (FOIA) revealed mass deaths of sea life, burials of toxic chemicals and the possible exposure of workers at Camp Kinser. The incidents, which occurred from the 1970s through the 1990s, involved heavy metals, pesticides, insecticides, PCBs and dioxin among other substances.[15] A second FOIA investigation by the same reporter found at least 270 environmental accidents at U.S. Marine bases in Okinawa between June 2002 and June 2016. Only six of the incidents were reported to Japanese authorities, in three cases because the Americans needed help cleaning up the spill. Many of the accidents involved the release of pollutants into waters near the bases.[16]

The Senkakus

Known to the Chinese as the Diaoyus and the Taiwanese as the Diaoyutais, the Senkaku Islands are a collection of eight, small un-inhabited islands in the East China Sea. The Senkakus are important because large deposits of oil and gas are believed to be nearby.

In 2012, the Japanese government bought three of the islands from the Kurihara family, to prevent them from being purchased by a nationalist group led by former Tokyo Governor Shintaro Ishihara, who wanted to demonstrate Japan's control over the Senkakus by building telecommunications and meteorological stations on the islands.

Since the purchase, China has increased the frequency of what it describes as "routine" air and sea patrols nearby. Intended to demonstrate China's jurisdiction over the area, the patrols provoked reciprocal actions by Japan and have the potential to escalate tensions between the two countries.

The situation is further complicated by the fact that—while the United States does not have a position on which nation has sovereignty over the islands—the Senkakus are included in the Treaty of Mutual Cooperation and Security Between Japan and the United States.[17]

Demographics

Okinawa Prefecture has a population of 1.4 million. Most people live on Okinawa Island, which, at 1,207 square kilometers, is the prefecture's largest landmass.

Okinawa has Japan's youngest population, with an average age of 41.8 years in 2016. It is also one of the few prefectures in which the population and number of households are growing. Between 2010 and 2035, Okinawan households are expected to increase 13.1%, versus a 4.4% decline nationwide.[18] Furthermore, Okinawa and Tokyo are the only prefectures where the population in 2035 is forecast to exceed that of 2005.[19] Okinawa is also a "blue zone"—a place where residents have unusually long life spans.

Transport

Naha Airport is Okinawa's main aviation gateway, with flights to cities in Japan as well as Mainland China, Hong Kong, South Korea, Taiwan and Thailand. There are also flights from Hong Kong and Taipei to Ishigaki Airport. Within Okinawa, there are air services to the islands of Ishigaki, Miyako, Kumejima, Aguni, Minami-Daito and Kita-Daito and Tamara.

Nonstop flights now operate between Ishigaki and Hong Kong.

A monorail links Naha Airport with Naha city.

A ferry service links ports in Kobe and Osaka with New Naha Port. In addition, there is a ferry from Kagoshima to Naha Port, via Motobu Port. Ferries sail between many of Okinawa's inhabited islands.

Commerce and industry

White sand beaches, clean air and an average temperature of 22.7°C make Okinawa an attractive tourist destination. The islands attracted 8.6 million visitors in 2016 and the government hopes to attract 10 million tourists by 2021 and 15.2 million by 2030.[20]

Despite the high cost of flying inside Japan, domestic travelers comprise the bulk of Okinawa's tourists. However, there are growing numbers of tourists from Taiwan, South Korea, Mainland China and Hong Kong who are capitalizing on new and improved airline services. In 2016, for example, twice-weekly nonstop flights started between Hong Kong and Ishigaki.

In 2014, Prime Minister Shinzo Abe named Okinawa a special strategic zone for international tourism. Okinawa has excellent scuba diving, and Prime Minister Abe's announcement allows divers to take examinations in languages other than Japanese.[21]

Infrastructure and development

The government is improving Okinawa's infrastructure, particularly on the outlying islands. In January 2017, for example, an undersea optical fiber cable was laid between Okinawa Island and Yonaguni, as part of a program to improve internet service. A new hospital opened on Ishigaki in 2017.

Numerous hotels and resorts are under construction in Okinawa.

Futenma relocation—In 2017, work began on a project to move Marine Corps Air Station Futenma from a crowded residential part of Ginowan to a 205-hectare site adjacent to Camp Schwab, near Nago.

Over five years, 160 hectares of Oura Bay will be reclaimed, using 21 million cubic meters of earth and sand.[22] The environmental and political aspects of this project have created controversy in and outside Japan.

Hotels and resorts—More than 20 hotels and resorts are now under development on Okinawa, Miyako and Ishigaki islands. The projects are backed by well-known Japanese companies, including Mori Trust, Mitsui Fudosan and Tokyu Liveable, as well as firms from Malaysia, Taiwan and Thailand. Some developments are new, while others have been revived after being abandoned during the global financial crisis.

Naha Airport expansion—A second runway at Naha Airport is expected to open in March 2020, increasing the number of annual departures and arrivals from 135,000 to 185,000.[23]

Naha–Nago rail line—Plans for a 69-kilometer train line between Naha and Nago have been announced. Construction is scheduled to start in 2019, with operations beginning in 2029.[24]

MONEY

MORTGAGES

Mortgages, which are also known as home loans or housing loans, are available in Japan through city, regional, trust and online banks; finance companies; and foreign banks. Most mortgages are sold through direct channels, such as bank branches, rather than intermediaries.

The Bank of Japan's low interest rate policy has kept mortgage rates affordable. In November 2017, variable-rate mortgages were available from 0.477% per annum, while 35-year, fixed-rate mortgages were 1.02%.

Mortgage basics

In fiscal 2015, 56.5% of new mortgages were variable rate; 30.0% were hybrids in which the interest rate floats after an initial fixed period, typically 3, 5 or 10 years; and 13.5% were fixed rate.[1] Variable-rate mortgages—where the interest rate is reviewed daily, monthly, bi-annually or annually—generally offer the lowest interest rates, with borrowers paying a premium for the security of a fixed rate for the duration of the mortgage.

Reverse mortgages, which allow elderly people to use their home as security for a nonrecourse loan that is repaid when the home is sold after the borrower and his spouse die, are becoming more common in Japan, where many elderly people are asset rich, but cash flow poor. Japan's three largest banks—Bank of Tokyo-Mitsubishi UFJ, Sumitomo Mitsui Banking Corporation and Mizuho Bank—offer reverse mortgages, and a 2016 survey by the Japan Housing Finance Agency indicated that more than one-fifth of Japanese lenders either offer reverse mortgages or plan to make them available.[2]

Mortgage repayment schedules can be tailored to the annual or semi-annual bonuses that many salaried workers receive. It is common for borrowers to make a modest mortgage payment for 10 or 11 months of the year with a large payment in June and/or December when bonuses are paid.

You can qualify for a mortgage with three years of continuous employment and an annual income of ¥2 million. If you are self-employed, lenders require three years of operating history and profitability. However, these numbers are bare minimums. Self-employed people and company presidents face more scrutiny than salaried employees. Military personnel covered by the U.S.–Japan Status of Forces Agreement need a guarantor when applying for a mortgage. Banks generally do not lend to foreigners with diplomatic status because of the legal protections diplomats receive.

In Japan, most residential mortgages are recourse loans. If you default, the lender can foreclose on and force the sale of the mortgaged property. The foreclosure process can take a year or more. If the sale proceeds do not repay the mortgage, the lender can pursue you for any remaining debt.

The default rate for residential mortgages has remained low, typically between 0.1% and 0.2%, even during the 2008 global financial crisis.[3] This makes mortgages an attractive business for lenders, who benefit from Japan's modest levels of unemployment and divorce, two common default triggers.

Applying for a mortgage

Relationships are important in Japan, and an introduction can smooth the way when you apply for a mortgage. Real estate agents and developers typically work with multiple lenders and are a useful source of introductions. They will know the lender's policies and have a relationship with loan officers that facilitates informal communication. That won't guarantee success, but it will ensure your application is presented in the right format and with the correct documents.

Agents and developers use introductions to sell property. One potential drawback to this approach is that the lenders with which they have a relationship may not offer the best deal. You can check the rate against those posted on several aggregators' websites. See the "Information Sources" chapter for more information.

The Bank of Japan's low interest rate policy has kept mortgages affordable.

It can take 30–60 days to arrange a mortgage. There are two steps in the process, although it is possible to skip the first step and go directly to a full application:

▲ **Pre-approval**. You complete an application form and provide supporting documents about your job, residency and finances. The lender indicates how much it is willing to lend and at what rate. The estimate is not binding, but you can begin shopping for a home with confidence that the mortgage will be approved. Because you have not identified the home you wish to buy, your application can be rejected if the lender has an issue with the property (see below). Many lenders' websites let you input your details and receive a preliminary loan assessment.

▲ **Full application**. You complete an application and provide sup porting documents about yourself and the home you want to buy. After reviewing the documents, the lender makes a binding offer that you can accept or reject. Waiting for full approval puts you at a disadvantage if you are competing with a cash buyer, dealing with a vendor who wants a quick sale or bidding for an attractively priced home.

Mortgage applications are refused for many reasons, including the borrower's advanced age, poor health or indebtedness. Property-specific issues can also cause the lender to reject a mortgage application. These include a home outside the lender's geographical or policy limits, such as a ski chalet in Hokkaido; missing documents, such as a certificate of post construction (*kensa zumisho*); a discrepancy between the purchase price and the appraised value; or new zoning that reduces a home's redevelopment potential. Some lenders will tell you the mortgage application has been approved but the property has been rejected and suggest that you find another. Others will simply reject your application outright.

Your ability to obtain a mortgage can be influenced by branch-level quotas, changes to a lender's credit rating and underwriting guidelines, the Bank of Japan's policies and global economic or political events.

Paying cash can be an effective strategy because it lets you complete the transaction quickly. You can then refinance the property, but you must have all the documents you would have gathered to obtain a mortgage. Without a full set of documents, you may be unable to arrange refinancing.

Over the past decade, Japanese real estate has become a popular investment for buyers from Mainland China, Hong Kong, Singapore and Taiwan. Some developers make financing available to nonresidents buying new homes in Japan. Loans to nonresidents for existing homes remain rare.

Credit bureaus

Japan has three national consumer credit bureaus. Each bureau retains data for five years from the date of the credit event and records events throughout Japan. Not all members share all their data.

Operated by the Japanese Bankers Association, the Personal Credit Information Center (PCIC) represents 1,180 banks, other financial institutions, bank-affiliated credit card issuers and guarantee companies. The PCIC collects both positive and negative information about consumer loans, current account transactions, guarantees and credit card transactions. As of March 2017, the PCIC's database contained 93.9 million contracts. Consumers can check their PCIC file by mail.

The Credit Information Center (CIC) has 946 members, including department stores and credit card, finance, consumer credit, leasing, insurance and credit guarantee companies. The CIC tracks credit card transactions, installment credit sales, leasing contracts, guarantees, loans and mortgages. Of the three bureaus, the CIC has the largest database, with 697.5 million contracts. You can check your credit record by mail, by internet or in person at the CIC's offices in Sapporo, Sendai, Tokyo, Nagoya, Osaka, Okayama and Fukuoka.

The Japan Credit Information Reference Center (JCIRC) has 1,421 members, including credit card, consumer credit, guarantee and finance companies, as well as banks and credit cooperatives. The JCIRC records consumer loans, guarantees and credit card transactions and has a database of 356.6 million contracts. You can check your credit record by mail or in person at the JCIRC's offices in Osaka and Tokyo.

Choosing a lender

Your choice of lender will be determined by your residency status, language ability and credit history. A Japanese-speaking permanent resident (PR) who is employed by a well-known Japanese company and has an established credit record can usually borrow from a large local bank. A less-fluent resident who doesn't have PR status will have more success with a midsize bank, such as Suruga or Shinsei. A person buying a home outside Japan's large cities may find a local or regional bank is helpful, particularly with an introduction from someone with good community connections.

The best interest rates come from internet banks, which have the lowest overheads, and from Japan's largest banks, which have the lowest cost of funds.

There are several other costs that borrowers should consider. For instance, lenders charge an administrative fee for setting up the mortgage, which can be a flat rate or a percentage of the loan amount, and may charge a fee if you prepay your loan. Banks usually require borrowers to join a group life insurance plan, and some lenders require you to purchase fire insurance on your home. Banks may charge a guarantee fee of about 2% of the mortgage amount, which is usually paid to a subsidiary or an affiliated company. The guarantee fee varies from lender to lender, and you can usually pay a slightly higher interest rate for the duration of the mortgage instead of the guarantee fee. This reduces your initial outlay, but costs more over the life of the mortgage.

You should also consider whether you want the lender to provide day-to-day banking services. For example, Bank of Tokyo-Mitsubishi UFJ has 766 domestic and 75 international branches, while Shinsei Bank has 28 domestic branches. Shinsei has no branches in Okinawa or outside Japan. Similarly, it is worthwhile investigating the bank's automated teller machine (ATM) network.

Foreign perspectives

If you are a non-Japanese borrower dealing with a Japanese lender, it helps to understand their perspective on you and your application. You represent a tiny proportion of most lenders' business, and few have systems and policies to accommodate your needs. Furthermore, banks are conservative organizations and it is often easier for a loan officer to say "no" than to bend the rules or do something different.

Unless you have lived in Japan for a long time, your local credit record will be brief. This makes it difficult for banks to evaluate your creditworthiness, because your financial history outside Japan is usually seen as irrelevant. Lenders focus on income rather than assets when evaluating your ability to repay a loan, which is rational given the volatility of the Japanese stock and real estate markets over the past 30 years. Lenders prefer borrowers with little or no outstanding debt.

Some lenders will refuse your application if you cannot read and speak Japanese. Even if you are fluent, there may be questions about your ability to understand the nuances of the loan documents, which will be in Japanese. If they are provided, translations of the Japanese documents are not legally enforceable.

Your mortgage application must be letter-perfect and internally consistent. Minor variations in usage, spelling or capitalization that a native English speaker would ignore—for example, one document referring to you as "Christopher" and another as "Chris"—can cause your application to be delayed or rejected. You may also be asked to produce original or notarized copies of documents.

It is easier to get a mortgage for a new condominium in Osaka than for an organic vegetable farm in Okinawa.

Despite these challenges, many foreign residents have obtained mortgages. Here's how to increase the likelihood that your application will be approved.

▲ **Become a permanent resident.** Meeting the government's PR requirements tells the bank you are a person of good character and are creditworthy. It also suggests you have strong ties to Japan and are unlikely to flee.

▲ **Speak and read Japanese.** Fluency in Japanese makes it easier for the bank to serve you.

▲ **Demonstrate ties to the community.** Having a Japanese spouse, having children living in Japan and applying for PR (even if it has not yet been approved) demonstrate that you are in Japan for the long term and are a good risk.

▲ **Exude stability.** Banks like borrowers who have worked for the same employer (ideally a large, well-known Japanese company) for a long time. Having three jobs in as many years, even with increases in salary and responsibility, is a negative. Entrepreneurs are seen as poor risks because their incomes are more volatile than those of salaried employees.

▲ **Have your paperwork in order.** You will save time and make it easier for the bank to approve your application if you have all of the documents (see below) the lender needs in their preferred format.

▲ **Be conventional.** You are more likely to get a mortgage for a new condominium than an organic vegetable farm. For face-to-face appointments, dress appropriately and avoid visible piercings or tattoos.

▲ **Use introductions.** A referral from your real estate agent, developer, employer, spouse's family or even a politician can open doors that would otherwise remain shut.

▲ **Make the numbers work.** Ensure your loan-to-value ratio (mortgage amount divided by the property's value), debt-to-income ratio (annual mortgage repayment divided by your annual income), mortgage amount and term are within the ranges specified by the bank. The larger your down payment, the less risk the lender perceives.

▲ **Leave some wiggle room.** Add 7%–8% to the purchase price for closing costs and incidentals and budget for repairs and maintenance. Japanese interest rates are low, but they may increase over the life of a 35-year mortgage. Buying a little less than you can afford is sensible.

The Herman case

No overview of financing a property purchase in Japan would be complete without mentioning Steven L. Herman, an American journalist who lived in Japan from 1990 to 2007.

In June 1999, Herman signed a contract to purchase a ¥75 million condominium in Tokyo's Shibuya-ku. Herman—who had been dealing with Asahi Bank (now part of the Resona Group) in a personal and corporate capacity for several years—applied to Asahi Bank for a ¥68.5 million mortgage for his new home.

At the time, Herman was a senior executive at a multinational media organization and was earning a salary he describes as several times that of a typical Japanese manager. He had a solid credit history, had lived in Japan for nearly a decade and spoke Japanese, but was not a permanent resident.

Despite his credentials, he was unsuccessful. "I wasn't turned down for a mortgage," observes Herman. "They refused to accept the application."

Herman says that when his then-fiancée met Asahi Bank representatives to ask why they wouldn't consider his application, they told her it was because "Foreigners run away."

As he explains, "If I had filed an application and they turned me down and said, 'No, we've reviewed your application and we don't want to give you a loan,' then that's their right. I thought they were extremely insensitive and were being blatantly discriminatory and that's why I decided to file the suit."

In October 1999, he sued Asahi Bank in Tokyo District Court seeking ¥11 million in damages. His attorney argued that Asahi Bank's lending practices were discriminatory, unconstitutional and violated Herman's human rights under international law.

Asahi Bank claimed it was against their policy to provide loans to foreigners without permanent resident status because they would not be able to recover the outstanding money if the borrower fled overseas.

In November 2001, the Tokyo District Court ruled in favor of Asahi Bank. Herman filed an appeal with the Tokyo High Court, which was dismissed in August 2002. He then appealed to Japan's Supreme Court, which declined to hear the case. The case was subsequently cited in a United Nations report on the prevention of discrimination against noncitizens.[4]

Herman believes the effort was worthwhile. "Even though we lost at every level from a legal point of view, we did apparently change the mindset of banks in Japan," says Herman, who later became a permanent resident and purchased a home in Tokyo's Ota-ku with a loan from Fuji Bank (now Mizuho Bank).

And despite spending "many, many thousands of dollars," Herman believes it was a Pyrrhic victory for Asahi Bank. "This must have cost them an enormous amount of money. In fact, I'm sure the legal case from their side cost them more money than if I had taken a loan and defaulted on it."

Funding sources

Large Japanese banks
Japan's big banks offer fixed-rate, hybrid, variable-rate and Flat 35 mortgages for the purchase of new and used residential property (i.e., detached houses and condominiums), construction of new homes, refinancing, repairs and improvements such as making homes barrier-free. Equity release mortgages are available, and many banks offer lower interest rates for energy-efficient and low-CO_2 homes. Banks also offer mortgages that include health insurance riders, a repayment holiday in the event of a natural disaster and revolving credit lines.

These banks offer competitive interest rates. However, they typically require you to be a permanent resident, to have an established credit record and a stable employment history in Japan, and to speak Japanese.

Internet banks

Since the government began deregulating Japan's financial markets in the late 1990s, the number of internet banks has grown. Some, like Sony Bank and Rakuten Bank, are part of larger nonbank organizations. Others are joint ventures, like Jibun Bank, which was formed by Bank of Tokyo-Mitsubishi UFJ and telecommunications company KDDI, and SBI Sumishin Net Bank, which is owned by SBI Holdings and Sumitomo Mitsui Trust Bank.

Internet banks have lower overheads than conventional banks. They have fewer staff and don't own or rent branches in expensive, high-traffic locations. Internet banks pass these savings along to customers as higher interest rates on deposits and lower rates on loans. In the current low interest rate environment, the difference between a mortgage from an internet bank and a conventional bank is typically less than 0.1 percentage points. But over 20–30 years, the savings can add up.

Internet banks offer fixed-rate, hybrid, variable-rate and Flat 35 mortgages. Some conduct their business online or by mail and do not require face-to-face meetings. Internet banks are particularly suited to refinancing, which is a simpler process than arranging a new mortgage.

Flat 35

From 1950 to 2003, the Government Housing Loan Corporation (GHLC) provided mortgages directly to individuals and was the main lender for the government's housing policies. In 2007, the GHLC was succeeded by the Japan Housing Finance Agency (JHF), which withdrew from the direct lending business. JHF now purchases and securitizes mortgages originated by private lenders, underwrites mortgage insurance and provides loans for urban redevelopment projects and the construction of rental housing for the elderly and families with small children. JHF also supports housing-reconstruction loans in areas affected by the Great East Japan Earthquake and other natural disasters.

Flat 35 is a long-term, fixed-interest mortgage offered by banks and other lenders in collaboration with JHF, which buys claims on the mortgages from lenders and then issues securities using the mortgages as collateral. When the borrower draws down the mortgage, the lender sells its claim against the mortgage to JHF. However, the interest rate, repayment schedule and other terms and conditions remain unchanged and the borrower makes payments to the lender where he obtained the mortgage. There is no guarantee fee or penalty for early repayment of a Flat 35 mortgage.

Flat 35S is a variant of Flat 35 that offers reduced interest rates for borrowers buying homes that are energy-efficient, earthquake-resistant, barrier-free and durable. JHF also offers Flat 50, a 50-year, fixed-rate mortgage for long-life homes that includes a "relay" feature allowing the child of a borrower to take over the mortgage. Flat 35 and Flat 50 are available to qualified permanent residents.

The interest rate for Flat 35 mortgages varies among lenders because it comprises three components: the coupon rate of the mortgage-backed security issued by JHF; JHF's operational cost; and a service fee, which is set by the financial institution that originates the mortgage. In addition, some lenders have introduced complexities, such as loan fees and interest rates that change over the course of the mortgage term, making it difficult to compare offers from different financial institutions.[5]

Midsize Japanese banks

Three midsize banks—Shinsei Bank, Suruga Bank and Tokyo Star Bank—offer mortgages to permanent residents and have English-language marketing materials.

Shinsei offers hybrid, fixed- and variable-rate mortgages for the purchase of a new or used home, building a new house or refinancing an existing dwelling. Mortgage amounts range from ¥5 million to ¥100 million with terms of 5–35 years. Shinsei does not charge a guarantor fee or an early repayment fee and operates an English-speaking call center, and bilingual ATMs and online banking services. Shinsei will lend to permanent residents and to nonpermanent residents who are married to Japanese citizens or permanent residents. Borrowers must join a group life insurance plan selected by Shinsei and pay a ¥54,000 handling fee if the mortgage is approved. Borrowers must be over age 20 and under 65 when the loan is originated and under 80 when the last payment is due.

Suruga provides mortgages for the purchase of residential property or land for personal use, home improvements and refinancing. Mortgages are variable rate, with amounts of ¥1 million to ¥100 million and terms of 1–35 years. A guarantor is not necessary, but the borrower must join a group life insurance plan selected by Suruga. A sliding scale of prepayment charges applies for the life of the loan, and Suruga charges a ¥108,000 handling fee if the mortgage is approved. Suruga requires borrowers to have some competence in Japanese. Borrowers must be over age 20 and under 65 when the loan is originated and under 76 when the last payment is due.

Tokyo Star Bank offers variable-rate, fixed-rate and deposit-linked mortgages to permanent residents and to foreign nonpermanent residents who are "capable of understanding contract provisions in Japanese." Funds may be used to purchase or build a new home, or to renovate or refinance an existing dwelling. Loan amounts range from ¥5 million to ¥100 million, with terms of 1–35 years and maximum loan-to-value ratios of 90% if the funds are used to buy or build a home. Borrowers must be between 20 and 65, and the loan must be repaid by the borrower's 75th birthday. Guarantors are not required and the bank charges an administrative fee of 2.16% of the loan amount. Borrowers must sign on to a "maintenance pack" that includes enrollment in group life insurance, early repayment options and other items, and adds between 0.3% and 0.702% to the annual interest rate.

In addition to their small branch networks, the main disadvantage to dealing with these banks is that their interest rates are usually higher than those of internet banks and large Japanese banks.

Foreign banks
When the first edition of this book was published in 2010, Commonwealth Bank of Australia, HSBC and National Australia Bank offered residential mortgages in Japan. All have since left the Japanese mortgage market. In November 2015, Citibank's retail

operations were integrated into those of SMBC Trust Bank under the "PRESTIA" brand.

The foreign banks were noteworthy for providing English-language websites and marketing materials and English-speaking staff. They also considered borrowers' financial history and assets outside Japan; used foreigner-friendly, Western-style credit scoring systems; and would lend for investment properties and equity release. These advantages were offset by higher interest rates and smaller branch networks.

As of late 2017, the Bank of China and the Bank of Taiwan offered loans to people speaking Japanese or Putonghua (Mandarin). Both lenders focus on their respective nationals, and their interest rates, loan tenors and loan-to-valuation rates are less attractive than those of large Japanese banks.

Mortgage brokers
Brokers know many financial institutions and use this knowledge to match your circumstances with the lender that is most likely to accept your application and offer a competitive deal. Brokers can also "polish" your application to make it more attractive to lenders and ensure you have all the necessary paperwork.

Brokers charge borrowers a fee for their services. Typically, brokers offer a free initial consultation, where they explain their services and screen the borrower to ensure the loan application has a reasonable chance of success. If the application is viable and the borrower wants to proceed, she supplies her personal details, indicates the amount she wants to borrow and pays an application fee. The broker submits mortgage applications to several lenders, and if the application is successful, charges the borrower a percentage of the mortgage amount. There is usually a minimum charge and, aside from the initial application fee, borrowers only pay the broker when the mortgage is drawn down.

Brokers add value when they arrange a mortgage from a lender that would not ordinarily consider your application. They can also be helpful if your situation is complex or unusual, or if you lack the time or inclination to search for a lender. Ask the broker for client references and examples of mortgages he has arranged from different lenders to gauge the breadth of his contacts.

Financing for nonresidents

The Japanese real estate industry knows the lack of financing options is hurting its ability to sell to nonresidents. Options remain limited, but the following companies lend to nonresidents.

ORIX Asia offers fixed- and variable-rate loans to Hong Kong identity card holders and Hong Kong–incorporated companies buying commercial and residential property in Tokyo and Osaka. Property purchased for investment and self-use qualify. The minimum loan amount is ¥20 million with a maximum tenor of 15 years.

Shinsei Investment & Finance offers loans to Hong Kong passport holders—but not Hong Kong identity card holders—who live in Hong Kong for new and used homes in Tokyo, Osaka and Nagoya. The minimum loan size is ¥10 million, with a maximum 20-year tenor and a ¥30,000 prepayment penalty. Borrowers must be between 20 and 70 at the time of the loan and under 75 at the time of the final payment. There is a 1.5% or ¥150,000 loan establishment charge, whichever is larger.

Singapore's UOB offers loans to people buying residential investment property in Tokyo, Yokohama, Osaka, Kyoto and Fukuoka. Loan-to-value ratios of up to 70% are available with a maximum tenor of 35 years. Loans are not available to Japanese citizens or residents of Japan.

Supporting documents

Here is a list of the documents a lender is likely to request with your mortgage application. Different documents will be required depending on the lender, type of property, whether you are an owner-occupier or investor, and your country of residence. Original documents or notarized copies may be required, and some documents have expiry dates.

You will need to complete a mortgage application form and a consent form that allows the lender to check your references. The consent form may authorize the lender to retrieve official documents on your behalf. There will be a life insurance application, if you are joining a group plan through the lender.

Identification

▲ Valid passport with valid visa, and/or valid driver's license for you and your spouse, if applicable.

▲ Residence card (*zairyu* card; 在留カード) for you and your spouse, if applicable.

▲ Resident's registration certificate (*jumin hyo*; 住民票), which is needed if you or your spouse is a Japanese national or if your Japanese spouse will act as guarantor. The certificate should include all family members in the household registered to that address and the loan applicant's relation to the guarantor. The certificate is valid for three months from the date of issue and is available from the ward or city office.

▲ Registered seal (*jitsu in*; 実印). This is purchased from a stamp (*hanko*) shop and registered with your local ward office.

▲ Three certified copies of the specimen of your seal (*inkan toroku shomeisho*; 印鑑登録証明書). Available from the ward or city office where your seal is registered, this is valid for three months from the date of issue.

▲ Valid national health insurance card (*kenko hoken sho*; 健康保険証).

▲ Name, address, phone and fax numbers and email address of your real estate agent and judicial scrivener (*shiho-shoshi*; 司法書士).

Financial

▲ Pay slips or bank statements showing three months of salary history. An employment report may be needed if you have been with your employer for less than three years.

▲ Employment contract (*koyou keiyakusho*; 雇用契約書). This is usually needed if you have been with your employer for less than one year.

▲ Statement of withholding tax paid for the past two years (*gensen choshuhyo*; 源泉徴収票). Available from your employer.

▲ Inhabitants tax certificate (*juminzei kazei shomeisho*;住民税課税証明書) or inhabitants tax notice (*juminzei kettei tsuchi sho*; 住民税決定通知書). Available from your ward or city office.

▲ Special income tax return (*kakutei shinkoksho hikae*; 確定申告書控え). People who are self-employed or have multiple income sources or income over ¥20 million must file this document with the regional tax office each year.

▲ Tax payment certificate (*nozei shomeisho*; 納税証明書その1、その2). Available from your ward or city office, this includes a set of two documents for the past two years and is needed if you filed your own income tax return (*kakutei shinkoku;* 確定申告).

▲ Schedule of repayments and outstanding balance for other mortgaged property you own.

▲ Account statements for other debts, such as credit cards or car loans.

▲ If you are self-employed or using a company to apply for the mortgage, you will need the company registration (*tokibo tohon*; 登記簿謄本) and two or three years of financial statements (*kessan sho*; 決算書) and tax returns.

Property

▲ Sale and purchase agreement (*baibai keyakusho*; 売買契約書). Available from the real estate agent.

▲ Construction contract (*ukeoi keyakusho*; 請負契約書) or cost estimate (*oyobi mitsumorisho*; 及び見積もり書). Available from the vendor, developer or builder.

▲ Explanation of important matters (*juyou jikou setsumeisho*; 重要事項説明書). This is available from the real estate agent, who reads it aloud before the contract is signed.

▲ Certificate of post construction (*kensa zumisho*; 検査済証 ［建物］). Available from the vendor, developer or builder.

▲ Building permit (*kakunin zumisho*; 確認済証 ［建物］). Available from the vendor, developer or builder.

▲ Building plan layout (*tatemono haichizu*; 建物配置図). Available from the vendor, developer or builder.

▲ Land registration certificate (*tokijikou shomeisho [tokibo tohon]*; 登記事項証明書 ［土地］). Available from the Legal Affairs Bureau (*houmukyoku*; 法務局).

▲ Building registration certificate (*tokijikou shomeisho [tokibo tohon]*; 登記事項証明書 ［建物］). Available from the Legal Affairs Bureau.

▲ Official land map (*kouzu*; 公図). Available from the Legal Affairs Bureau.

▲ Property brochure (*bukken gaiyo [hanbai zumen]*; 物件概要 ［販売図面］). Available from the real estate agent or developer.

▲ Statement of income and expenses (*shushi meisai*; 物件収支明細). Available from the vendor or management company.

▲ Property location map (*bukken annaizu*; 物件案内図). Needed for new condominiums and houses, this is available from the real estate agent.

▲ Acreage survey map (*chiseki sokuryouzu*; 地積測量図). Available from the Legal Affairs Bureau.

▲ Building floor plan (*tatemono heimenzu*; 建物平面図). Available from the builder or the Legal Affairs Bureau.

▲ Building inspection certificate (*tatemono kensazumishou*; 建物検査済証). Needed for new condominiums and houses, this is available from the builder or real estate agent.

▲ Original title deed (*kenrisho*; 権利書原本). Available from the vendor after the title is transferred.

Insurance

▲ Proof of fire insurance, including the insurer's name, policy number and insured amount.

▲ Proof of earthquake insurance, including the insurer's name, policy number and insured amount.

▲ Proof of life insurance, including the insurer's name, policy number and insured amount, if the insurance is not provided by the lender.

INSURANCE

Earthquake insurance

Despite Japan's reputation as a seismic hot spot, earthquake insurance for residential buildings is readily available. In 2016, just over one-third of the 18.2 million households in the Tokyo Metropolitan Area had earthquake insurance.[1]

Earthquake insurance premiums are higher for wooden homes than for dwellings made from steel-reinforced concrete.

Until recently, Japanese homes had short life spans and depreciated rapidly. Local earthquake insurance is structured and priced accordingly.

Earthquake insurance in Japan
Under the Law Concerning Earthquake Insurance, coverage is sold by non-life insurance companies, which are reinsured by the Japan Earthquake Reinsurance Company (JER). JER, in turn, has retrocession agreements under which it is reinsured by the non-life insurance companies and the Japanese government.

As of April 2016, there was an aggregate liability limit of ¥11.3 trillion for any one earthquake, with the contribution of JER, the non-life insurance companies and the government varying according to the amount of claims payable. If total losses exceed ¥11.3 trillion, insurance companies can reduce their payouts to policyholders. To put the liability cap into perspective, as of March 31, 2017, ¥1,275 billion in reinsurance claims had been made in relation to the 2011 Great East Japan Earthquake (GEJE). The GEJE remains the most expensive earthquake in Japanese history.

Buying earthquake insurance

Earthquake insurance is sold as a rider to fire insurance policies and is not available separately. Fire insurance does not cover losses from fires caused or spread by an earthquake. You can add earthquake coverage to a valid fire insurance policy, but you may not be able to do so if an earthquake warning is in effect. Earthquake insurance policies are available in terms of one to five years, and discounts are available for multiyear contracts. You can buy separate earthquake insurance riders for your building and for your personal property.

Coverage

Earthquake insurance covers loss or damage to residential buildings and personal property through fire, destruction, burial or flooding caused directly or indirectly by an earthquake, a volcanic eruption or a tsunami. Loss or damage is excluded if it is caused by gross negligence, willful or illegal acts, war or insurrection, or if it occurs 10 or more days after an earthquake.

Buildings used as factories or offices are not insurable, as are precious metals, gems or antiques valued at ¥300,000 or more per piece, currency, securities, automobiles and certain other items. Claims are not payable for loss or damage caused only to gates, walls, fences and other items that are not major structural parts.

The sum insured ranges from 30% to 50% of the amount of the fire insurance policy to which the earthquake rider is attached. Coverage is limited to ¥50 million for a building and ¥10 million for personal property. For policies with an inception date on or after January 1, 2017, losses are categorized as total (up to 100% of the depreciated value of the insured object), large half loss (up to 60%), small half loss (up to 30%) or partial loss (up to 5%).

Read your policy carefully to ensure the coverage matches your needs. Many homeowners in Urayasu, Chiba, were surprised to learn their earthquake insurance did not cover the liquefaction that hit the city during the GEJE.[2]

Premiums

Earthquake insurance premiums are standardized and based on the dwelling's location and construction material.

For example, ¥10 million of earthquake insurance on a non-wooden dwelling in Fukuoka Prefecture built in 1980 costs ¥6,800 per year. In Tokyo, ¥10 million of coverage on a wooden dwelling built in 1980 is ¥36,300 per year. Both examples exclude the cost of fire insurance and earthquake coverage for personal property.[3]

A 10% discount is available for buildings constructed after June 1981. Earthquake resistant buildings qualify for a 10%–50% discount, while seismically isolated buildings receive a 50% reduction. Discounts cannot be combined, but earthquake insurance premiums are tax deductible.

Premiums for earthquake insurance rose by an average of 5.1% on January 1, 2017, in response to new risk projections. This will be followed by a series of additional increases that will see premiums in some prefectures rise 50%.[4] If you plan to live in Japan for the long term and see earthquake insurance as being valuable, it could make sense to lock-in current prices and take advantage of the discount available for a five-year policy.

Fire insurance

Lenders generally require fire insurance for the duration of the mortgage.

Life insurance

Many lenders will not approve a mortgage unless you enroll in a group life insurance plan. The lender usually specifies the insurer, pays the premium and is named as the policy's beneficiary.

If you have had a major health problem, such as cancer or a heart attack, within the past three years, you are unlikely to qualify for life insurance. Chronic conditions such as diabetes mellitus, hypertension, cirrhosis or renal disease will also cause you to be disqualified. Shopping around is pointless because different insurers use the same terms. Your insurance coverage can be revoked if you are discovered to have omitted information on your application.

Minpaku insurance

A unit of security company Secom offers home contents insurance for hosts, while Airbnb is partnering with Sompo Japan Nipponkoa to develop insurance products for minpaku operators. Both Secom and Sompo have 24-hour call centers to help guests and hosts deal with security issues as well as noise- and garbage-related disputes.

Warranties for new and pre-owned homes

The Organization for Housing Warranty (OHW) provides defect liability insurance to real estate agents and builders selling new homes, and to individuals and agents selling pre-owned homes.

The OHW also offers completion insurance for unfinished homes, foundation and subsidence insurance, and renovation insurance.

TAXES

Individuals and companies that buy, own, sell or earn rental income from property in Japan are subject to Japanese taxes. The tax obligation will depend on whether the property is owner-occupied or held as an investment; on the owner's residency status; on the length of time the property is held; and on whether the property is acquired by an individual or a company. Consumption tax is payable on buildings and most services associated with buying and selling real estate. Allowances and deductions are available for many taxes.

Japanese tax law is complicated, and the level of complexity increases rapidly when multiple tax jurisdictions are involved. If you own property in Japan, get professional tax and estate planning advice.

Tax basics

Appraised values
Taxes on acquiring and holding property are based on four government-sponsored appraisals. A property's appraised value bears little relationship to its market price.

The "Land Market Value Publication" (also known as the official land price) is based on an annual nationwide appraisal by the Ministry of Land, Infrastructure, Transport and Tourism (MLIT).[1] Prices are effective January 1. In 2017, 26,000 sites were appraised.

The "Market Values of Standard Sites" (aka the prefectural land price) is derived from an annual nationwide appraisal by prefectural governments. Prices are effective July 1. In 2017, 21,644 sites were appraised.[2]

The "Road Rating" (aka the roadside or *rosenka* price) is conducted annually by the National Tax Agency and appraises one square meter of land along major roads. Results are used to calculate inheritance and gift taxes. The road rating price is typically about 80% of the land market value publication price and is effective on January 1. In 2017, about 333,000 plots were surveyed.[3]

The *rosenka* value is an annual appraisal of land along major roads.

The "Land Appraisal for Fixed Assets Tax" is assessed by municipal governments every three years along selected streets throughout Japan. It is effective January 1 and is used to calculate the registration and license tax, fixed assets tax, real estate acquisition tax and urban planning tax. The land appraisal for fixed assets tax is approximately 70% of the land market value publication.

Residency

In Japan, the way your income is taxed depends on whether you are a nonresident, a permanent resident or a nonpermanent resident. These categories only reflect your tax status; it is possible to be a permanent resident for tax purposes without having permanent resident status from the Immigration Bureau.

For tax purposes, you become a permanent resident when you have lived in Japan for five years (60 months) or more in the previous 10 years.[4] Permanent residents are taxed on their worldwide income and are subject to national income tax and local inhabitants tax.

Nonpermanent residents have resided in Japan for more than one year but less than five years in the past 10 years. Nonpermanent residents are taxed on income earned in Japan and on income earned offshore and paid in or remitted to Japan.[5]

Nonresidents have lived in Japan for less than one year. They are taxed on income earned in Japan and on capital gains from the sale of property in Japan.

Income earned in Japan may be subject to special measures to prevent double taxation. As of July 2017, Japan was a signatory to 55 tax conventions with 66 countries.[6] Double taxation agreements do not usually offer relief from withholding tax on rental income or capital gains tax from the sale of property in Japan. But, for example, an Australia resident can generally claim a tax credit in Australia for taxes paid on rental income or capital gains in Japan.[7]

How to pay

Taxes can be paid at the tax office, at banks and other financial institutions and at convenience stores. You can also pay taxes using designated automated teller machines, smartphones and personal computers, and with credit cards.[8]

Acquisition taxes

Consumption tax

An 8% consumption tax is payable on buildings, construction contracts, real estate agents' commissions and most services associated with buying and selling property. Comprising a 6.3% national tax and a 1.7% local tax, consumption tax is not payable on the sale of land, on residential rents or on mortgages. The consumption tax rate is scheduled to rise to 10% in October 2019.

Real estate acquisition tax

Buyers of land and buildings are subject to a 4% acquisition tax, which is based on the value from the land appraisal for fixed assets tax. This one-off prefectural tax is due within a few months of your purchase and does not apply to inherited property. You are required to notify the tax office of your purchase within a period set by the prefecture.

Registration and license tax

Based on the valuation from the land appraisal for fixed assets tax, this 2% national tax is paid when real estate is purchased. This tax also applies when property is reregistered as a result of inheritance, corporate merger or partition. Registration and license tax is payable on mortgages at a rate of 0.4% of the loan amount.[9]

Stamp tax

This national tax is levied on contracts, including those for mortgages, leases, construction and the sale of property. Stamp tax is based on the contract amount and is paid by the buyer or borrower.[10] Stamp tax is assessed in bands, with rates ranging from ¥1,000 for the purchase of a property valued at ¥1 million or below to ¥45,000 for property valued at ¥100 million or below.

Ownership taxes

Fixed assets tax

This municipal tax is based on the valuation from the land appraisal for fixed assets tax. The standard rate is 1.4% of the value of the building and land, but there are numerous deductions.

The fixed assets tax is payable in four installments each year. Owners of property on the tax register on January 1 must pay this tax for the fiscal year beginning April 1, even if the property is sold on January 2.

Urban planning tax

This municipal tax is capped at 0.3% of the land appraisal for fixed assets tax. Urban planning tax is collected with the fixed assets tax and is payable in quarterly installments.

Income and disposal taxes

Capital gains

For individuals who are residents of Japan, gains on the sale of real estate that has been held for less than five years are taxed at a minimum rate of 39.63%: a 30.63% national tax plus a 9% local inhabitants tax. Gains on property that has been held for more than five years are taxed at 20.315%: a 15.315% national tax plus a 5% local inhabitants tax.[11]

To calculate the five-year period, count backward from January 1 of the year the property was sold. For example, if you bought a property on January 2, 2014, and sell it on December 31, 2019, you will be taxed at the 39.63% rate.

Capital gains made by nonresidents of Japan are not subject to the 9% or 5% local inhabitants tax.[12] However, a 10.21% withholding tax is assessed on the proceeds from the sale of real estate in Japan by nonresidents. The withholding tax is creditable against the vendor's final tax bill.[13]

A deduction of ¥30 million is available on capital gains from the sale of residential land and buildings owned for more than 10 years. In some circumstances, capital gains can be offset against capital losses of a similar nature.

Rental income

For residents, rental income from property in Japan is generally included with the owner's other income and taxed at the current marginal rate.

For nonresidents, rental income is subject to a 20.42% withholding tax, which is treated as a prepayment of the investor's tax bill. Nonresident investors are required to file a tax return between February 16 and March 15 of the following year.[14] Owners who live outside Japan can deduct some travel-related expenses from their rental income.

If you are a citizen of another country, you may be able to claim a credit for taxes paid in Japan (see "Residency," above).

Earthquake reconstruction surtax

An earthquake reconstruction surtax is in effect from January 2013 to December 2037. During this period, individuals are subject to a 2.1% surtax that is applied to any national income tax due during the year. An additional ¥1,000 charge is levied on individuals when they pay their local taxes each year.[15]

Inheritance tax

In 2015, Japan's inheritance tax system was amended to cut the basic exemption from ¥50 million to ¥30 million and to reduce the additional exemption from ¥10 million to ¥6 million. At the same time, the maximum gift and inheritance tax rates were increased to 55%.[16]

Other taxes

The government recently introduced changes to its tax laws that could affect high net worth individuals and long-term foreign residents. For example:

- ▲ Effective January 1, 2017, income from the sale of nonpermanent residents' property (excluding real estate) located outside Japan is taxable in Japan, even if the proceeds remain offshore.[17]

- ▲ An exit tax was introduced that levies a 15.315% income tax on unrealized gains on financial assets over ¥100 million. Due to a transition period, this tax will not be collected from departing foreigners until 2020.

- ▲ The worldwide assets of foreigners who have lived in Japan for more than 10 of the last 15 years are subject to Japanese gift and inheritance taxes. Furthermore, the transfer of assets located outside Japan could be subject to Japanese taxes for five years after the foreign donor or decedent has left Japan.[18]

- ▲ Individuals who are residents of Japan for tax purposes and who have assets outside Japan with a value of ¥50 million or more must declare those assets to the tax office each year in a foreign asset report.

- ▲ Tax residents with income of ¥20 million and assets of ¥300 million or more are required to submit an annual statement of assets and liabilities to the tax office.

Deductions and allowances

The following is a sample of the tax deductions and allowances available to homeowners. Many of these incentives are available for a limited time, require professional inspection or certification and have caps on the amount of money that can be claimed. Equipment manufacturers and renovation companies promote their products and services around these initiatives. Read the fine print carefully to ensure your purchase qualifies for the tax break.

The cost of improvements, such as solar power systems, can be deducted from your income tax and fixed assets tax.

Insurance and improvements
Earthquake insurance premiums are deductible from your income tax and local inhabitants tax. Deductions are available for improvements that make your home barrier-free or increase its ability to withstand earthquakes, and for renovations that allow three generations to live together.

Mortgages and related loans
The government offers a 1% tax credit on the balance of mortgages for a period of 10 years from the date of a home's first occupancy. Proceeds from the loan can be used to build, to acquire or to improve a home. Homes that are categorized as "Long-life Quality Housing" qualify for a higher maximum tax deduction. In some cases, deductions that cannot be applied to income tax can be applied to local inhabitants tax.

Energy conservation and solar power

Deductions from income tax and fixed assets tax are available for retrofits that increase your home's energy efficiency. There are extra deductions for installing solar power systems. For owner-occupied homes erected before January 1, 2008, energy saving retrofits qualify for a discount on the fixed assets tax.[19]

Tax-efficient structures

Investors can use a legal entity such as a *tokumei kumiai* (TK) or *tokutei mokuteki kaisha* (TMK) to reduce their tax liability. TKs and TMKs involve extra cost and complexity and must be structured correctly to ensure they withstand the scrutiny of the tax authorities. These structures are usually inappropriate for individuals with one or two properties.

Tokumei kumiai

In a TK, an individual or a company invests in a Japan-based real estate operator in exchange for a share of the operator's profits. TK investors are silent partners with no direct control of the operator's business.

TK distributions to nonresident investors are subject to a 20.42% withholding tax. This tax is final, and nonresident investors are not required to file an income tax return in Japan. In some circumstances, it is possible to structure a TK so distributions to nonresident investors are exempt from withholding tax.

Tokutei mokuteki kaisha

A TMK is a special-purpose vehicle used to securitize real estate and other assets. TMKs are more complex and expensive to set up and run than TKs, and are usually used for large transactions. Investors in a TMK benefit from limited liability and can take an active role in managing the investment.[20]

SPECIAL CASES

A CUSTOM-DESIGNED HOME

With prices starting at about ¥1.2 million per *tsubo* (3.3 square meters), plus land, custom-designed homes are expensive. Planning and building a custom home can easily take two years and require thousands of decisions. The results, however, can be spectacular.

To build a custom home, you will need the services of an architect/building engineer (*kenchikushi*). In addition to planning and designing your home, an architect can arrange bids, negotiate with contractors and suppliers and supervise the construction process. An architect can also help you achieve your environmental goals, make the most of an unusual building site, overcome drainage problems and ensure your home complies with shadow restrictions (*nichiei kisei*) and other regulations.

Defining the project

Building a custom home starts with a budget, which includes land, design and construction services, furniture and appliances, taxes, insurance, maintenance and contingencies. A realistic budget will prevent you from running out of money halfway through the project or building something that you cannot afford to occupy.

Next, decide what you want. This includes physical and functional requirements, such as the home's overall size, the number of bathrooms (most Japanese homes only have one, with separate rooms for the bathtub [*ofuro*] and toilet) and bedrooms, and your storage and parking needs. Consider your hobbies and interests, and whether you want a home theater, home office, Western kitchen, garden or basement. Think about the future, especially if you plan to have children or if your kids will be moving out. List your aesthetic preferences: Do you want a modern or traditional design? Finally, address environmental issues, such as rainwater collection or the use of solar power. These factors may also influence your choice of a site.

Understanding your needs, wants and preferences will help you find an architect whose style and experience are compatible with your vision. This process also forms the basis for the brief (see below) that you use to explain your project to the architect.

Hiring an architect

When you have defined your priorities, start looking for an architect. The Japan Institute of Architects and the Japan Federation of Architects & Building Engineers Associations have lists of practitioners.

Assemble a short list of candidates and contact them. Describe your project, goals, schedule and budget. If the firm is interested and has capacity to work on your project, arrange a meeting. Discussions with three to five firms will give you a sense of what is possible, without consuming too much time.

In the meeting, you will learn about the firm's technical credentials, design philosophy and attitude toward customer service. Ask if the firm has professional liability insurance; many in Japan do not. Meet the architect who will design your home—not just the salesperson—so you can gauge the chemistry between you. A good working relationship is vital, because you and the architect will spend a lot of time together, and it will not be pleasant or productive if you dislike or distrust each other. Check to see if there is a gap between your Japanese and the architect's English skills. Ask for references, talk to previous clients and visit the architect's finished projects. Smart architects interview their clients, so don't be surprised if she asks to visit your building site or your home. As part of the selection process, you may ask the architect to prepare preliminary sketches for which you will be charged a fee. Finally, ask how the architect charges for her work: as a percentage of the total building cost (excluding land), on an hourly basis or as a lump sum.

When you have selected an architect, notify her and the unsuccessful candidates as soon as possible. The winning architect will ask you to sign a contract, which will specify the schedule and the services she will provide. Depending on how the contract is structured, you will make four to six payments over the life of the project. Typically, there is a small initial payment for preliminary work, several larger ones as the project progresses and a small, final payment when minor defects and outstanding issues are resolved.

The brief

A well-organized, unambiguous brief is the foundation of a success-ful project. Use words, sketches, pictures from books and magazines, videos, paint samples, fabric swatches and anything else that conveys your goals, tastes and preferences. The more detail, the better.

The brief explains your preference for features like a Western-style kitchen.

Producing an effective brief takes time and effort. But with a clear brief, the architect will understand what you want and achieve your goals more quickly and efficiently. Creating the brief will help you clarify your thinking and may reveal gaps between your and your spouse's preferences. These differences are best resolved early in the design process, before changes become expensive.

In addition to your functional requirements and aesthetic preferenc-es, tell the architect what features you consider essential and which ones are negotiable. If you are unsure about something, say so. Don't forget to give the architect creative "breathing space," so she can use her training and skill to turn your vision into a home you can both be proud of.

Other considerations

Since the 2005 discovery that architect Hidetsugu Aneha had faked earthquake-resistance data for 99 buildings, the process for approving building plans has become more strict. According to Astrid Klein of Klein Dytham Architecture in Tokyo, in 2017 it can take up to 70 days to have designs approved by the government, up from 21 days before the Aneha scandal. When your plans have been accepted, only minor changes to items such as finishes are allowed. Previously, architects could simultaneously send project plans to tender and for approval, and then amend the plans after they were accepted. This is another reason to avoid changes late in the design process.

It can be difficult to arrange financing for a custom home, because many banks do not offer mortgages for vacant land. In addition, banks sometimes see a mortgage on a custom home as having higher risk, believing the home's unique design will make it harder to sell if you default.

With a custom-built home, you can include wiring for a computer network, satellite TV, home theater, intercom or burglar alarm. You can also consider new technologies, such as electronic door locks and smart thermostats. Extra electrical outlets and telephone jacks reduce clutter.

Green buildings

Japan's dependence on imported energy, post-Fukushima electricity shortages and heightened environmental awareness have given added impetus to the green building movement.

Environmental technologies such as photovoltaic cells are becoming cheaper, more efficient and more reliable. Utilities buy surplus electricity at above-market rates, known as the feed-in tariff, although rates have fallen as incentives expire.

Previously, green buildings cost more to design and erect than conventional structures. That cost differential is narrowing as architects and construction companies gain experience. Despite these advances, architect Mark Dytham notes that many people ask for green features in their initial designs, but drop them when they see the cost.

As more green buildings are erected, people are becoming more aware of their benefits. By combining sensors, energy-efficient designs and abundant natural light, green buildings cost less to operate than conventional designs.

Furthermore, people occupying green buildings experience better objective and subjective health outcomes. This includes fewer sick building syndrome symptoms, fewer respiratory symptom reports in children and better physical and mental health. In green office buildings, people report improved productivity, reduced absenteeism and fewer work hours affected by asthma and allergies. Green buildings are also associated with lower employee turnover and a decrease in the length of open staff positions.[1]

Corporate sustainability strategist Charles Lockwood believes that green building techniques can be used in all buildings. But rather than using experimental technologies, he recommends proven, relatively inexpensive solutions like adding thermal insulation and installing double-glazed windows. For example, replacing a 60-watt incandescent light bulb with a 12-watt light-emitting diode (LED) produces a 75%–80% energy savings. Incandescent bulbs typically have a life span of 1,000 hours, versus 25,000 hours for an LED.[2]

While it is possible to retrofit buildings, it is generally cheaper and easier to use an environmentally friendly design from the start. One way to do this is through the Comprehensive Assessment System for Built Environment Efficiency (CASBEE), a method for evaluating and rating the performance of buildings, including homes. CASBEE spans a building's life-cycle, from predesign and new construction to existing buildings and renovation, and includes English-language checklists.

Architects in Japan

Japan is home to many internationally renowned architects, including Tadao Ando, Shigeru Ban and Toyo Ito. Japan also has a history of attracting talented practitioners from abroad. In the late 1880s, U.K. native Josiah Conder designed the National Museum in Tokyo and was elected honorary president of the Architectural Institute of Japan. Frank Lloyd Wright, who opened an office in Japan in 1915, was responsible for several homes in Tokyo as well as the Imperial Hotel. More recently, Le Corbusier designed the National Museum of Western Art in Tokyo.[3] Today, numerous foreign architects practice in Japan. For a partial list, see the Japan chapter of the American Institute of Architects.

Nikken Sekkei designed Tokyo Skytree, the world's tallest tower.

In Japan, architects work for two broad categories of employer. The first is the big organizations that build big projects. This group includes Nikken Sekkei Ltd., which employs more than 1,100 first-class architects and designed Tokyo Skytree, the world's tallest tower. Large construction companies also have in-house architects, which helps them win jobs by bundling design and construction services. Construction companies usually focus on delivering practical, low-maintenance structures at competitive prices, rather than setting new aesthetic standards.

The second group comprises ateliers, most of which have fewer than 30 staff. Ateliers are design-driven firms with a signature style shaped by the founder or founders, whose names are often on the front door.

Ateliers focus on smaller projects, such as stores, public buildings and individual homes. Both Japanese and foreign architects are well represented among the ateliers.

There are three classes of kenchikushi—first, second and *mokuzo*—which determine the projects the license-holder may undertake. As of September 2015, there were 360,003 first-class kenchikushi, who are permitted to design and perform construction administration on any kind of building, regardless of its size, structure or use. There were 752,251 second-class kenchikushi, who are limited to smaller, general-purpose buildings. Finally, 17,534 mokuzo kenchikushi design and administer the construction of small wooden structures.[4]

Architects may work as a representative of the construction company or the building owner.

Contractors and architects

In Japan, design and construction services are often bundled into a single package that takes advantage of a longstanding relationship between an architect and contractor. Knowledge of each other's staff, approach and philosophy allows the two companies to start work quickly without the "getting to know you" phase that is common in new partnerships.

The drawback to this arrangement is that the client is quoted a single price for design and construction services, which can be disconcerting for customers expecting a clear demarcation between the two. Not all architects and contractors work this way, but it is common even for detached houses.

Design and construction work was often undertaken using a simple written order or even a verbal agreement. The use of contracts has become more common and the contracts have become more detailed. But contracts continue to be regarded as a statement of intent rather than a checklist that covers every possible eventuality. In Japan, relationships are important, and agreements assume that if there is a problem, a solution will be reached that is fair to both parties.[5]

During the planning and construction phases, the line between architects and contractors can become blurred. It is not unusual for Japanese architects to spend time on-site, inspecting the construction and liaising with suppliers. Contractors, on the other hand, make design suggestions that save time and money and reduce risk. Project deadlines are often seen as targets. Compliance within a few days is usually acceptable as long as the other party is not inconvenienced.

Many architects' designs test the boundaries of what is technically possible. Contractors—who must implement architects' ideas and make a profit—tend to be conservative. However, in Japan the relationship between architects and contractors and between contractors and subcontractors is usually cordial and cooperative. This is in stark contrast with the United States and other countries where litigation and antagonism are the norm.

This cooperative approach reflects Japan's nonconfrontational culture and its legal system, which is based on civil law and where the outcome of a mediated settlement is usually very close to one delivered by the courts. Mediated settlements have the added advantage of arriving faster and at a much lower cost.

Alternatives

There are several alternatives for people who want a distinctive home but prefer not to hire an architect. These approaches are complicated and require hands-on involvement.

One option is to purchase building plans from a company such as Hometta or Houseplans, import or buy building materials in Japan and hire a contractor to erect the house for you. Plans start at about $1,000, and a variety of designs are available. This approach requires a contractor who is comfortable working from Western-style drawings and adapting the design to meet Japanese regulations and conditions.

Wooden kit homes, which are known in Japan as log houses, are another option. Lindal Cedar Homes, Sweden House and other companies import these kits from Canada, Finland, Sweden and the United States. Many importers offer assembly services, but you can erect these homes yourself or hire a contractor to do it for you. It is also possible to buy log homes directly from manufacturers such as Lake Country Log Homes in Canada.

Finally, if you have the time and are looking for an adventure, you can design and build your own home. See the Build-it-yourself entry in the "Information Sources" chapter for more information.

Zoning

In Japan, zoning regulations were introduced to existing communities where mixed use was the norm. As a result, rules tend to be flexible and to focus on maintaining the current land use pattern.

The following national zoning categories apply to land in urbanization promotion areas. Japan also has urbanization control areas, where development is not permitted.[6]

Zone	Permitted uses
Category I: Exclusive low-rise residential	Houses; small shops and offices; schools; temples, shrines and churches; clinics.
Category II: Exclusive low-rise residential	As above, plus shops and restaurants up to 150 square meters.
Category I: Mid/high-rise residential	As above, plus hospitals and universities; shops and restaurants up to 500 square meters; independent garages up to 300 square meters.
Category II: Mid/high-rise residential	As above, plus shops, restaurants and offices up to 1,500 square meters.
Category I: residential	As above, plus shops, restaurants, offices and hotels up to 3,000 square meters; auto repair shops up to 50 square meters.
Category II: residential	As above, plus karaoke lounges.
Quasi-residential	As above, plus movie theaters; warehouses; garages up to 300 square meters, auto repair shops up to 150 square meters.

Zone	Permitted uses
Neighborhood commercial	As above, plus movie theaters, shops and restaurants over 10,000 square meters; auto repair shops up to 300 square meters.
Commercial	As above, plus bathhouses with private rooms.
Quasi-Industrial	As above, plus factories posing some danger or environmental risk. Bathhouses are excluded.
Industrial	Houses; temples, shrines and churches; clinics; shops, offices and restaurants; karaoke lounges; garages; warehouses; auto repair shops; factories posing a strong risk of danger or environmental degradation.
Exclusive industrial	Shrines, temples and churches; offices; karaoke lounges; garages; warehouses; auto repair shops; factories posing a strong risk of danger or environmental degradation.
Areas without a designation	All of the above, except bathhouses with private rooms and movie theaters, shops and restaurants over 10,000 square meters.

Custom built in Tokyo

In 2004, California native John Kirch and his Japanese wife Chiharu decided it was time to become homeowners.

John and Chiharu looked at neighborhoods in and around Tokyo for about a year before a Japanese friend introduced them to Shimouma in Setagaya-ku. Shimouma is a green, quiet area with more than 10 parks within a 10-minute bicycle ride, including Setagaya Park with its miniature steam engines and Komazawa Olympic Park, which was a site for the 1964 games. Most of the homes in the area are two- or two-and-a-half stories tall, and Shimouma has convenient public transit links, with Shibuya Station just two stops away on the Toyoko train line. With a well-stocked supermarket, several excellent restaurants, a neighborhood pub and three bakeries nearby, John describes Shimouma as "One of the best neighborhoods I've found in Tokyo."

In Japan, it is not uncommon for industrial facilities to be near residential and commercial zones.

Before the Kirchs were introduced to Shimouma, they used a shotgun approach to learn more about homes and housing. They read books and magazines, talked to friends and family and attended seminars organized by the American Chamber of Commerce in Japan and by architect Kisho Kurokawa, who designed the Nakagin Capsule Tower and National Arts Center in Tokyo. These experiences shaped the Kirchs' thinking and helped them determine what they wanted in their new home.

After the Kurokawa seminar, the Kirchs began considering the relationship between their future home, the family's needs and the activities—such as barbecues, bicycle and ski outings and John's passion for motorcycles—that make up their lifestyle. After discussions with Chiharu's parents, they looked at the long-term implications of their choices and how to find a house that they could grow into over time.

As a result, the Kirchs decided they didn't want to pay condominium fees, which topped ¥100,000 a month for some properties. John was also keen to avoid the drawbacks of apartment living, especially for their son Christopher, who was born in 2003. "I wanted a garden outside where Chris could play whenever he wanted," says John.

That meant a house, and John viewed several existing homes, including one where the owners refused to let him perform a prepurchase structural survey, without finding anything that fit his family's requirements. He briefly considered erecting a log house, but felt the cost savings did not justify the design compromises that would be required. John even looked into moving an old house down from the mountains, an idea that was ultimately rejected as too expensive and impractical. In the end, a new home built to the family's specifications was the best solution.

Through an ad in a real estate magazine, John met an agent from Unihouse, who showed him a vacant plot in a neighborhood near Shimouma. While the property wasn't a good fit, the agent's willingness to understand John's preferences and find something suitable convinced John to continue working with him.

That proved to be a smart decision, as the agent later found an affordable 50-tsubo lot on a quiet cul-de-sac in Shimouma. "I got lucky," says John with a smile, noting that the land, which represented about two-thirds of the project's budget, has appreciated significantly since he bought it in 2005.

John spoke to several banks about a mortgage, a process he found frustrating. "I had one banker tell me, 'I'm sorry, we don't make loans on property, only on property with buildings on it. Once you build something on it, you can get a loan from us.'" In the end, the real estate agent introduced him to Sumitomo Mitsui Banking Corporation. "SMBC rolled out the red carpet for us. They made us feel welcome and comfortable coming to ask them for a little bit of money," he says. With a 50% down payment, it took less than three weeks to arrange the mortgage.

While the agent was searching for a suitable lot, the Kirchs were busy planning their new home. They met and interviewed several architects before settling on Isa Homes, a company that had been recommended by their real estate agent. John and Chiharu say they liked the employees' communication skills, dedication and the quality of the homes they had designed for other clients. Isa Homes' lead architect, Tanimoto-san, and associate architect, Oya-san, helped the Kirchs maximize the floor space and height of their new home, while ensuring that it complied with the shadow restrictions, which prevent people from erecting buildings that leave their neighbors permanently in the shade.

The architect also incorporated a fireplace into the Kirchs' design, a late change that added about ¥2 million to the project cost and required structural reinforcements, heat proofing and a chimney. John says he was glad he added the fireplace, which he uses frequently during the winter months.

One of John's few regrets is not having a basement. Although it would have added approximately ¥2.5 million to the budget, the architects advised him that it could cause problems with mold, mildew and water leakage. "Having a foosball, pool or ping-pong table in the basement is very appealing, especially when its pouring rain outside," notes John.

The architect agreed to separate the design and construction aspects of the project. John wanted separate contracts to ensure he was getting the best price and to provide transparency. He also had a local attorney review both contracts.

John interviewed and received quotes from several general contractors before settling on one recommended by Isa Homes. After initially submitting the most expensive quote, the architect's contractor produced a more competitive bid. John hired the contractor based on the lower bid, the contractor's close working relationship with the architect and the temple-grade carpentry he had seen at the contractor's other projects.

Before construction began, John arranged a traditional Shinto ceremony, known as a *jichinsai*, to purify the land, pacify the spirits, protect the workers from injury and prevent the building from being affected by structural problems.[7]

As construction progressed, John maintained a contingency fund to pay for changes like the new fireplace. He also received monthly updates from the contractor, who provided a 10-year guarantee on his work, which is standard under the Housing Quality Assurance Act. Six months later, the Kirchs' house was delivered on time and on budget.

After more than a decade, the Kirchs remain happy with their home. John offers the following advice to potential home buyers:

▲ Think long and hard about what you need and want in your new home. When you are spending that much money, you really should get what you want. But that will not happen unless you understand your needs and desires.

▲ Find a real estate agent who you are comfortable with, who knows your target neighborhood and who listens to you, and then give him a clear brief and a budget.

▲ As long as you are making progress, stick with the agent, even if you do not like the first few properties he shows you.

▲ Get a good local lawyer to review the contracts.

▲ Maintain open communication with your agent, architect and contractor. Have a contingency fund of about 10% of the house's total projected cost. This will cushion you against unforeseen problems and last-minute changes.

▲ Hold regular meetings with your architect during the planning and design process. A 90-minute session every two weeks should be sufficient to review the architect's progress and make structural and design decisions.

INVESTMENT PROPERTY

As a resident or nonresident, you can buy and hold investment property in Japan. However, Japan's rental market and regulatory environment have several distinctive characteristics that will shape your investment approach.

The residential rental market

Renting is a popular choice in Japan. In 2013, rented homes represented 33.4% of the total housing stock, with the balance made up of owned homes (61.7%) and company supplied housing (2.2%).* Local governments, public corporations and bodies such as the Urban Renaissance Agency supplied rental accommodations equaling 5.4% of the total housing stock, with private landlords providing 28.0%.[1]

Inspecting signs in real estate agents' windows is a good way to learn about local rents.

Rental accommodations are small. In 2013, the average owner-occupied detached house was 131.7 square meters, versus 83.2 for a

---

* Totals do not equal 100% because some respondents did not indicate the type of housing they occupied.

rented house. Similarly, owner-occupied apartments averaged 71.6 square meters, compared with 41.1 square meters for rented apartments.[2] Single people and couples often live in rented dwellings. But when couples start a family, they must buy a home in order to have space for their children.

The need to pay "key money" and limits on landlords' ability to raise rents (see below) discourage people from moving. A survey published in 2003 found that just 8.3% of Japanese renters move each year, compared with 25.6% in the United Kingdom and 30.1% in the United States.[3]

But Japan's residential rental market is changing. The growing number of empty homes (*akiya*) throughout the country, and the added transparency provided by online listing services are strengthening tenants' bargaining position. This is particularly true for desirable tenants—younger, financially secure people with good employment and rental histories—who can avoid or negotiate exemptions to key money and lease renewal fees.

Peak moving season is from January to March, when new hires, employees who have been transferred to new locations and university entrants look for apartments.

Renting in Japan

Renting a home in Japan is expensive. Before a tenant moves in, they pay up to six months' rent, which breaks down as follows:

- ▲ Key money (*reikin*), which is a nonrefundable "gift" to the landlord equal to one or two months' rent

- ▲ Deposit (*shikikin*) of one or two months' rent. This is refunded at the end of the tenancy, less any cleaning and repair charges

- ▲ Agent's commission (*chukai tesuryo*) of one month's rent, plus consumption tax

- ▲ The first month's rent

▲ Property insurance, which typically costs ¥10,000–¥20,000 for a two-year lease. This is optional on smaller properties.

▲ A lock replacement fee, which typically costs ¥10,000–¥20,000. This is also optional on smaller properties.

In what are known as "zero-zero" rentals, some landlords do not charge key money or a deposit, but require the tenant to cosign a lease with a guarantee company. Such arrangements are often decidedly disadvantageous to the tenant.[4] Other landlords forego key money in return for higher monthly rent.

Tenant protection laws

In exchange for high initial costs, tenants enjoy considerable legal protection. However, as with most aspects of Japanese life, real estate disputes are usually resolved through discussion, not legal channels. The majority of tenants are responsible and law abiding, and issues between landlords and tenants are usually resolved quickly and amicably.

Most homes are rented using a regular lease (*futsu shakuya keiyaku*), which does not have a fixed termination date and may be written or oral. A regular lease is automatically renewed, even if there is no renewal clause in the contract. Landlords who do not renew a lease must have a valid reason. Rents are set at the beginning of the tenancy, and tenants may request a reduction if the rent is later found to be above market rates. Similarly, landlords may ask for a rent increase if taxes or other costs have increased. When a lease is renewed, the rent may not exceed the rent for a new lease on a comparable home. If a sitting tenant refuses to accept a rent increase, the case can go to court. While this is uncommon, courts generally find in favor of the tenant.[5]

There are few justifications, such as nonpayment of rent, for a landlord to evict a tenant, and a relatively small number of people abuse Japan's legal protections to live rent-free. The eviction process is slow—taking a year or longer—and expensive. It is not unusual for a landlord to pay a tenant ¥5 million or more to leave. As a result, landlords focus on screening and avoiding problem tenants. Owners also prefer to rent small homes to singles and couples, who move more frequently than families.

This legal environment discourages owners from improving or re-developing their properties and can make it difficult for landlords to recover the cost of essential repairs, such as seismic reinforcements.[6] It also creates opportunities for the yakuza, who unscrupulous owners hire to evict tenants.

Residential lease terms

A regular lease typically includes the following terms:

- ▲ The lease is for a two-year term. (The lease is automatically extended at the end of the term.)

- ▲ The tenant may terminate the lease with 30 days' notice or by paying rent in lieu of notice.

- ▲ Rent is payable on the last business day of the preceding month (i.e., February's rent is payable on the last weekday in January). Rent is usually paid by bank transfer.

- ▲ The landlord and tenant may enter discussions to revise the rent if the rent becomes unreasonable because of changes in property values, taxes or economic factors, or if the rent is inappropriate in relation to other buildings in the vicinity.

- ▲ The tenant agrees to pay the monthly condominium management fee. (This is usually paid to the landlord, who pays it and the building repair fee to the owners' committee each month.)

- ▲ The tenant may not alter the interior of the property.

- ▲ At the end of the lease, the tenant must return the property to the landlord in its original condition. The tenant is not responsible for wear and tear caused by normal use.

- ▲ The landlord is responsible for keeping the property in habitable condition. The tenant is responsible for any damage he causes; for replacing damaged shoji and tatami mats and burned-out light bulbs and fuses; and similar minor repairs.

▲ The tenant may not sublet the property.

▲ People who are not listed on the lease are not allowed to occupy the property.

▲ The tenant agrees to use the property only for residential purposes. (This is negotiable, as apartments are often used as offices for small businesses.)

▲ The tenant agrees to pay the landlord a security deposit, which the landlord agrees to promptly return to the tenant at the end of the tenancy. The tenant may not use the deposit to offset outstanding rent or condominium management fees. Interest is not payable on the deposit. At the end of the tenancy, the landlord may deduct the cost of cleaning and repairs from the deposit. If these costs are deducted from the deposit, the landlord must give the tenant a breakdown of the expenses.

▲ The tenant may not do anything that will annoy or endanger other tenants.

▲ The landlord may cancel the lease if the tenant fails to pay the rent or condominium management fees or violates any of the other terms of the lease.

▲ The tenant will notify the landlord if the home will be vacant for one month or more.

▲ The tenant may not place personal items, signs or advertisements in the building's common areas.

▲ With the tenant's prior approval, the landlord may enter the property to conduct maintenance and repairs and to show the home to prospective tenants.** The tenant may not withhold reasonable requests for access by the landlord.

---

* According to one source, asking a tenant for permission to show their home to a prospective tenant would be seen as extremely rude.

▲ The landlord may enter the property without the tenant's prior approval in an emergency, such as to prevent the spread of a fire. The landlord must advise the tenant of any such entry.

▲ The tenant's guarantor is jointly responsible for any unpaid rent, condominium management fees or damage.

▲ Issues not addressed above will be handled in accordance with the Japanese Civil Code and other laws and trade practices for the real estate industry. The landlord and tenant will discuss and try to resolve any disputes through good-faith consultations.

Fixed-term leases

In 2000, fixed-term leases (*teiki shakuya keiyaku*) were introduced. A fixed-term lease is similar to a regular lease, except that it is not automatically extended at the end of the term. Fixed-term leases must be in writing and include a separate, notarized document stating that the lease will not be renewed and will end when it expires. A 2015 survey by the Ministry of Land, Infrastructure, Transport and Tourism found that only 3.2% of leases used fixed-term contracts.

For both regular and fixed-term leases, the real estate agent reads an explanation of important matters (*juyou jikou setsumeisho*) to the tenant. This document describes the property; outlines the facilities and equipment that are included in the property and their condition; explains the terms of the tenancy; and identifies the landlord, real estate agent and property manager. The tenant signs the explanation to indicate that he understands and agrees to the terms in it.

Renewal fees and guarantors

Lease renewal fees (*koshinryo*) of up to two months' rent are also common in Tokyo and other cities. In July 2009, the Kyoto District Court ruled that these charges, which the landlord typically splits with the real estate agent, were illegal.[7] The following month the Osaka High Court upheld an earlier ruling in favor of a man who sued his landlord for the return of renewal fees he had paid for his Kyoto apartment. Most Japanese tenants continue to pay renewal fees, while some expatriates try to exclude them when negotiating a lease. If, as a landlord, you plan to collect renewal fees, this should be explicitly stated in the explanation of important matters.

Landlords normally insist that tenants provide a guarantor (*hosho-nin*), who will be responsible if the tenant damages the property or fails to pay the rent or condominium management fee. Typically, the tenant's parents (regardless of the parents' age, income or employment status) or employer act as the guarantor. Increasingly, renters without family or a full-time job turn to rental guarantee companies (*yachin hosho kaisha*), which provide this service. The companies typically charge 30%–50% of the monthly rent plus ¥10,000 to act as a guarantor for a two-year lease. This is not insurance: If the tenant defaults, the guarantee company pays the landlord and pursues the tenant for the outstanding money. According to one estimate, about 40% of renters use these companies.

Open-ended leases and complex eviction procedures make landlords cautious. Before renting a home, prospective tenants complete a detailed application form, which lists their personal data, income, employment history, rental history, guarantor and the names of the people who will be living in the property.

Difficult tenants

The elderly, the disabled, foreigners and families with small children frequently have difficulty finding rental accommodations. Landlords are reluctant to rent to these groups for a variety of reasons.

Some disabled tenants require special facilities, such as barrier-free designs, while families with small children may damage the property or disturb the neighbors. The rental yields on family-sized homes are generally lower than on small apartments.

The elderly
Landlords frequently discriminate against the elderly, citing worries about older tenants having accidents, starting fires, becoming ill or having difficulty finding a guarantor. Furthermore, elderly tenants are often long-term residents who are unlikely to move out and let the landlord raise the rent.

However the biggest concern is that older tenants are more likely to die in a property, reducing its resale and rental value. *Kodokushi*, or lonely death, occurs when a person lives and dies alone. Kodokushi victims may not be discovered until neighbors notice a bad smell, or the deceased's bank account, from which rent and utility payments are automatically deducted, is empty. In some instances, skeletal remains are found years after the person's death.

Estimates put the annual number of kodokushi deaths in Japan at nearly 30,000, although some experts believe the actual number is much higher. In a study conducted at a public housing estate in Chiba Prefecture between 2000 and 2007, 60.3% of kodokushi deaths were men, with a mean age of 61.3 years. Female victims had a mean age of 71.3. Men are believed to be at greater risk because they are more socially isolated than women.[8]

Kodokushi has become so common that companies now specialize in discretely cleaning up after the police have removed the tenant's remains. Firms typically charge ¥80,000–¥350,000, depending on the apartment's size.

Foreigners

Landlords also discriminate against non-Japanese renters, fearing that foreigners may upset xenophobic neighbors and fail to observe local rules, such as sorting garbage. Westerners have a reputation for throwing loud parties, while some landlords worry that Asian tenants will invite their extended family to move in with them.

A 2016 survey of 18,500 foreign residents conducted for the Ministry of Justice found that 39.3% of respondents who had applied to rent apartments over the past five years had their applications rejected because they were not Japanese. Another 41.2% said their applications were rejected because they could not find a Japanese guarantor.[9] This represents an opportunity for landlords who are able to meet the needs of foreign tenants.

Unlike many countries, where locals and foreigners live side-by-side, there is little crossover between the expatriate** and domestic

---

*   "Expatriate" refers here to an employee who has been dispatched to Japan (often with family in tow), receives a housing allowance and lives in a Western-style home. This is in contrast to foreign nationals who have been hired on local terms and pay their own housing and living expenses. Both are foreigners, but they are distinct markets.

markets in Japan. The Western-style bathrooms, gourmet kitchens and wall-to-wall carpet preferred by expats do not appeal to most Japanese renters.

What and where to buy

For many renters, a compact apartment near their workplace, shops and restaurants is preferable to a larger home and a longer commute. In a 2003 survey by the Tokyo Metropolitan Government, 80% of respondents said one hour was the maximum tolerable commuting time.[10]

In general, small pre-owned apartments offer low risk and high returns. Medium-sized new and secondhand homes are low risk and low return. Large properties, such as family homes, are often high risk and low return.

In Tokyo, prices per square meter for very small apartments tend to be high. Prices drop for units in the 35- to 100-square-meter range, and then increase for larger units. Newer units command a higher price than older ones, with 30- to 40-year-old apartments selling at significant discounts.

Homes near train and subway stations command higher prices and rents.

There is usually an inverse relationship between a property's rental yield and its desirability as a residence. In Greater Tokyo, homes in desirable areas like Kamakura and Kichijoji have lower yields than those in grittier neighborhoods like Ueno and Higashi Chiba. That said, working-class neighborhoods in Japan are generally clean, safe and well served by public transit. Apartments in these districts can make excellent investments.

Rents are lower in areas identified on hazard maps as having a high earthquake risk. Homes in high-risk districts that were erected before the seismic standards were tightened in 1981 rent at a discount, compared with those built after 1981.[11]

Look for homes that are bland, unexceptional and near other residential complexes. These homes are easy for real estate agents and tenants to understand, and appeal to a broad audience, making them simpler to rent and sell.

Proximity to train and subway stations is important. Almost everyone in Japan commutes by rail, and a short walk to the nearest station makes your apartment more desirable.

Government offices, universities and hospitals are recession-proof employers that create demand for rental housing. Universities and teaching hospitals have the added advantage of attracting students who stay for a short tenancy, giving you the possibility of a rent increase for new tenants.

Single women are security-conscious. They prefer homes close to busy, well-lit streets and near restaurants and businesses that stay open well into the evening.[12]

Tenanted homes are desirable, because there is no need to pay a real estate agent to find a renter. However, if there is a sitting tenant you will almost certainly buy the apartment without seeing the interior, as tenants are not obliged to show their homes to prospective purchasers.

If you buy a property with a sitting tenant, you assume the vendor's obligation to repay the tenant's security deposit. The buyer deducts the tenant's security deposit from the purchase price.

Many real estate agents provide property management services. These range from basic plans to full-service packages that guarantee the landlord will receive the rent, even if the tenant doesn't pay.

The Foreign Exchange and Foreign Trade Act (Act No. 228 of 1949) requires nonresidents to file a "Report Concerning Acquisition of Real Property in Japan or Rights Related Thereto," with the Bank of Japan if they buy real estate for investment purposes. The report must be filed within 20 days of the purchase and is not required if the property is used as a residence for the buyer, his relatives or employees; to house a business or nonprofit business; or if the property is purchased from another nonresident.[13]

An income property in Tokyo

After publishing the first edition of *Landed Japan* in May 2010, it was time to use what I had learned to buy an apartment in Tokyo.

With Erik Oskamp, an agent I had met researching the book, I spent the afternoon of September 30, 2010, looking at apartments in Nakano-ku, in Tokyo's western suburbs, and in Itabashi-ku, Adachi-ku and Katsushika-ku in the north. The apartments were 16–42 square meters in size and 22–36 years old. Some buildings had hundreds of units, while others had fewer than 40, and the group included buildings made of steel-reinforced concrete as well as steel frame construction. All were priced at less than ¥6 million and served by a train or subway line, although one apartment was a 20-minute walk from the nearest station.

In Japan, prospective buyers cannot view the inside of tenanted apartments. But we were able to walk around the neighborhoods, some of which were quasi-industrial. Overflowing mailboxes indicated buildings with high vacancy rates, while rust stains and peeling paint suggested maintenance problems.

I short-listed three apartments and, on October 1, made an offer for one in Itabashi-ku. The offer, which was 5% less than the asking price, was rejected, and I subsequently met the original ¥4.2 million asking price. When that offer was accepted, I started doing the paperwork, which included a notarized declaration that I was not a resident of Japan. I also signed two powers of attorney, one authorizing Erik's company to purchase the apartment on my behalf and a second enabling a judicial scrivener, Kawanabe-san, to register the property in my name. Erik also began the due diligence process to ensure that there were no problems with the building, title or tenant.

Located in Tokyo's Itabashi-ku, this apartment was built in 1974 from steel-reinforced concrete.

This was followed by two video chat sessions on Skype. One was with Kawanabe-san, who needed to verify my identity and confirm that I was buying the property. The second was with Wakabayashi-san, a licensed real estate agent employed by Erik's company, who read me the explanation of important matters.

The recitation took 70 minutes and degenerated into comedy when the agent told me that the tenant, a retired civil servant, "had a problem with his waist." I asked for clarification, wondering if he was confined to a wheelchair or if there was a trash-related problem. After consulting a dictionary and much discussion among the office staff,

Wakabayashi-san told me that the tenant had a severe case of hemor-rhoids, which was the reason he had retired.

The sale closed on November 15, 2010, and the tenant has remained in the apartment. Built in 1974 from steel-reinforced concrete, the unit is 21 square meters, plus a six-square-meter balcony. The apartment is adjacent to the Shuto Expressway and is a 10-minute walk to the Mita subway line, from which it is 30 minutes to central Tokyo.

I paid cash for the apartment, which I still own. With all taxes and fees, the total purchase price was ¥4.6 million. In calendar 2016, the apartment generated revenue of ¥424,701, after management fees, maintenance charges, repairs and taxes.

As a nonresident Canadian living in Hong Kong, rental income from the apartment does not create a tax liability in Canada or in Hong Kong.

Purchase	
Purchase price	¥4,200,000
Agent's fee	195,300
Judicial scrivener's fee	118,400
Stamp tax	10,000
Acquisition tax	63,500
Total	**¥4,587,200**

2016 Revenue	
Rent	¥639,000
Management fee	(34,506)
Maintenance fee	(142,560)
Repairs	(4,172)
Fixed assets tax	(23,900)
Income tax	(9,125)
Total	**¥424,737**

OTHER OPPORTUNITIES

In addition to buying a residence or a conventional rental property, there are several ways to gain exposure to the Japanese real estate market.

Commercial property

Unlike places such as Hong Kong, where you can buy individual offices and shops, most commercial real estate in Japan is sold on an en bloc (whole building) or multi-floor basis. Prices for small office buildings in the Tokyo area start at about ¥120 million. Pocket listings, where the property is not advertised for sale, are common, so it helps to have a strong relationship with a broker.

Individual apartments in commercial districts, near train and subway stations, are commonly rented by small and medium-sized businesses and used as offices. Depending on the unit's age, size, location and condition, these apartments can be purchased for as little as ¥10 million.

In addition, there are real estate investment trusts (J-REITs) listed on the Tokyo Stock Exchange that invest in Japanese offices, hotels, and retail and industrial property.

Foreclosures

Buying foreclosed property in Japan is a well-established process. However, in recent years, the number of foreclosed properties has declined as the economy has improved. Most foreclosures are now located in secondary and tertiary cities and in rural areas.

To buy foreclosed property in Japan:

1. Check the listings on the Broadcast Information Tri-set System or 981 websites, or watch for foreclosure notices published each month in your local newspaper. Typically, about half the foreclosed properties are detached homes and 20% are condominiums. Vacant land and commercial properties make up the balance.

2. Next, visit the courthouse listed in the notice and complete a series of forms that identify you, the property you want to buy and the amount of your bid.

3. You will need to make a deposit—typically 20% of the reserve price set by the court—which is applied to the purchase price if your bid is successful. The deposit is refunded in full if your bid is unsuccessful, but is forfeited if you are the winning bidder and fail to complete the purchase. In some jurisdictions, the court retains the runner-up bidder's deposit until the winner has completed the purchase.

4. A week after the end of the bidding period specified in the notice, the bids are opened in public. The highest bidder then has four to six weeks to pay the outstanding balance and purchase the property. Once the purchase is completed, it is final. The former owner cannot reclaim the property.

The process and all of the documents are in Japanese. If you are not fluent, you can enlist a company like Foreclosed Japan to guide you through the bidding process. Steven Windholz, a consultant with Foreclosed Japan, says his company can provide market data to ensure that you don't overbid, explain the documents, help you complete the purchase and manage the property afterward.

Banks are reluctant to offer mortgages on foreclosed property, so buyers pay cash. Bidders do not have to be permanent residents of Japan, and some courts maintain a file on the foreclosed property that includes photos of the interior, diagrams of the property and other information that can give a prospective buyer a better idea of the property's condition.

Buying foreclosed property involves several challenges:

▲ Japan is a mature market, and many experienced investors have access to cash. The most desirable properties have usually been picked over by professional investors.

▲ Tenant protection laws prevent you from inspecting the interior of a property before you bid on it. Furthermore, it is almost impossible to cancel a lease if the occupants want to continue living in a fore-closed property that you have purchased.[1]

▲ The yakuza are active in real estate and frequently occupy build-ings to depress auction prices.

It's important to have a clear understanding of what is and is not cov-ered by the foreclosure process. If you buy a foreclosed property with a tenant, you will be responsible for returning the tenant's deposit at the end of their tenancy. You may also be expected to cover other unpaid fees.

Foreclosed property in Yamanashi

American David Markle speaks fluent Japanese and has made Japan his home for nearly four decades. He currently lives in a small town in Yamanashi Prefecture with his wife and children. Since 2004, he has bought five foreclosed properties—known as *keibai bukken*—including a farmhouse, undeveloped agricultural land and three apartments in "mansions," the Japanese term for upmarket, multistory residential buildings that are usually built using reinforced concrete.

Markle's first foreclosed property was an 800-*tsubo* (2,645-square-meter) site that included an old farmhouse; a second, smaller home; a garage and several outbuildings. He bought the property, which had an estimated value of ¥8 million, for ¥1.5 million after his wife spotted a foreclosure notice in the newspaper.

Markle notes that the staff in his local courthouse were very helpful. "They answered our questions, helped us complete the paperwork and were very welcoming to us as nonprofessionals."

After buying five properties for cash and finding stable tenants, he refinanced three of them. "I still own the properties and collect rent from them, which is paying off the mortgages and then some, and I get the benefits of having the cash available for doing other things."

Markle and his wife, who is from the Kanto region, have lived in Yamanashi for nearly 20 years. They appreciate the prefecture's fresh air, good quality of life and access to services and transportation. However, he notes that outsiders are sometimes viewed with suspicion. The situation was exacerbated by the fact that Markle isn't Japanese and was buying foreclosed property—an activity that some see as shameful or disreputable.

"There was a sense of, 'Oh, what's going on here? What's this guy up to?'" says Markle, who admits to being anxious about how his neighbors would react to a foreigner buying foreclosed property. The situation was made more complicated because the former owners were living in the farmhouse, the first of his purchases, when the property was foreclosed.

Markle consulted a lawyer and considered a range of options, including coming to an agreement with the former owners or hiring someone to evict them. In the end, he let them stay in the house for three years rent free, until the husband died and the wife decided to move on. While this may not have been the most profitable approach, it did help to build goodwill with his neighbors, something that can be important in a small, tightly knit community.

He had fewer difficulties with the three mansions he purchased. "The first one was kind of rundown, but not unlivable," he says. "It was empty, and we needed to put in new kitchen cabinets and repair one of the walls, but that was no big deal."

The second was fully furnished and slightly more complicated. "At the auction, I bought the property but not the furniture. So I called the former owners and asked them if they wanted to come and pick up their furniture. They said I'd have to pay them if I wanted to keep the furniture. I told them to send a truck over, and I'd help them load it. They hung up on me and I never heard from them again."

The third mansion was more of a textbook foreclosure, where the former owners walked away leaving dirty dishes in the sink. After giving the unit a thorough cleaning and making some minor repairs, Markle said he had no trouble finding a tenant.

Neighbors can also be an issue. At one point, Markle purchased agricultural land that had been rezoned as residential. The access road to the property was agricultural land that had never been rezoned as a road, and the farmer who owned the land tried to charge Markle a fee to access his property. After several confrontations, Markle and the farmer ended up in mediation. Ultimately, the farmer backed down and let him use the road.

Despite these challenges, Markle believes it is possible to find value in foreclosed property, especially if you do your research. He points out that you are competing with local investors and real estate agents who know how much things cost and are hoping to flip the property for a quick profit. If you are planning to use the property yourself, hold it for the long term or rent it out, you may be able to make a profit on a property that real estate agents pass up.

"Every situation is different," he concludes, "and it doesn't always go by the book. It helps to be prepared for the long haul and to be tenacious. If you don't expect everything to be perfect, you won't be disappointed."

Homes for the elderly

With people aged 65 and above estimated to represent 29% of the population by 2020 and 40% by 2060, Japan faces a shortage of homes for the elderly.[2] In 2017, 366,000 people were waiting for places in special nursing homes, which are government-subsidized facilities that provide round-the-clock care to individuals who are unable to care for themselves.[3]

Nursing homes are operated by companies such as Nichii Gakkan and Benesse. Large insurers, including Sompo Japan Nipponkoa, have purchased nursing home operators, as have private equity firms, such as CVC Capital Partners. There are public and semipublic homes, many of which are spartan and located in suburban and rural areas where costs are lower. According to a 2015 survey by Kyodo News, 15,000 people live in over 1,600 unauthorized care facilities.[4]

Japan's senior care industry faces numerous challenges, including reductions in government funding and difficulty hiring and retaining staff, due to low wages and poor working conditions. In 2016, a record 108 nursing care companies went bankrupt, including 48 home nursing care companies.

The industry has seen a growing number of abuse cases, with 328 employees accused of abusing elderly residents in fiscal 2014.[5] Worse, staff have murdered residents. Hayato Imai confessed to throwing three elderly patients off the fourth-floor balcony of a home in Kawasaki in 2014. Two years later, Satoshi Uematsu stabbed 19 patients to death at a home for the physically and mentally disabled in Sagamihara.

Love hotels

Japan has about 10,000 love hotels, where amorous couples can escape for a few hours of privacy. Also known as leisure hotels, love hotels are an accepted part of life in a nation where homes are small and many people live with their parents into middle age.

Love hotels have two rates: A "rest" price of around ¥3,000 per hour and an overnight rate that can range from ¥6,000 to ¥30,000. This pricing structure allows well-managed properties to rent a room three times a day and generate revenues of ¥400,000 to ¥800,000 per month, per room.

The industry is estimated to have annual revenues of more than ¥2 trillion.[6] But the number of hotels has declined from 20,000–25,000 a decade ago, as demand has been diminished by an aging, less frisky population.

Due to their association with prostitution and organized crime, love hotels have traditionally been outside the mainstream hospitality industry, and operators have had difficulty arranging financing. However, the government now sees love hotels as part of the solution to Japan's accommodation shortage and has instructed state-run lender Japan Finance Corporation to make money available to owners who wish to convert their properties into conventional hotels.[7]

Converted love hotels have found a new audience among budget-conscious travelers, including backpackers and the growing number of Chinese tourists visiting Japan.[8]

Minpaku

Japan's growing popularity as an international tourist destination, its shortage of hotel rooms and upcoming sporting events, including the 2019 Rugby World Cup and 2020 Olympics, have inspired investors to buy homes for use as short-term, Airbnb-style rentals, known as *minpaku*.

In 2017, the national government passed legislation to legalize minpaku. The specifics of the law, which is expected to take effect in June 2018, continue to be refined.

For *minpaku* hosts, proximity to popular attractions, such as shrines and temples, is essential.

Before the law was passed, minpaku was only legal in Tokyo's Ota-ku, in Osaka Prefecture and in the city of Fukuoka. Despite this restriction, there were an estimated 40,000 Airbnb locations in Japan, almost all of which were illegal.[9]

Under the new law, after registering with the local government, hosts may rent their homes for up to 180 days per year.[10] Hosts must maintain a guest register, display a sign and ensure their facilities are safe and clean. Absentee hosts are required to appoint a property manager.

Local governments are introducing their own regulations. For example, Ota-ku will prohibit minpaku hosts from operating in residential neighborhoods where hotels and inns are banned. Tokyo's Shinjuku-ku plans to ban hosts from accepting guests between noon Monday and noon Friday. Other jurisdictions are preparing local regulations based on factors ranging from record keeping to proximity to temples and schools.[11]

In 2017, the Travel Agency Act was revised to raise fines for illegally running a minpaku service from the current ¥30,000 to ¥1 million. Licensed operators who fail to obey record keeping rules could be fined up to ¥500,000.[12]

Buying a home for minpaku
If you are buying a home for minpaku use, ensure that you comply with national and local laws. Places such as Kyoto that are popular with tourists often have the toughest minpaku regulations.

Ask your real estate agent to check the building's rules to see if short-term rentals are banned. In response to Airbnb's popularity, many owners' committees have prohibited rentals of less than 30 days. Owners committees in desirable buildings claim to scan listings on sites like Airbnb in search of owners who are violating the regulations.

Some operators evade the short-term rental ban by offering a minimum stay of 30 days and targeting students and long-term business travelers. While returns from guests staying 30–90 days are lower than from shorter stays, they are higher than from regular residential leases. In addition, 30–90 day rentals require less administration and maintenance than shorter stays.

Location is important. Your home should be near destinations that are popular with guests, whether that is business centers like Tokyo's Marunouchi and Shinjuku districts, universities or tourist attractions like Universal Studios in Osaka and Tokyo Disneyland. The size of the home will be determined by nearby attractions. Families visiting theme parks will want two- and three-bedroom homes, while students and couples prefer one-bedroom or studio apartments. Proximity to major train and subway lines is a key selling point.

Japan's confusing addresses make clear maps and directions essential. Google Maps and similar services are helpful, but contain gaps and mistakes. Guests who have gotten lost following flawed directions on a steamy July afternoon are unlikely to rate your home highly. Worse, they may knock on neighbors' doors or visit the local police box in search of assistance. Don't forget that your guests may have just arrived on a long flight and may be jet-lagged. If in doubt, over-communicate.

Guests appreciate maps showing nearby services, such as train and subway stations, grocery and convenience stores, automated teller machines that accept international bank cards, laundromats and restaurants.

Typically, appliances in Japan only have Japanese-language markings. Translating and labeling the main controls on the hot-water heater, air-conditioner and other appliances will help your guests get settled. Many domestic appliances are exported with English-language controls, and you can sometimes find the English manual online. Other devices have multilingual operating systems and a user interface that can be switched from Japanese to English.

Around the world, security and the presence of strangers is a concern for people living near short-term rental accommodations. Japanese people also worry about foreigners sorting and disposing of their trash correctly. Sorting trash isn't complicated, but foreign guests need to understand that Japanese people take it seriously. Many ward offices produce multilingual instructions that you can leave in the apartment, with an ample supply of approved trash bags. Don't forget to explain where the trash is to be left.

Noise complaints are another common problem. One Airbnb host solved this problem by installing thick carpets and removing everything that could possibly annoy a neighbor. There was no radio, television or even an alarm clock.

A portable Wi-Fi hot spot can provide internet access in the home and while guests are visiting nearby attractions.

Finally, review your insurance policy to see if it covers acts by guests, such as a fire or overflowing bathtub, or injuries to guests on your premises.

The Olympic effect

Previous Olympics have created strong demand for short-term rentals, as tourists seek an alternative to expensive hotel rooms during the games. As noted in the "Market Drivers" chapter, Japan has a serious shortage of hotel rooms, which is likely to exacerbate this effect during the 2020 games.

People are also buying homes ahead of the games in the hope of achieving capital gains. But not everyone is bullish. Some analysts predict a post-Olympic correction, with falls of up to one-third in Japan's land prices.

A 2010 study by the University of British Columbia found no evidence of a post-Olympic boom or bust. The study, which covered the Summer Olympics cities of Atlanta (1996), Los Angeles (1984) and Sydney (2000), and the Winter Olympic cities of Calgary (1988), Salt Lake City (2002) and Vancouver (2010), concluded that "while construction employment dramatically increases in the period prior to the games, house prices are the same as they would be in the absence of the games."[13]

Recreational property

Japan offers a wide array of recreational property, ranging from ski chalets in the hills of Hokkaido to beachfront resorts in Okinawa. Much of this is new, expensive and built for international tourists.

Japan also has tens of thousands of empty resort condominiums that were built during the 1980s and early 1990s. Many were built in ski resorts like Yuzawa, Niigata Prefecture, about 90 minutes by Shinkansen northwest of Tokyo. Seaside towns such as Atami, Shizuoka Prefecture, just over an hour by Shinkansen southwest of Tokyo, were also fashionable. Onjuku, a community in Chiba Prefecture that is about 80 minutes by train from the capital, was another popular, if less expensive, destination.

At the market's peak, resort condominiums sold for ¥50 million or more. But as the economic bubble burst, many owners realized they couldn't afford a second home. Ski resorts suffered because Japan's aging population had fewer and fewer skiers. Many units were abandoned, and their owners' whereabouts remain unknown.

Recreational properties, ranging from condominiums to estates, are available throughout Japan.

Today, resort condominiums can be purchased for as little as ¥1 million. But there are several catches. First, many developments include upmarket amenities, such as swimming pools, *onsen* baths and exercise rooms, that are expensive to operate and maintain. Monthly management and repair fees for a small condominium can easily total ¥50,000.[14]

Second, the units often come with unpaid tax, management and repair bills that the new owner is expected to pay. These costs can range from hundreds of thousands to millions of yen.

Third, because property taxes are based on the condominium's original value and not its current market price, property taxes are high. In some instances, taxes for a small-town resort condominium are comparable to those for a condominium in Tokyo.

However, economics and demographics may pose the biggest challenges. As Japan's population continues to age and people move to cities like Tokyo, the enclaves in which these resorts are located become increasingly dependent on government subsidies. Events like Fuji Rock, an annual music festival held outside Yuzawa, attract tourists but are not enough to sustain a community year round.

A vacation home in Gunma

While Niseko is becoming an international destination to rival Whistler, Vail and St. Moritz, there are other ways to invest in and enjoy recreational property in Japan, as Dale Willetts and his wife, Alyssa, discovered.

The Willetts have never lived in Japan and don't speak Japanese, but they did spend several ski vacations in Niseko, starting at Easter 1999. "We had a great time," says Dale. "The snow was fantastic and the place was brilliant." They also found the trip from their home in Hong Kong was easier and less expensive than flying to a ski resort in Dale's native Canada.

Dale, Alyssa and their son, Benjamin, returned to Niseko several times until the area's growing popularity became a disadvantage. "We stopped going because you had to book a year ahead for Christmas or Chinese New Year," explains Dale, who also mentions rising hotel prices and difficulty in reserving direct flights from Hong Kong to Sapporo as drawbacks.

In 2007, the Willetts wanted a Christmas ski holiday. A friend told them about Minakami in Gunma Prefecture, where he owned a vacation home. Over Christmas, Dale and his wife rented a two-story mountain chalet in Minakami and, after a couple of days, decided to buy it. "It was exactly what we were looking for: peaceful and away from it all, yet very convenient to get to and reasonably priced," says Willetts.

A 75-minute Shinkansen ride from Tokyo, the three-bedroom chalet sits on a 700-square-meter lot. Skiing, hiking, biking, rafting, paragliding and sport fishing are nearby, as are golf courses and numerous hot springs. The Willetts bought the chalet from a Japanese-speaking American, who built it in the 1970s.

Dale estimates the chalet cost about one-third of a comparable property in the Niseko area. He made a 10% deposit on signing the sale and purchase agreement and paid 50% three months later and the balance on registration. He paid cash for the chalet, because he felt his non-resident status would make it difficult to get a mortgage.

Several aspects of the transaction were unusual. Because the Willetts' friend knew the chalet's owner, the sale was completed without a real estate agent. The vendor introduced the Willetts to a local judicial scrivener (*shiho-shoshi*), who handled the transaction documents, which were scrutinized for the Willetts by a Tokyo-based attorney. And since the buyer and seller were native English speakers, the sale and purchase agreement was written in English and then translated into Japanese. Both versions were then registered with the town office.

Alyssa, who is a furniture designer, imported a 40-foot container of furniture from China for the vacation home. She traveled to Japan and completed a declaration that the container was unaccompanied baggage, which allowed the furniture to be imported free of taxes and duties. Alyssa then gave the declaration to a freight-forwarder, who handled the shipping arrangements.

One thing that Dale had not counted on was the need for a certificate of alien registration, which is now known as a residence (*zairyu*) card. "It's impossible to open a bank account, register your utilities and arrange other services without one," he says.

The Willetts family is happy with their vacation home and its four-season appeal. They also appreciate its proximity to Tokyo and the frequent flights between Hong Kong and Tokyo, which are available even during peak travel periods.

Dale counsels anyone contemplating a similar purchase to ensure they have help with the language. "To get anything important done requires fluency in Japanese," he says.

Rural real estate

As outlined in the "Demographics" chapter, rural areas are suffering the worst effects of Japan's shrinking, aging population. This includes large numbers of empty and abandoned homes (*akiya*).

In response, the national, prefectural and local governments are encouraging people to return to their hometowns or to move to rural areas. Governments use public relations campaigns showing people who have happily relocated, financial incentives for migrants and subsidies for people renovating old houses. Bodies such as the Furusato Kaiki Shien Center, a Tokyo-based nonprofit organization, provide resources for people relocating to the countryside, including information about abandoned homes.

One challenge facing migrants is that, despite the glut of empty homes, there are few houses available for rent. That makes it difficult for people to sample rural living before making a commitment to move permanently.

Another issue is the decline of Japan's agricultural sector as farmers age, retire and die. In fiscal 2010, more than 60% of Japan's farmers were over age 65.[15] The number of farm households has dropped from 1.6 million in 2011 to 1.3 million in 2016. Over the same period, the number of business farm households (as opposed to households where farming is a hobby or a sideline) has fallen from 356,000 to 285,000.[16] Many farms are dependent on government subsidies.

Meanwhile, a growing proportion of Japan's rural real estate has unclear ownership. A 2017 survey by the Ministry of Justice found the ownership of 32.4% of forests, 23.4% of farmland and 10.5% of housing lots in rural areas had not changed in at least 50 years, suggesting that the property has been abandoned.[17] In total, the ownership of about 11% of Japan's landmass, or about 40,000 square kilometers, is unknown.[18]

Despite the glut of empty houses, there is a shortage of rental accommodations in rural parts of Japan.

Many people who inherit rural real estate don't bother to claim it, due to the property's low value and potential for tax liabilities. The lack of clear ownership makes it difficult to collect property taxes, to consolidate farmland into more functional, regularly shaped plots, or to use land for public projects, such as highways.

Japan's agricultural sector is dominated by large numbers of small farms. While there have been amendments to the Agricultural Land Act, the pace of reform is glacial, and it remains difficult for farmers to achieve the economies of scale that could revitalize these communities.

Reforming Japan's agricultural sector will not be easy. Farms and farmers occupy a special place in the national psyche, and there are powerful government, industry and community groups with an interest in maintaining the present system. This includes rural committees that must approve the sale or lease of farmland.[19]

Share houses

Japan has many share house operators, including Borderless Japan, House-Zoo, Oakhouse and Parenting Home. These organizations offer people with a common bond—such as pets, the arts or single parenthood—the ability to share a house. Each resident has a private room and access to common areas and amenities, such as childcare. Rents are usually comparable to those for a small apartment, but residents enjoy more space and the company of like-minded individuals. Some share house operators are social enterprises, while others are businesses that are attracted to the potential for higher rental yields.

In addition, there are share houses catering to students, "freeters" and other budget-conscious tenants seeking inexpensive accommodations.

Solar power

After the 2011 Great East Japan Earthquake, Japan faced serious electricity shortages. In response to the shortages and growing antinuclear sentiment, the government intensified efforts to conserve energy and encourage the development of alternative sources, including solar, wind, geothermal and biomass.

Solar power installations sprang up throughout the country, encouraged by feed-in tariffs (FITs), which are regulations requiring power companies to buy electricity from green suppliers at fixed, above-market rates.[20]

More than 1.5 million Japanese households now have solar power systems, and investors have built large solar farms to capitalize on the subsidies.[21] However, the cost of this program has been passed on to consumers in the form of higher electricity bills. Electrical utilities have rebelled against the program, claiming the FITs undermine their business model.[22]

Japan now faces a shortage of land suitable for solar installations,[23] and the government is reducing the FITs, making solar power less attractive for independent producers. At the same time, Panasonic and other solar equipment manufacturers are focusing on batteries that allow electricity producers to store power for their own use, rather than selling it back to the grid.

Stocks and other investments

If you prefer not to buy physical property, there are several other ways to gain exposure to Japanese real estate. You can:

▲ Buy shares in housebuilders such as Daiwa House, Misawa Homes or Sumitomo Forestry, or in developers such as Mitsubishi Estate, Mitsui Fudosan or Sumitomo Realty & Development.

▲ Invest in a J-REIT. See the Association for Real Estate Securitization for more information.

▲ Buy shares in companies that supply or support Japanese real estate. For example, asset managers such as Star Mica, building material manufacturers like Lixil and mortgage lenders including Mizuho Bank.

▲ Invest in an exchange traded fund (ETF), such as those operated by Vanguard, iShares or State Street, that tracks an international real estate index.

▲ Buy a mutual fund, such as those offered by Fidelity and Schwab, that invests in global real estate.

Institutions and wealthy individuals can also invest through private equity firms. These companies, which finance everything from warehouses to software start-ups, typically require a multiyear investment horizon and a minimum commitment of $250,000.

RESOURCES

INFORMATION SOURCES

This chapter features resources to help you buy and own a home in Japan. The entries are arranged alphabetically and include English-language content, unless noted with "JO" (Japanese only). Many sites have information in Chinese and other languages.

Most of these resources are free of charge. Since organizations often restructure their websites, the addresses given are generally for the main page, which may be in Japanese with an English (or "Global") option. The Japanese section of these websites often has information that is more detailed and more current than the English pages.

The inclusion or omission of a company should not be taken as a recommendation that you use or avoid them. Government organizations with an interest in housing and real estate are included. Additional information about entries marked with an asterisk can be found in the Government section.

Finally, things change quickly. Consider this information a starting point, not the last word.

A

Air pollution*

Real time air-pollution maps for cities in Japan and elsewhere are available at http://aqicn.org/map.

Antiquities*

The Agency for Cultural Affairs is responsible for antiquities and archaeological relics. Your local city or ward office has maps showing the location of archaeological sites in their administrative area.

Japan has 4,775 Important Cultural Properties, including the Mikasa Hotel in Karuizawa.

Appraisal services

Many English-speaking real estate appraisers work in Japan, and most have a website. Prices range from ¥20,000 for a one-page appraisal of a vacant lot to more than ¥200,000 for a detailed report covering the rental of a building.

The Japan Association of Real Estate Appraisers' website has links and information on a range of topics (www.fudousan-kanteishi.or.jp).

The Tokyo Association of Real Estate Appraisers' website includes a glossary (www.tokyo-kanteishi.or.jp, JO).

Architects and designers

The American Institute of Architects has a chapter in Japan (http://aiajapan.org).

Arch Daily features the work of architects from around the world, with many examples from Japan (www.archdaily.com). London-based Dezeen has similar content (www.dezeen.com).

The Architectural Institute of Japan is an academic association with 35,000 members, including architects, building engineers and researchers (www.aij.or.jp).

The Japan Architectural Education and Information Center conducts examinations of building designers and construction engineers (*kenchikushi*) and supervises their training. The center also certifies interior planners. The center's website explains how architects are certified and the services that various grades of architects may provide (www.jaeic.or.jp).

The Japan Federation of Architects & Building Engineers Associations' website includes links to each prefecture's architectural association (www.kenchikushikai.or.jp, JO).

The Japan Institute of Architects' website has a search function for architects (www.jia.or.jp).

The Japan Interior Architects/Designers' Association maintains a website with a members' directory (www.jid.or.jp, JO).

The Japan Interior Industry Association represents companies supplying the decoration and construction industries (www.interior.or.jp, JO).

The Japan Interior Planner Association's website explains the role of interior planners and has links to regional associations (www.jipa-official.org).

Klein Dytham Architecture is a Tokyo-based multidisciplinary design studio known for retail outlets, restaurants, resorts, offices and private residences (www.klein-dytham.com).

RIBA offers information about how to hire and work with an architect (www.architecture.com).

Riccardo Tossani Architecture has offices in Tokyo, Niseko, Beijing and Los Angeles and experience in hotels and resorts, residential, office, interior design and master planning (www.tossani.com).

The World Architects website (www.world-architects.com) includes a directory of Japanese architects with photographs of their work (www.japan-architects.com).

B

Building components and systems

Building components and systems are available through dealers and dedicated showrooms. Design-oriented complexes, such as Ozone (www.ozone.co.jp) and the Tokyo Design Center (www.design-center.co.jp), feature local and international brands.

Appliances and electronics
▲ Bang & Olufsen; audiovisual equipment (http://stores.bang-olufsen.com/japan)

▲ Bosch; appliances (www.bosch.co.jp)

▲ Carrier; heating, ventilation and air-conditioning systems (www.carrier.com/carrier/en/jp)

▲ Crestron; lighting and home automation systems (http://crestronjapan.com)

▲ Electrolux; appliances (www.electrolux.co.jp)

▲ Fujitsu; air-conditioning systems (www.fujitsu.com)

▲ Haier; appliances (http://haier.co.jp)

▲ Hitachi; audiovisual equipment and appliances (www.hitachi.com)

▲ Kyocera; photovoltaic systems (www.kyocera.co.jp)

▲ Leviton; lighting and home automation systems (www.leviton.com)

▲ LG; audiovisual equipment and air-conditioning systems (www. lg.com/jp)

▲ Lutron; lighting and home automation systems (www.lutron.jp)

▲ Miele; appliances (www.miele.co.jp)

▲ Mitsubishi Electric; audiovisual equipment, photovoltaic systems and appliances (www.mitsubishielectric.com)

▲ Panasonic; audiovisual equipment, photovoltaic systems and appliances (www.panasonic.com)

▲ Philips; audiovisual equipment and appliances (www.philips.co.jp)

▲ Samsung; audiovisual equipment and appliances (www. galaxymobile.jp)

▲ Sharp; audiovisual equipment, photovoltaic systems and appliances (www.sharp.co.jp)

▲ Siemens; appliances, lighting and home automation systems (www. siemens.com)

▲ Smeg; appliances (http://smeg-shop.net)

▲ Sony; audiovisual equipment (www.sony.com)

▲ Toshiba; audiovisual equipment and photovoltaic systems (www. toshiba.co.jp)

Bathrooms and kitchens

▲ Blum; kitchen systems (www.blum.com/jp)

▲ Boffi; kitchens and bathrooms (http://www.interiors-inc.jp)

▲ Bulthaup; kitchen systems (http://kc-kitchen.com)

▲ Duravit; sanitary ware (www.duravit.co.jp)

▲ Gaggenau; kitchens and appliances (www.gaggenau.com/jp)

▲ Hansgrohe; plumbing (www.hansgrohe.co.jp)

▲ Kohler; sanitary ware (www.jpkohler.com)

▲ Lixil; plumbing, sanitary ware and building components (www. lixil.com)

▲ Noritz; water heaters (www.noritzglobal.com)

▲ Poggenpohl; kitchens and appliances (www.tokyo.poggenpohl. com)

▲ Toto; sanitary ware (www.toto.co.jp)

▲ Viking; appliances (www.vikingrange.com)

Floors and windows

▲ Armstrong; ceilings and floor coverings (www.armstrong.co.jp)

▲ Hunter Douglas; window coverings (https://jp.hunterdouglas.asia)

▲ YKK AP; doors, windows and architectural components (www. ykkap.co.jp)

Furniture

▲ Armani Casa; furniture and accessories (www.armanicasa.com)

▲ Cassina; Le Corbusier and Frank Lloyd Wright furniture (www. cassina-ixc.jp)

▲ Conran; furniture and accessories (www.conranshop.jp)

▲ Herman Miller; Eames and Aeron chairs (www.hermanmiller.co.jp)

▲ Ikea; furniture and accessories (www.ikea.co.jp)

Build-it-yourself

Arudou Debito (formerly David Aldwinckle), a naturalized Japanese citizen, bought land and built a house in the Hokkaido countryside in 1997 (www.debito.org/residentspage.html#HOUSEBUILDING).

Philip Brasor and Masako Tsubuku—authors of the Home Truths column in *The Japan Times*—built a home outside Tokyo between 2013 and 2016. That experience is detailed in their blog, Cat Foreheads & Rabbit Hutches (https://catforehead.com).

Hometta (www.hometta.com) and Houseplans (www.houseplans.com) sell professionally designed building plans for single-family homes.

Paperhouses is a group of architects offering free downloads of home blueprints. Similar to the open-source software movement, Paperhouses' network includes partners who can customize designs to meet users' needs and local conditions (www.paperhouses.co).

The U.K.–based National Custom & Self Build Association offers reports, videos, technical information and other resources for people who are building their own homes (www.nacsba.org.uk).

Several organizations in the United States offer courses for people interested in learning to build a home: Rocky Mountain Workshops (www.rockymountainworkshops.com), the Shelter Institute (www.shelterinstitute.com) and the Yestermorrow Design/Build School (www.yestermorrow.org).

C

Consumer protection*

The Center for Housing Renovation and Dispute Settlement Support provides information and telephone counseling on housing-related issues (www.chord.or.jp).

The National Association for Real Estate Transaction Guaranty (NARETG) settles disputes in property transactions handled by agents who are members of the National Federation of Real Estate Transaction Associations. NARETG ensures a buyer's "earnest money" (deposit) is refunded if a transaction becomes invalid (www.hosyo.or.jp, JO).

The National Consumer Affairs Center of Japan provides consumer counseling, conducts research and publishes an English-language newsletter (www.kokusen.go.jp).

The Organization for Housing Warranty provides warranties for new and pre-owned homes, as well as renovations (www.mamoris.jp).

Oshimaland operates a website where people can post the location of "stigmatized properties," such as homes where people have died (www.oshimaland.com).

E

Earthquakes*

The Disaster Reduction and Human Renovation Institution in Kobe is a useful resource for anyone wanting to learn more about the Great Hanshin Earthquake, earthquakes in Japan and disaster preparation (www.dri.ne.jp).

The Japan Building Disaster Prevention Association offers information for professionals and homeowners about evaluating and retrofitting buildings (www.kenchiku-bosai.or.jp).

The Tokyo Metropolitan Government (TMG) published a 320-page guide entitled *Disaster Preparedness Tokyo* that includes useful information, even if you live elsewhere (www.metro.tokyo.jp/ENGLISH/GUIDE/BOSAI/). The TMG also offers a map of Tokyo's medical facilities, emergency shelters and evacuation areas (http://map.bousai.metro.tokyo.jp/en/pc/).

The Disaster Reduction and Human Renovation Institution in Kobe has an earthquake display and a large library.

The U.S. Geological Survey has general background on earthquakes (http://earthquake.usgs.gov).

The elderly*

The Foundation for Senior Citizens' Housing researches and certifies housing for the elderly, promotes universal design and publishes reports, books and design manuals (www.koujuuzai.or.jp, JO).

Energy conservation

The Comprehensive Assessment System for Built Environment Efficiency (CASBEE) is a method for evaluating and rating the performance of buildings—including homes—and cities (www.ibec.or.jp/CASBEE).

The Energy Conservation Center, Japan, provides information about national energy policies, government subsidies, tax incentives and related resources for businesses and individuals (www.eccj.or.jp, JO).

The Green Home Guide is produced by the nonprofit U.S. Green Building Council (http://greenhomeguide.com).

The Japan Photovoltaic Energy Association offers case studies, statistics, background information and checklists for people thinking of installing a residential solar power system (www.jpea.gr.jp). See the Building Components and Systems entry for a list of photovoltaic equipment manufacturers.

Passive House Japan (http://passivehouse-japan.org, JO) is affiliated with the Passive House Institute, an independent research body in Germany that champions the development of energy-efficient sealed homes (http://passivehouse.com).

The Renewable Energy Institute researches, develops and advocates policies to promote renewable energy in Japan (www.renewable-ei.org).

Environmental resources*

The Asbestos Center provides information about asbestos-related issues, including books, a telephone hotline and more (http://asbestos-center.jp).

Asbestos Disaster: Lessons from Japan's Experience (Kenichi Miyamoto, Kenji Morinaga and Hiroyuki Mori, editors; Springer 2011, ISBN 978-4-431-53914-8) offers a detailed account of the social, economic, legal and political impact of asbestos in Japan.

The Building Center of Japan has information about standards for building materials as they relate to sick house syndrome and sells translations of the Building Standard Law (www.bcj.or.jp).

The Geo-Environmental Protection Center website has a list of companies providing soil testing and remediation services (www.gepc.or.jp).

The U.S. Centers for Disease Control and Prevention operates the Agency for Toxic Substances and Disease Registry, which has clear explanations of hazardous chemicals such as polychlorinated biphenyls (PCBs) (www.atsdr.cdc.gov).

The U.S. Environmental Protection Agency has information about indoor air quality, mold, lead, radon, volatile organic compounds and more (www.epa.gov).

F

Finance*

Lenders

The following organizations offer housing loans. This is not an exhaustive list, as it excludes all but two of Japan's 105 regional banks, which may be worth considering if you are buying property in their operating area.

Deregulation has seen nontraditional lenders—such as telecommunications company KDDI and retailer Rakuten—enter the mortgage market. The Japan Bankers Association (see below) has a list of banks licensed to operate in Japan.

Japanese banks

▲ AEON Bank (www.aeonbank.co.jp)

▲ Aozora Bank (www.aozorabank.co.jp)

▲ Bank of Tokyo-Mitsubishi UFJ (www.bk.mufg.jp)

▲ Japan Net Bank (www.japannetbank.co.jp)

▲ KDDI (www.au.com/finance)

▲ Mitsubishi UFJ Trust and Banking (www.tr.mufg.jp)

▲ Mizuho Bank (www.mizuhobank.co.jp)

▲ Mizuho Trust & Banking (www.mizuho-tb.co.jp)

▲ ORIX Group (www.orix.co.jp)

▲ Rakuten Bank (www.rakuten-bank.co.jp)

▲ Resona Group (www.resona-gr.co.jp)

▲ SBI Sumishin Net Bank (www.netbk.co.jp)

⏶ Shinsei Bank (www.shinseibank.com)

⏶ Sony Bank (http://moneykit.net)

⏶ Sumitomo Mitsui Banking (www.smbc.co.jp)

⏶ Sumitomo Mitsui Trust Holdings (http://smth.jp)

⏶ Suruga Bank (www.surugabank.co.jp)

⏶ Tokyo Star Bank (www.tokyostarbank.co.jp)

Foreign banks

Citibank, Commonwealth Bank of Australia, HSBC and National Australia Bank no longer offer housing loans in Japan. In late 2017, the Bank of China (www.bankofchina.com) and the Bank of Taiwan (www.bot.com.tw) were making home loans to people who could speak Japanese or Chinese.

Lenders outside Japan

⏶ ORIX Asia is the Hong Kong branch of the Japanese finance company (www.orix.com.hk).

⏶ Shinsei Investment & Finance is a subsidiary of Shinsei Bank that lends to Hong Kong passport holders (www.shinsei-if.com, JO).

⏶ UOB is a Singapore-based bank that lends to people who are not resident in Japan (www.uobgroup.com).

Other resources

Aggregators and brokers

⏶ AP Advisers is a Tokyo-based mortgage broker (www.ap-advisers.com).

⏶ The E-LOAN website aggregates mortgage information from 100 lenders (www.eloan.co.jp, JO).

▲ Jutapon lets you enter your details once and simulate mortgage applications to multiple lenders. The service works with or without identifying a property and for refinancing (www.jutapon.com, JO).

▲ The Mortgage Comparison Dictionary lets you compare the offerings of different lenders, including terms and conditions (http://loan1192ya.com, JO).

Credit bureaus
▲ The Credit Information Center (www.cic.co.jp)

▲ The Japan Consumer Credit Association (www.j-credit.or.jp)

▲ The Personal Credit Information Center (www.zenginkyo.or.jp)

The Japanese Bankers Association
The Japanese Bankers Association website provides background on Japan's banking laws and regulations and a list of banks licensed to operate in Japan (www.zenginkyo.or.jp).

Reverse mortgages
Mitsubishi UFJ Trust and Banking Corp., Mizuho Bank, Sumitomo Mitsui Banking Corp. and Tokyo Star Bank offer reverse mortgages on Japanese homes.

Fire*

The International Fire Service Information Center's website has detailed reports on firefighting and fire prevention in Japan, as well as links to fire-related laws and regulations (www.kaigai-shobo.jp).

The Tokyo Fire Department (TFD) maintains a multilingual website with fire and safety information (www.tfd.metro.tokyo.jp).

The TFD also operates the Life Safety Learning Center, which features a smoke-filled maze, simulations of earthquakes and rainstorms, first-aid and fire-prevention courses and information for children (www.tfd.metro.tokyo.jp/hp-hjbskan, JO).

G

Government: municipal

Tokyo
The Tokyo Metropolitan Government's website includes a guide for foreign residents as well as information about public safety, transportation, health care, education, tourism and other topics (www.metro.tokyo.jp).

Tokyo's 23 wards have websites with English-language content ranging from brief summaries to monthly newsletters. Many sites include maps showing disaster evacuation routes, as well as seismic and flood hazards (http://www.metro.tokyo.jp/ENGLISH/ABOUT/LINKS/municipalities.htm).

Other cities and towns
▲ Chiba (www.city.chiba.jp)

▲ Fukuoka (www.city.fukuoka.lg.jp)

▲ Hiroshima (www.city.hiroshima.lg.jp)

▲ Kawasaki (www.city.kawasaki.jp)

▲ Kitakyushu (www.city.kitakyushu.lg.jp)

▲ Kobe (www.city.kobe.lg.jp)

▲ Kyoto (www.city.kyoto.lg.jp)

▲ Nagasaki (www.city.nagasaki.lg.jp)

▲ Nagoya (www.city.nagoya.jp)

▲ Naha (www.city.naha.okinawa.jp)

▲ Niseko (www.town.niseko.lg.jp)

▲ Okayama (www.city.okayama.jp)

▲ Osaka (www.city.osaka.lg.jp)

▲ Saitama (www.city.saitama.jp)

▲ Sakai (www.city.sakai.lg.jp)

▲ Sapporo (www.city.sapporo.jp)

▲ Sendai (www.city.sendai.jp)

▲ Yokohama (www.city.yokohama.lg.jp)

Government: national

Land, real estate and related issues fall under the jurisdiction of many agencies, ministries and bureaus. Here are some key bodies.

The Agency for Cultural Affairs is responsible for antiquities and archaeological relics (www.bunka.go.jp).

Although, technically, it is not a government agency, the Bank of Japan sets and implements the nation's monetary policy and publishes the quarterly *tankan* survey of business trends (www.boj.or.jp).

The Cabinet Office produces reports on social, business and economic topics (www.cao.go.jp).

The Consumer Affairs Agency promotes consumer rights through the Household Goods Quality Labeling Law, the Real Estate Transaction Act and the Money Lending Control Act (www.caa.go.jp).

The Financial Services Agency is responsible for the stability of Japan's financial system. The agency's website includes lists of licensed banks, insurance companies and other providers of financial services, as well as English translations of finance laws (www.fsa.go.jp).

The Geospatial Information Authority of Japan produces topographical, land use, coastal and hazard maps, which show areas likely to be affected by floods, earthquakes, liquefaction, lava flows and tsunamis (www.gsi.go.jp).

The National Diet Building is located in Nagatocho, Tokyo.

The Headquarters for Earthquake Research Promotion provides information about current seismic activity, threat assessments, maps and other data (www.jishin.go.jp).

Japanese Law Translation, operated by the Ministry of Justice, has English versions of Japanese laws, keyword search capabilities and translations of legal terms (www.japaneselawtranslation.go.jp).

The Japan Housing Finance Agency (www.jhf.go.jp) collaborates with commercial lenders to offer Flat 35 (www.flat35.com, JO), Flat 35S (www.flat35.com/loan/flat35s, JO) and Flat 50 (www.flat35.com/loan/flat50, JO), which are long-term, fixed-rate mortgages.

The Japan Meteorological Agency provides information about weather and operates an earthquake early-warning system. The agency's website includes information about local seismic activity, tsunami warnings and the JMA Seismic Intensity Scale (www.jma.go.jp).

The Japan Seismic Hazard Information Station website has detailed interactive maps showing earthquake fault lines and subduction zones (www.j-shis.bosai.go.jp).

The Justice Department's Legal Affairs Bureau has instructions for registering the sale and purchase of real estate, discharging mortgages and demolishing buildings (http://houmukyoku.moj.go.jp, JO).

The Ministry of Agriculture, Forestry and Fisheries administers farmland and forests and promotes the development of rural areas (www.maff.go.jp).

The Ministry of the Environment handles issues relating to agrochemicals, asbestos, contaminated soil and PCBs. The ministry's website has background information, statistics and English translations of environmental laws (www.env.go.jp).

Each year, the Ministry of Finance produces a draft budget and statistical summary. The ministry's website includes *The Comprehensive Handbook of Japanese Taxes 2010* and *Learning More About Taxes (July, 2017)* (www.mof.go.jp).

The Ministry of Health, Labour and Welfare is involved in environmental, aging and pension issues (www.mhlw.go.jp).

The Ministry of Land, Infrastructure, Transport and Tourism (MLIT) features the following information and resources on its website (www.mlit.go.jp):

▲ Historical sales data starting from fiscal 2005 for residential, commercial and industrial property, and for farmland and forests throughout Japan. Updated quarterly, the site includes detailed English-language maps (www.land.mlit.go.jp/webland).

▲ The annual *White Paper on Land, Infrastructure, Transport and Tourism in Japan* covers land use and demand trends, real estate industry and policy initiatives, and price and transaction data (www.mlit.go.jp/en/statistics/white-paper-mlit-index.html).

▲ Basic information about Japanese real estate transactions, including laws, taxes and buying and registering property (www.mlit.go.jp/en/report/press/totikensangyo13_hh_000003.html).

▲ A searchable database of building products containing asbestos (www.asbestos-database.jp, JO).

▲ A page where you can conduct background checks on companies and people in the real estate and construction industries (www.mlit.go.jp/nega-inf, JO).

The National Diet Library has searchable databases as well as statistics and information about Japan (www.ndl.go.jp).

The National Institute of Population and Social Security Research publishes demographic data and research in English, Chinese and Korean (www.ipss.go.jp).

The National Research Institute for Earth Science and Disaster Resilience investigates landslides, floods, volcanoes and earthquakes (www.bosai.go.jp).

The National Tax Agency publishes an annual income tax guide for foreigners that includes a directory of tax offices and an explanation of Japan's tax system (www.nta.go.jp).

NHK, Japan's national broadcaster, maintains a website with news in text, podcast and video formats. NHK is funded by mandatory annual receiving fees, which range from about ¥14,000 for terrestrial reception to ¥25,000 for terrestrial and satellite services (www.nhk.or.jp).

The Statistics Bureau of Japan, which is part of the Ministry of Internal Affairs and Communications, compiles data on life in Japan. The bureau produces the detailed *Japan Statistical Yearbook* and a more user-friendly annual *Statistical Handbook of Japan*. The bureau also conducts a census every five years, most recently in 2015 (www.stat.go.jp).

The Supreme Court of Japan's website explains Japan's legal system, the structure of the nation's courts and the procedures for criminal, civil and family law cases (www.courts.go.jp).

Government: prefectural

Japan's 47 prefectures have websites that include content in English and other languages. Links to the websites can be found at www. japan-guide.com/list/e1002.html.

H

Hay fever

Detailed local pollen forecasts can be found at https://tenki.jp/pollen (JO).

Home builders

Domestic

▲ Asahi Kasei Homes (www.asahi-kasei.co.jp, JO)

▲ Daikyo (www.daikyo.co.jp)

▲ Daiwa House (www.daiwahouse.co.jp)

▲ Higashi Nihon House (www.higashinihon.co.jp, JO)

▲ Hosoda (www.hosoda.co.jp, JO)

▲ Misawa Homes (www.misawa.co.jp)

▲ Mitsubishi Estate Home (www.mitsubishi-home.com, JO)

▲ Mitsui Home (www.mitsuihome.co.jp, JO)

▲ PanaHome (www.panahome.jp)

▲ Sanyo Homes (www.sanyohomes.co.jp)

▲ Sekisui Heim (www.sekisuiheim.com, JO)

▲ Sekisui House (www.sekisuihouse.co.jp)

▲ Selco Home (http://selcohome.jp, JO)

▲ Shin-Nihon Tatemono (www.kksnt.co.jp)

▲ Sumitomo Forestry (http://sfc.jp)

▲ Sumitomo Realty & Development (www.sumitomo-rd.co.jp)

▲ Tokyu Homes (www.tokyu-homes.co.jp, JO)

▲ Toyota Home (www.toyotahome.co.jp, JO)

▲ Yamada SXL Home (www.sxl.co.jp, JO)

Log houses

In Japan, a log house refers to an imported wooden home. This can include post-and-beam homes as well as houses made from stacked logs, like a traditional log cabin.

Two of the largest log home companies are Lindal Cedar Homes (www.lindaljapan.com, JO, but www.lindal.com has information in English) and Sweden House (www.swedenhouse.co.jp, JO). There are numerous smaller companies, including Akane Planning (www.akane-plan.co.jp, JO), Bess (www.bess.jp, JO) and East Loghouse (www.eastloghouse.jp, JO), that import log houses.

Industry associations

The Imported House Industries Organization has a list of member companies and information about imported homes (www.ihio.or.jp).

The Japan Prefabricated Construction Suppliers and Manufacturers Association has a website that explains how prefab homes are designed and built and offers tips about care and maintenance (www.purekyo.or.jp).

The Japan 2×4 Home Builders Association's website explains how wood-frame homes are built and the benefits of 2×4 construction (www.2x4assoc.or.jp, JO).

The United States–based Log Home Builders Association offers classes and information for people interested in building a log home (www.buildloghomes.org).

The Real Estate Companies Association of Japan represents builders and related companies (www.fdk.or.jp).

Housing information

The Association of Living Amenity has information about choosing and maintaining housing components, including roofs, windows, bathrooms and kitchens (www.alianet.org, JO).

The Center for Better Living provides testing and certification for building components and systems, ranging from elevators and windows to kitchens and bathrooms. Products bearing the BL logo are covered by a warranty of between two and 10 years (www.cbl.or.jp).

The Condominium Management Center offers information about maintaining and managing condominiums, and offers training and certification programs (www.mankan.or.jp, JO).

The Housing Information Provision Council features consumer-oriented links and information about laws, anti-seismic treatments, reform, security, sick building syndrome and sustainability (www.sumai-info.jp, JO).

The Japan Federation of Housing Organizations has information about environmentally friendly designs, urban planning, financing and more (www.judanren.or.jp).

Infestation

The Japan Termite Control Association's website includes photos of termites and the damage they cause and a members' directory (www.hakutaikyo.or.jp, JO).

The National Pest Management Association's website includes a pest identification section and contacts for exterminators in Japan (www.pestworld.org).

The University of Florida's Entomology and Nematology Department has detailed information about termites and other insects (http://entomology.ifas.ufl.edu).

Insurance

The Foreign Non-Life Insurance Association of Japan maintains a list of international companies licensed to provide non-life insurance in Japan (www.fnlia.gr.jp).

The General Insurance Association of Japan's website explains how non-life insurance works in Japan and includes a members' directory (www.sonpo.or.jp).

The General Insurance Rating Organization of Japan publishes the exhaustive *Earthquake Insurance in Japan* (www.giroj.or.jp). For a more reader-friendly summary, see the annual reports of the Japan Earthquake Reinsurance Company (www.nihonjishin.co.jp).

The Independent Insurance Agents of Japan has a consumer-oriented explanation of Japan's non-life insurance sector (www.nihondaikyo.or.jp, JO).

The United States–based Insurance Information Institute offers an exhaustive glossary of insurance terms and other resources (www.iii.org).

L

Law

The Japan Commercial Arbitration Association provides dispute resolution services, including mediation and arbitration, in English and Japanese, under the United Nations Commission on International Trade Law (UNCITRAL) rules (www.jcaa.or.jp).

The Japan Federation of Bar Associations' website offers multilingual fee-based legal counseling for foreigners from local bar associations throughout Japan (www.nichibenren.or.jp). The federation also operates the Japan Legal Support Center telephone hotline (0570-07-8374).

The Japan Federation of Shiho-Shoshi Lawyer's Associations' website explains the services provided by judicial scriveners (*shiho-shoshi*), including the transfer of land and building titles. The Japanese section of the site includes a directory of local associations (www.shiho-shoshi.or.jp).

The National Center for Removal of Criminal Organizations' website provides information about the yakuza and contacts for local police departments (www1a.biglobe.ne.jp/boutsui/, JO).

The University of California Hastings College of the Law maintains a comprehensive list of Japanese legal resources (http://library.uchastings.edu).

M

Machiya

The Machiya Information Center (www.kyomachiya.net, JO) and the Kyoto Center for Community Collaboration (http://kyoto-machisen.jp/fund) offer information and resources for people buying or renovating these historic homes.

Machiya are an important part of Kyoto's architectural heritage.

Maps*

The David Rumsey Map Collection includes more than 150,000 historical maps and aerial photos from around the world, more than 80,000 of which are online. The collection can provide useful clues about how a neighborhood or city has changed over time (www.davidrumsey.com).

The Japan Map Center sells maps of the active earthquake faults in Japan's urban areas, as well as places at risk of liquefaction. The center also sells maps covering everything from land use and floods to subsidence and volcanoes (www.jmc.or.jp, JO).

Old Maps Online makes more than 400,000 maps available on the web, including historical maps of Japan (www.oldmapsonline.org).

Media

Japan-based media
The Asia-Pacific Journal: Japan Focus is a peer-reviewed online publication providing critical analysis of the forces shaping Asia and the world (http://apjjf.org).

The ACCJ Journal is a free online monthly magazine published by the American Chamber of Commerce in Japan that occasionally publishes articles about real estate (http://journal.accj.or.jp).

The Asahi Shimbun, a leading Japanese daily, publishes an English-language edition that is available free on the company's website (www.asahi.com/ajw).

Cat Foreheads & Rabbit Hutches is a blog about real estate in Japan (https://catforehead.com).

Fukuoka Now is a free monthly magazine with news and information about Fukuoka City. The magazine's website carries translations of stories from Japanese newspapers (www.fukuoka-now.com).

The Japan News is the English edition of the *Yomiuri Shimbun*, Japan's largest circulation daily newspaper. News stories and limited archive access are available free on the paper's website (http://the-japan-news.com).

Japan Inc is an online business magazine with a searchable archive (www.japaninc.com).

The Japan Times is Japan's leading English newspaper. Reading the on-line version and limited archive searches are free (www.japantimes.co.jp).

Japan Today is an online newspaper featuring Japan-focused stories from wire services such as Kyodo News and the Associated Press, as well as original content (www.japantoday.com).

Japan Update publishes general and business news about Okinawa, and has background on Okinawa's history and culture (www.japanupdate.com).

Kyoto Journal is a quarterly, nonprofit magazine founded in 1986. Covering Kyoto, Japan and Asia, the magazine is a valuable reference for Kyoto's history and traditions (www.kyotojournal.org).

The Mainichi is the English edition of the *Mainichi Shimbun*. News stories and limited archive access are available on the paper's website (http://mainichi.jp/english).

Metropolis is a Tokyo-based, free monthly magazine that occasionally covers real estate (http://metropolis.co.jp).

Nikkei Inc. is Japan's preeminent source of business news. Nikkei publishes the English newspaper *Nikkei Asian Review* (http://asia.nikkei.com) and *Nikkei Real Estate Market Report* for corporate users and institutional investors (http://realestate.nikkeibp.co.jp).

Niseko.com is a free magazine focusing on the Hokkaido ski resort (www.niseko.com).

The Okinawa Times is a Japanese-language newspaper that offers some English content (www.okinawatimes.co.jp).

The Real Estate Economic Institute produces a weekly English-language summary of real estate news (www.fudousankeizai.co.jp). The summary is searchable and available by subscription.

Ryukyu Shimpo produces an online, English-language version of its newspaper, which covers Okinawa (http://ryukyushimpo.jp).

Shinkenchiku-sha Co. publishes books and magazines in Japanese and English about design and architecture (www.japan-architect.co.jp).

International
Major international newspapers including the *Financial Times* (www.ft.com), *The New York Times International Edition* (www.nytimes.com) and *The Wall Street Journal* (www.wsj.com) report on Japanese property.

Japanese real estate is also covered by wire services such as Bloomberg (www.bloomberg.com) and Reuters (www.reuters.com), which offer searchable archives. Yahoo! News compiles stories from wire services, including Reuters, Agence France-Presse and the Associated Press (http://news.yahoo.com).

N

Nuclear Power

The Citizens' Nuclear Information Center is one of Japan's leading antinuclear organizations (http://cnic.jp).

ENEnews aggregates reports about nuclear energy, including Fukushima, from government, media and academic sources around the world (www.enenews.com).

The Federation of Electric Power Companies of Japan's website includes information about Japan's nuclear plants (www.fepc.or.jp).

The Nuclear Waste Management Organization of Japan is planning to build a large underground storage facility for high-level radioactive waste (www.numo.or.jp).

The Tokyo Electric Power Company's website has detailed information about the Fukushima accident and the decommissioning of the Fukushima Daiichi plant (www.tepco.co.jp).

The World Nuclear Association's website contains extensive information about the Japanese nuclear industry (www.world-nuclear.org).

O

Olympics

The official site of the Tokyo Organizing Committee of the Olympic and Paralympic Games can be found at http://tokyo2020.jp.

The Tokyo Metropolitan Government's Bureau of Urban Development has information about government-driven Olympic projects (www.toshiseibi.metro.tokyo.jp).

R

Real estate agents

Japan's real estate industry has four key associations—*Zennichi, FRK, Zentakuren* and *Zenjukyo*—that collaborate on the Fudosan listing service (see below).

The All Japan Real Estate Federation (known in Japanese as Zennichi) is the parent of the Real Estate Guarantee Association, which resolves transaction-related complaints made against Zennichi members by other real estate agents (www.zennichi.or.jp). Zennichi operates an internet-based listing service, Rabbit Net Real Estate (http://rabbynet.zennichi.or.jp JO).

The Association of Real Estate Agents of Japan (*Fudosan Ryutsu Keiei Kyokai*, or FRK) produces standard sales forms for its members. PDF versions of the forms, along with Japanese explanations, can be found on the FRK website (www.frk.or.jp).

Real estate agents focus on specific neighborhoods, or on market segments like student housing or income properties.

The National Federation of Real Estate Transaction Associations, known in Japanese as Zentakuren, claims 100,000 members or about

80% of the licensed real estate agents in Japan (www.zentaku.or.jp, JO). Zentakuren operates the Hato Mark listing service (see below) and the Zentaku Housing Loan website, through which its members arrange loans for home buyers (www.zentakuloan.co.jp, JO).

The National Housing Industry Association represents developers, builders and related companies throughout Japan. The association's website includes a list of members, links to related organizations and news updates (www.zenjukyo.jp, JO).

Multilingual agencies
In addition to the Japan-based companies listed below, many large Japanese firms (and smaller local brokerages) have offices selling Japanese real estate in cities such as Hong Kong, Singapore and Taipei. Property roadshows—usually co-organized with a local agency and held in a luxury hotel—are also common.

Akasaka Real Estate focuses on investment properties in the Tokyo area (www.akasakarealestate.com).

Century 21 has franchises throughout Japan. Its website lists franchises with multilingual staff (www.century21japan.co.jp).

Daiwa House sells residential and investment property in the Tokyo area (www.propertyinvestmentjapan.com).

Katitas buys old, unwanted homes, renovates them and resells them (http://katitas.jp).

Ken Corporation sells and rents property in Tokyo and Yokohama (www.kencorp.com).

List Sotheby's International Realty operates the Sotheby's International Realty franchise in Japan and sells real estate in Tokyo and Kanagawa (www.listsothebysrealty.co.jp).

Mitsubishi Jisho Residence sells new condominiums in central Tokyo (www.mecsumai.com).

Mitsui Fudosan Realty sells new and pre-owned homes in central Tokyo (www.rehouse.co.jp).

Nippon Tradings International is a proxy and buyers' agency based in Fukuoka that works throughout Japan (http://nippontradings.com).

Nomura Real Estate Urban Net sells residential and investment property throughout Japan (www.nomu.com).

Open House sells new and pre-owned homes in Tokyo and Yokohama (https://oh.openhouse-group.com).

Plaza Homes sells and rents commercial and residential property in Tokyo (www.realestate-tokyo.com).

Provident Investment provides property sales and management services (www.provident-investment.com).

Sinyi sells new and preowned properties from offices in Tokyo and Osaka (www.sinyi.co.jp).

Sumitomo Real Estate Sales offers sales and leasing services in Japanese, English and Chinese throughout Japan (http://global.sumitomo-res.com).

Real estate investment trusts

The Association for Real Estate Securitization operates a website called Real Estate Investment Trust in Japan that explains how J-REITs (Japanese real estate investment trusts) are structured, lists the J-REITS that are available and offers investment performance data (http://j-reit.jp).

Real estate listings

Individual buyers and sellers can access listings on several internet sites, most of which include rentals and sales. There is considerable overlap in the listings on the mainstream sites. The primary difference between the sites is in how the listings are organized and whether a site specializes in a specific type of property or geographical area.

INFORMATION SOURCES   283

Mainstream listings
E-Life lists residential property, including vacant land, and new and used condominiums and houses and investment properties in Tokyo, Chiba, Kanagawa and Saitama (www.e-life.jp, JO).

Fudousan lists all types of real estate and includes news, tips for buyers and legal information (www.fudousan.or.jp, JO).

Goo is operated by NTT and aggregates information from several other listing sources. Goo lists vacant land, and new and used condominiums and houses and investment properties nationwide (http://house.goo.ne.jp, JO).

The Hato Mark site lists property for sale and rent throughout Japan (www.hatomarksite.com, JO).

Home4U is operated by NTT Data and includes listings of vacant land as well as new and used houses and condominiums throughout Japan (http://home4u.jp, JO).

Home's lists vacant land and new and used houses and condominiums throughout Japan (www.homes.co.jp, JO).

Suumo is a nationwide listing site operated by Recruit (http://suumo.jp, JO).

Yahoo! Real Estate lists vacant land and new and used houses and condominiums nationwide (http://realestate.yahoo.co.jp, JO).

Specialist agents and listings
981 is a bilingual site operated by the Real Estate Auction Distribution Association that lists foreclosed property available for auction throughout Japan (http://981.jp).

The Broadcast Information Tri-set System is a searchable list of foreclosed properties for sale throughout Japan (http://bit.sikkou.jp, JO).

Foreclosed Japan helps people purchase foreclosed properties at auction (www.foreclosedjapan.com).

The Furusato Kaiki Shien Center is a Tokyo-based nonprofit organization that provides information about abandoned rural homes (www.furusatokaiki.net).

Kyoto-based Hachise Co. sells machiya, with prices beginning at ¥25 million (www.hachise.com).

Higashinihon Jutaku sells units in government-built condominiums (*kodan*) in the Kanto area from the 1960s and 1970s (www.higashinihonjutaku.co.jp, JO).

The Hokkaido Tracks Group provides property development, management and brokerage services in the Niseko area (http://hokkaidotracks.com).

Niseko Izumikyo sells property and land in the Niseko area (www.izumikyo.co.jp).

Niseko Property sells residential and commercial property as well as vacant land (www.nisekoproperty.com).

Reform (renovation)

As the Japanese government encouraged the construction of long-life homes, there has been increased interest in home renovations. Large builders—including Misawa Homes, PanaHome, Sekusui Chemical and Sumitomo Realty & Development—have subsidiaries and affiliates that provide reform services. In addition, companies such as Daikyo have begun buying 10- to 15-year-old apartments and apartment buildings, renovating them and reselling them to the public. People buying these apartments get a professionally renovated dwelling, with up-to-date appliances and fittings, at a significant discount to a new home.

The Housing Renovation Promoting Council is a trade association. Its website includes guides to renovation tax benefits and other resources (www.j-reform.com, JO).

Jerco Reform is a nationwide industry group. Its website has a supplier search function and information about planning renovation projects (www.jerco.or.jp, JO).

The Remodeling Promotion Committee for Condominium's website has themed sections for people carrying out life-stage renovations, like the arrival and departure of children (www.repco.gr.jp, JO).

Renoco is an online, fixed-price renovation service (www.renoco.jp, JO).

Rentals

Many real estate agents offer property management services, which allow them to earn commission on the sale and rental of property.

Japan has a local, Airbnb-style home-sharing (*minpaku*) service called Stay Japan, which describes itself as "the first website to offer legal short-term rentals in Japan" (https://stayjapan.com). Airdna provides paid and free statistics and background on short-term rental markets around the world, including Japan (www.airdna.co). Airbnb has a large presence in Japan (www.airbnb.com), and Rakuten operates a short-term rental company in Japan (www.rakuten-lifull-stay.co.jp).

The Japan Property Management Association represents property managers and provides training, support and advice. Its website includes a national directory of property managers (www.jpm.jp, JO).

The Property Manager Council provides training and certification to property managers. Its website includes a search function and an ethics charter (www.chintaikanrishi.jp, JO).

Research

Economic
Teikoku Databank provides corporate credit and market research services focusing on Japan. Highlights from the company's research, which includes monthly corporate confidence and bankruptcy statistics, are available in English from www.tdb.co.jp.

Tokyo Shoko Research sells credit information on Japanese businesses (www.tsr-net.co.jp).

General
The Building Center of Japan evaluates, researches and develops new building technologies. It also publishes an annual yearbook, *A Quick Look at Housing in Japan,* that features data about the nation's housing stock, housing policy and urban planning (www.bcj.or.jp).

The Japan Real Estate Institute offers research, appraisal and consulting services and produces surveys of land and house prices, and office and apartment rents (www.reinet.or.jp).

The Land Institute of Japan researches land issues and the real estate market. It produces a monthly report of sales volumes, housing starts and other data (www.lij.jp).

The Real Estate Companies Association of Japan publishes a free English yearbook, *Real Estate in Japan,* which includes trends, recent developments and statistics (www.fdk.or.jp).

Style Act Co. provides market research services about rents, vacancy rates, consumer preferences and market trends (www.styleact.co.jp).

Institutes and others
The Economist Intelligence Unit produces a range of paid and free research (www.eiu.com).

Fitch (www.fitchratings.com), Moody's (www.moodys.com) and Standard & Poor's (www.standardandpoors.com) provide research and data, including economic forecasts and sovereign and corporate debt rating services.

McKinsey & Company is a management consultancy that produces articles and research on a range of property-related topics (www.mckinsey.com).

The Urban Land Institute is a United States–based nonprofit organization that conducts research and publishes materials on real estate-related topics around the world (www.uli.org).

International agencies

International real estate agencies generally focus on Japan's office, industrial and commercial markets, but occasionally cover the residential sector.

⏶ CBRE (www.cbre.com)

⏶ Colliers (www.colliers.com)

⏶ Cushman & Wakefield (www.cushmanwakefield.com)

⏶ Jones Lang LaSalle (www.jll.com)

⏶ Knight Frank (www.knightfrank.com)

⏶ Savills (www.savills.com)

Japanese institutions

The following organizations produce English-language reports about real estate, economics and social trends:

⏶ Fujitsu Research Institute (www.fujitsu.com/jp/group/fri)

⏶ Mizuho Research Institute (www.mizuho-ri.co.jp)

⏶ Nippon Communications Foundation (www.nippon.com)

⏶ NLI Research Institute (www.nli-research.co.jp)

⏶ Nomura Research Institute (www.nri.com)

S

Software

Decoration

Adobe Color is a cloud-based service that lets you build color schemes and export them to Adobe products, such as Photoshop (https://color.adobe.com).

Colorjive lets you upload a photo and virtually "paint" it (http://colorjive.com).

Dow Chemical operates a site with information about paint, color and design (www.paintquality.com).

Pinterest (www.pinterest.com) can be useful for inspiration, as can Houzz (www.houzz.com).

Zillow Digs lets you see decoration ideas sorted by room, color scheme, price range and popularity (www.zillow.com/digs).

Design
Floorplanner is a free, web-based design tool that lets you create two- and three-dimensional room layouts and home designs (http://floorplanner.com).

Ikea offers an online design tool called Ikea Home Planner that may be useful if you are planning to use that company's furniture (www.ikea.com).

Sweethome is an open-source program that is similar to Floorplanner and available in 25 languages (www.sweethome3d.com).

Surveyors

Japan has two national organizations for surveyors: the Japan Association of Surveyors (www.jsurvey.jp) and the Japan Federation of Land and House Investigators' Associations (www.chosashi.or.jp). The federation's website contains contact information for regional associations, which have their own websites, and offers a boundary dispute resolution service.

T

Tax*

Accounting Asia Group's Japan Tax website contains useful information about structuring real estate investments in Japan (www.japantax.com).

International accounting firms, including Deloitte (www.deloitte.com), EY (www.ey.com), Grant Thornton (www.grantthornton.com), KPMG (www.kpmg.com) and PwC (www.pwc.com), produce real estate guides and bulletins about tax and accounting issues for residents and expatriates.

The Japanese Institute of Certified Public Accountants' website includes detailed information about accounting and auditing in Japan (www.hp.jicpa.or.jp).

The Japan Federation of Certified Public Tax Accountants' Associations represents 15 regional tax accountants' associations. In addition to assistance with taxes, certified public tax accountants offer property appraisal services (www.nichizeiren.or.jp).

The Tokyo Metropolitan Government's *Guide to Metropolitan Taxes 2017* includes information about real estate taxes (www.tax.metro.tokyo.jp/book/guidebookgaigo/guidebook2017e.pdf).

Translation

The Japan Association of Translators' website includes a members list with profiles and contact details (http://jat.org).

Japan Lumber Journal has a Japanese-English glossary of technical terms used in the housing and construction industries (www.jlj.gr.jp/database/glossary.html).

Transportation

Hyperdia is a rail and aviation database that shows the optimal route between destinations throughout Japan (www.hyperdia.com).

Japan's extensive rail networks define cities and neighborhoods.

U

Universal design

Buildings that incorporate universal design are aesthetically pleasing and usable by the greatest number of people possible, regardless of their age or ability.

A Practical Guide to Universal Home Design is available from the Easter Seals Iowa Assistive Technology Program (www.iowaat.org/udbooklet).

The Center for Universal Design at NC State University's College of Design has information for people who are building or renovating a home, including floorplans, checklists and design suggestions (www.ncsu.edu/ncsu/design/cud).

Universaldesign.com features news, links and information and is run by the Center for Inclusive Design and Environmental Access (www.universaldesign.com).

Utilities

Electricity
The Japan Electric Power Information Center is the trade organization representing the nation's generating and distribution companies. The center's website includes links to Japan's electric companies as well as technical data (www.jepic.or.jp).

The electrical supply in western Japan, including Kansai, is 100 volts, 60 hertz. This differs from eastern Japan, including Tokyo and Hokkaido, where the supply is 100 volts, 50 hertz. Most electrical equipment is unaffected by the frequency difference, but it can upset the operation of turntables and clocks.

Gas
The Japan Gas Association has detailed English-language information about the city gas industry, including a listing of all of the gas suppliers in Japan and safety and environmental information (www.gas.or.jp).

W

Weather*

Tropical Storm Risk combines the efforts of the British Meteorological Office and several insurance and reinsurance companies to map storms worldwide (www.tropicalstormrisk.com).

PROPERTY BUYER'S CHECKLISTS

The following checklists cover many of the problems you may encounter when buying a home in Japan. Not all of the questions apply to every property. Some information—for example asbestos and seismic tests—may be impractical or impossible to obtain, particularly for older, inexpensive homes.

Buildings and land

- ▲ Is the building being used for **Airbnb** or similar *minpaku* rentals?

- ▲ Has the building been **altered** or modified? Are plans available?

- ▲ How much is the **building repair fee** (*shuzen tsumitate kin*)?

- ▲ Are the **common areas** clean and well maintained? Do they need repairs?

- ▲ Has a **death,** suicide or violent crime occurred in the home?

- ▲ Are there any **easements** or rights of way on the property?

- ▲ What **facilities**—e.g., a gym, swimming pool or tennis court—are included in the complex? Are the facilities open, clean and well maintained?

- ▲ Does the home have bad *feng shui* or an inauspicious address?

- ▲ In Hokkaido, have **forest**- and **water**-related reporting requirements been observed?

- ▲ How much are the management **fees** (*kanri-hi*)? What do they include?

- ▲ Are there any **hidden fees** for parking, facilities, cable TV and internet, etc.?

⏶ Has the building been designated an **Important Cultural Property**?

⏶ Is the building mainly populated by **owner-occupiers** or tenants?

⏶ Is the relationship between the **owners' committee** and residents cordial?

⏶ Is a **parking** space included? Is guest parking available? Are electric vehicle charging facilities available?

⏶ How much are the **property taxes**?

⏶ Does the building have a reputation for **quality** problems, such as defective pilings?

⏶ Is the home built on **reclaimed land**?

⏶ Are there any problematic **regulations**, such as restrictions on pets, in the house rules?

⏶ Are major **renovations** planned? How much is in the building's repair fund?

⏶ Is the area affected by **subsidence** or soil contamination?

⏶ Has a land **survey** been conducted?

⏶ Are there any wells or **underground** pipes or tanks on the property?

⏶ Does the home include **universal design** features that would make it suitable for elderly or disabled people?

⏶ Does the unit have any **unusual liabilities**, like maintenance of a roof?

⏶ Are there many rental **vacancies** or units for sale in the building?

⏶ Does the home comply fully with **zoning** regulations? Has the zoning changed since the building was erected?

Developers and off the plan purchases

⬩ How long has the developer been in **business**?

⬩ Does the developer have a record of **completing projects** on time and on budget?

⬩ Is the developer **financially sound**?

⬩ At the **handover**, are the building and home constructed, finished and equipped as specified in the contract?

⬩ Is there anything **incongruous** or unusual about the developer, salesperson, building site, contract, marketing materials, etc.?

⬩ Is the developer facing **lawsuits** from unpaid suppliers and unhappy customers?

⬩ What is the **payment schedule**?

⬩ Does the developer have all of the required **permits** and permissions?

⬩ When will you take **possession** of your home?

⬩ Have the developer's **previous projects** aged well?

⬩ How long is the developer's **warranty** (in addition to the government warranty)? What is covered?

Home inspection

⬩ Do the **air-conditioners** work? How old are they? Is the refrigerant still available?

⬩ Is **aluminum wiring** installed in the home or building?

⬩ Has an **asbestos** survey been conducted?

▲ Is corrosion visible on the **balcony** ironwork? Are there missing tiles or grout, signs of accumulated water or blocked drains?

▲ Are the built-in **cabinets** complete? Is all of the hardware present and functional? Do the doors and drawers open smoothly? Is the finish free of blemishes?

▲ Are the **ceilings** flat and free from water stains, mold, gaps and cracks?

▲ Are the kitchen **counters** level and free from scratches and other defects?

▲ Do the **doors** close smoothly? Is there insect damage or gaps between the door and the frame? Is the finish acceptable and the hardware intact and functional?

▲ Is there visible **earthquake damage**, such cracks in the walls, floor or ceiling, or doors that don't close properly? Has the building been damaged in a fire?

▲ Do the switches, **electrical** outlets and lights work? Are there scorch marks on the outlets? Are the circuits on the breaker panel labeled correctly?

▲ Are the **floors** level? Are there gaps between the planks? Is water or insect damage visible?

▲ Is **galvanized steel pipe** present?

▲ Are the **gas** pipes or gas meter damaged?

▲ Are **plastered** and painted surfaces flat and free from cracks, mold, water stains and bulges?

▲ Does water flow smoothly through the **plumbing**, including the kitchen sink, floor drains and the sink, toilet and bathtub in the bathroom? Are there foul smells coming from the drains? Do the taps work?

▲ Has the home been tested for **radon**?

▲ Does the **roof** leak?

▲ Has the home undergone a **seismic** (earthquake) test?

▲ Has the home been inspected for **termites** and other pests?

▲ Are **tiled** surfaces flat? Are tiles set straight and free from excess grout?

▲ Does the home have any **unauthorized alterations**?

▲ Do **windows** and sliding doors open smoothly? Are the frames anchored solidly? Is the glass clear and free from chips and inclusions? Are water stains visible nearby?

Income properties

▲ How much is the management company's **fee**?

▲ What is the tenant's payment **history**?

▲ How will I receive rental **income**?

▲ How much time remains on the tenant's **lease**?

▲ How much does the management company charge to **recruit** tenants?

▲ Will the management company keep the tenant's **renewal fee**?

▲ Is the **rent** in line with market rates?

▲ How does the management company **report** its activities?

▲ What **services** does the management company provide? Can they file your taxes? Do they make repairs or contract them to another company?

▲ Is the property **tenanted**?

▲ What is the rental **yield** or capitalization rate?

Neighborhood

▲ Are there **abandoned** homes in the area? Is the neighborhood stable, decaying or being gentrified?

▲ Are sources of **air pollution** or bad smells nearby?

▲ Are their **archaeological** sites in the neighborhood?

▲ Is the neighborhood near a **brownfield** site or other source of soil pollution?

▲ Are nearby properties being **expropriated**?

▲ Are the local **government's finances** in order? Are tax increases or service cuts expected?

▲ Is **infrastructure** being built or demolished nearby?

▲ Are allergen-producing **Japanese cedar** trees nearby?

▲ Is the area at risk from **landslides** or volcanoes?

▲ Are **nuclear** power plants nearby?

▲ Do homes in the area have access to normal **services**: ambulance, broadband internet, cable TV, electricity, fire department, piped gas, police, public transportation, mail, restaurants, schools, sewerage, shopping, telephone and water?

▲ Is the area at risk from **storm surges** or floods?

▲ Are there **transportation** concerns, such a reliance on ferries, private roads or restrictions on the use of private vehicles? Does the local government have the funds to maintain roads, bridges, tunnels and other essential infrastructure?

⏶ Are **undesirable neighbors** nearby, such as cemeteries, crematoria, late-night entertainment, expressways, factories, incinerators, prisons or yakuza offices?

Title and transaction

⏶ Are the management fees, building repair fees, property taxes or utilities in **arrears**?

⏶ What are the estimated **closing costs**? When are the post-closing taxes due?

⏶ Are there liens or **encumbrances** on the property?

⏶ What decorations, appliances or **equipment** are included in the sale?

⏶ When is the **handover** date?

⏶ Is the property **price** consistent with the market valuation?

ENDNOTES

Demographics

1. "Summary Report of the 2010 Population Census," Statistics Bureau, Ministry of Internal Affairs and Communications, Government of Japan, 2013, 392–94.

2. "White Paper on the Aging Society (Summary) FY 2007," Cabinet Office, Government of Japan, December 1, 2008, 3.

3. "Statistical Handbook of Japan 2017," Statistics Bureau, Ministry of Internal Affairs and Communications, Government of Japan, 2017, 163–64.

4. "Population Projections for Japan: 2011 to 2060," National Institute of Population and Social Security Research, Government of Japan, 2012, 4.

5. "Seniors Living Alone in Japan Topped 6 Million for First Time in 2015," *The Japan Times*, July 13, 2016.

6. "Japan's Affluent and HNWI Markets Consisted of 903,000 Households and Amounted to ¥254 Trillion in 2007, While its Inheritance Market Will Expand to ¥102 Trillion by 2015," Nomura Research Institute, October 1, 2008.

7. "More Senior Citizens on Welfare," *The Japan Times*, June 16, 2016.

8. Tatsuya Ishikawa and Koichi Haji, "On the Financial Situation of Elderly Households: A Structural Analysis of Income, Expenditure and Wealth," NLI Research Institute, March 17, 2009.

9. Sachiko Miyamoto, "Bequests and Household Assets," *Nomura Capital Market Review* 9, no. 4, 2006, 41.

10. Aya Abe, "Poverty and Social Exclusion of Women in Japan," *Japanese Journal of Social Security Policy* 9, no. 1, March 2012.

11. Leo Lewis, "Why Japan's Elderly Are Turning to a Life of Crime," CNBC, March 27, 2016.

12. "Preliminary Counts of the 2015 Population Census of Japan Released," Statistics Bureau, Ministry of Internal Affairs and Communications, Government of Japan, April 20, 2016.

13. Kanoko Matsuyama, "In Japan, the Rising Cost of Elder Care—and Dying Alone," Bloomberg, March 1, 2013.

14. Akiko Oishi, "Child Support and the Poverty of Single-Mother Households in Japan," National Institute of Population and Social Security Research, Government of Japan, August 2013.

15. Mariko Tran, "Unable or Unwilling to Leave the Nest? An Analysis and Evaluation of Japanese Parasite Single Theories," *Electronic Journal of Contemporary Japanese Studies*, July 3, 2006.

16. "Japan Woman Held for Cashing Dead Parents' Pension for 50 Years," Agence France-Presse, May 8, 2015.

17. "Ehime Man Arrested for Burying Mother's Body in Garden of Home," Japan Today, August 29, 2015.

18. Akiko Funakoshi and Yuki Miyamoto, "Significant Factors in Family Difficulties for Fathers and Mothers Who Use Support Services for Children with Hikikomori," *Psychiatry and Clinical Neurosciences* 69, no. 4, April 1, 2015, 210–19.

19. "Population Statistics of Japan 2012," National Institute of Population and Social Security Research, Government of Japan, July 30, 2012, fig. 6.21.

20. Mizuho Aoki, "In Sexless Japan, Almost Half of Single Young Men and Women Are Virgins: Survey," *The Japan Times*, September 16, 2016.

21. "Statistical Handbook of Japan 2017," 17.

22. "Basic Plan for Immigration Control (5th Edition)," Ministry of Justice, Government of Japan, 2015, 5.

23. "2015 Immigration Control," Ministry of Justice, Government of Japan, 2015, 183–84.

24. David Green, "Japan's Highly Skilled Foreign Professional Visa: Too Little Too Late?," Social Science Research Network, October 4, 2015.

25. "Naturalization Trends," Ministry of Justice, Government of Japan, 2016.

26. David Green and Yoshihiko Kadoya, "English as a Gateway? Immigration and Public Opinion in Japan," Social Science Research Network, September 3, 2013, 15.

27. "Summary of the Results of Internal Migration in 2016," Statistics Bureau, Ministry of Internal Affairs and Communications, Government of Japan, 2017.

28. "Household Projections by Prefecture in Japan: 2010-2035," National Institute of Population and Social Security Research, Government of Japan, 2014.

29. "Social Indicators by Prefecture 2016," Statistics Bureau, Ministry of Internal Affairs and Communications, Government of Japan, 2016.

30. "Future Depopulation in Japan: A Cabinet Committee Report," *Population and Development Review* 41, no. 2, June 1, 2015, 369–72.

31. "9 Japan Prefs. Face Serious Obstetrician Shortages," Jiji Press, October 25, 2014.

32. "Japan Refiners Target Power Business as Profits Evaporate," Reuters, May 15, 2015.

33. Masashi Kato, "School Closures," NHK World, December. 17, 2014.

34. Rachel Martin, "Buddhism Is Waning In Japan," NPR, November 22, 2015.

35. "Bankrupt Mining Town Downsizes to Avoid Becoming a Ghost," Bloomberg, September 25, 2016.

36. "New Road to Recovery," NHK World, September 7, 2016.

The Buying Process

1. "Real Estate in Japan 2017," The Real Estate Companies Association of Japan, 2017, 59.

2. Chihiro Shimizu, Kiyohiko G. Nishimura and Yasushi Asami, "Search and Vacancy Costs in the Tokyo Housing Market: Attempt to Measure Social Costs of Imperfect Information," *Review of Urban & Regional Development Studies* 16, no. 3, November 1, 2004, 210–30.

3. "Real Estate in Japan 2017," 30.

4. Dan Ariely, *Predictably Irrational: The Hidden Forces That Shape Our Decisions,* HarperCollins, 2009, 8.

5. Akio Doteuchi, "Family and Residence in the Gracefully Aging Society—Integrating Housing and Community," NLI Research Institute, April 18, 2007, 4.

6. Tatsuya Ishikawa and Koichi Haji, "On the Financial Situation of Elderly Households: A Structural Analysis of Income, Expenditure and Wealth," NLI Research Institute, March 17, 2009, 4.

7. Akio Doteuchi, "Aging Issues in New Town Developments—The Tama New Town Case," NLI Research Institute, 1998.

8. Paul Previtera, "Tax Consequences of Cross-Border Investment in Japanese Real Estate," *Tax Notes International,* July 10, 2006, 151–75.

What to Buy

1. "Statistical Handbook of Japan 2016," Statistics Bureau, Ministry of Internal Affairs and Communications, Government of Japan, 2016, 157.

2. "A Quick Look at Housing in Japan," The Building Center of Japan, 2017, 18.

3. "A Quick Look at Housing in Japan," 54.

4. Kei Sakamoto, Hisato Okamoto and Toru Matsumoto, "A Study on the Life Cycle Cost and Environmental Burden of a Long-Life House," 22nd Pan Pacific Congress of Real Estate Appraisers, Valuers and Counselors, Taipei, 2004, 30–1.

5. "A Quick Look at Housing in Japan," 52.

6. "Property Tax Hike Eyed for Owners of Japan's Upper-Floor High-Rise Condos," *The Japan Times*, November 1, 2016.

7. Chihiro Shimizu, Kiyohiko G. Nishimura and Koji Karato, "Nonlinearity of Housing Price Structure: The Secondhand Condominium Market in the Tokyo Metropolitan Area," CSIS Discussion Paper no. 86, University of Tokyo, 2010, 18.

8. Masahide Tanaka and Yoshinobu Kumata, "Problems of Decrepit Condominiums Furthering Aggravation of Urban Environment: Is Rebuilding Possible by Means of Reverse Mortgage System?," *Studies in Regional Science* 29, no. 2, 1999, 58.

9. Toshiro Kojima, "Proposal to Offer Reverse Mortgages for Condo Reconstruction," Social Science Research Network, December 25, 2013, 4.

10. Shinichiro Iwata and Hisaki Yamaga, "Land Tenure Security and Home Maintenance: Evidence from Japan," *Land Economics*, August 2009, 429–41.

11. "A Quick Look at Housing in Japan," 23.

Market Drivers

1. "Panel Says Fukushima Power Plant's Cleanup Fees Are Now Almost Double the 2013 Estimate," *The Japan Times*, December 9, 2016.

2. "Nuclear Power in Japan," World Nuclear Association, December 28, 2016.

3. "Statistical Handbook of Japan 2016," Statistics Bureau, Ministry of Internal Affairs and Communications, Government of Japan, 2016, 107.

4. "Statistical Handbook of Japan 2017," Statistics Bureau, Ministry of Internal Affairs and Communications, Government of Japan, 2017, 106.

5. "Prospect of 40 Million Foreign Visitors to Japan Annually," Mizuho Securities, September 5, 2016.

6. "Expanding Tourist Accommodations," *The Japan Times*, January 4, 2016.

7. "Japan Copes with Shifting Demands in Tourism," *Urban Land*, May 16, 2016.

8. "MGM Resorts Ready to Bet up to $10 Billion on Japan Casino, Possibly via REIT," Reuters, October 31, 2016.

9. Yumi Yamaguchi, "Japan's Pachinko Industry Eyes a Big Gamble," Bloomberg, July 11, 2014.

Risk Factors

1. "Law for Forced Demolition of Derelict Houses Takes Effect," *The Japan Times,* May 26, 2015.

2. Eric Johnston, "Kansai Uses Subsidies to Fill Empty Homes, but Persuading Aging Population to Pull up Stakes Remains a Challenge," *The Japan Times,* September 25, 2016.

3. Robin Harding, "Is This the Solution to Japan's Glut of Empty Homes?," *Financial Times,* July 17, 2015.

4. Philip Brasor, "Abandoned Buildings Still House Problems," *The Japan Times,* December 3, 2016.

5. "Law for Forced Demolition of Derelict Houses Takes Effect."

6. "Policy of Cultural Affairs in Japan," Agency for Cultural Affairs, Government of Japan, 2016, 48.

7. Charles T. Keally, "Japanese Archaeology," February 15, 2003.

8. "Ancient Roman Coins Unearthed at Japan Castle," Yahoo! News/AFP, September 28, 2016.

9. "Summary of Countermeasures Against Asbestos in Japan," Ministry of the Environment, Government of Japan, 2011, 6.

10. Kenichi Miyamoto, Kenji Morinaga and Hiroyuki Mori, *Asbestos Disaster,* Springer Japan, 2011, 31.

11. A. Terazono, S. Sakai and H. Takatsuki, "The Great Hanshin-Awaji Earthquake of Japan 1995 and Asbestos Emission," *Air Pollution* VIII 42, no. 10, 2000, 8.

12. "High Asbestos Levels Detected at Disaster-Linked Sites," Jiji Press, January 11, 2013.

13. Miyamoto, Morinaga and Mori, *Asbestos Disaster,* 231.

14. "Social Report 2007," Kubota Corp., 2007, 26.

15. Takumi Kishimoto, "Malignant Pleural Mesothelioma in Parts of Japan in Relationship to Asbestos Exposure," *Industrial Health* 39, 2001, 66.

16. "28 Japanese Confirmed with Asbestos Injuries from Working at U.S. Bases," *The Japan Times,* January 8, 2014.

17. Emily A. Su-lan Reber, "Buraku Mondai in Japan: Historical and Modern Perspectives and Directions for the Future," *Harvard Human Rights Journal* 12, Spring 1999, 297–359.

18. Timothy Amos, "Asakusa 'Newtown': The Transformation of Outcaste Space in Early Modern Edo/Modern Tokyo," *Japan Forum* 27, no. 2, April 3, 2015, 213–34.

19. Richard Werly, "The Burakumin, Japan's Invisible Outcasts—Brief Article," *UNESCO Courier*, September 2001.

20. "Policy of Cultural Affairs in Japan," 40–41.

21. Emiko Kakiuchi, "Cultural Heritage Protection System in Japan: Current Issues and Prospects for the Future," National Graduate Institute for Policy Studies, 2014, 5.

22. Yasuyuki Fukukawa, "Solitary Death: A New Problem of an Aging Society in Japan," *Journal of the American Geriatrics Society* 59, no. 1, January 1, 2011, 174–75.

23. Toru Hanai, "A Lonely Death," Reuters, April 2, 2015.

24. "Bereaved Families of Suicide Victims Seek Protection from Landlords' Compensation Claims," *Mainichi Daily News*, December 22, 2010.

25. Akemi Nakamura, "Aneha Seen as Just Part of Problem," *The Japan Times*, December 27, 2006.

26. "A Quick Look at Housing in Japan," The Building Center of Japan, 2017, 86.

27. "Sumitomo Realty Proposes Total Rebuild at Another Tilting Condo Complex in Yokohama," *The Japan Times,* March 6, 2016.

28. "Seller of Tilting Condo Presents Compensation Package," Jiji Press, October 27, 2015.

29. "Piling Scandal Now Engulfs 7 Firms in Japan: Industry Group," Jiji Press, November 27, 2015.

30. "Understanding Earthquakes," The Earthquake and Disaster-Reduction Research Division, Research and Development Bureau, Ministry of Education, Culture, Sports, Science and Technology, Government of Japan, 2014, 4.

31. "Tables Explaining the JMA Seismic Intensity Scale," Japan Meteorological Agency, 2014.

32. "White Paper: Disaster Management in Japan 2015," Cabinet Office, Government of Japan, 2015, 85–91.

33. Hiroyuki Yoshida, "A Study of Earthquake Risk in Japan and Its Peripheral Problems," 23rd Pan Pacific Congress of Real Estate Appraisers, Valuers and Counselors, San Francisco, September 16–19, 2006, 5.

34. Etsuko Tsunozaki, "Disaster Reconstruction in Japan: Lessons Learned from the Kobe Earthquake," SAR Regional Conference on Hazard Risk Management, Mumbai, December 19, 2006.

35. "The Great East Japan Earthquake Damage Report," *The Japan Journal*, December 2011, 27.

36. "A Quick Look at Housing in Japan," 55.

37. Yuen-ting Yeung, "The Effect of Chinese Culture on the Implicit Value of Graveyard View in Hong Kong Residential Property Market," The University of Hong Kong, 2005, 108.

38. "Overview of the 2015 White Paper on Fire Service," International Fire Service Information Center, 2016, 12.

39. "A Quick Look at Housing in Japan," 85.

40. Kyoichi Kobayashi, "Effects of Fire Regulation Revisions on Building Fire Damage," *Fire Science and Technology* 32, no. 1, 2013.

41. "Outline of Measures for Fire Prevention and Safety under the Laws and Regulations of Fire Fighting," International Fire Service Information Center, 2015, 15.

42. James Singleton, "The Sneeze Trees: Ridding Japanese Forests of Pollen," Nippon.com, April 4, 2015.

43. "Japanese Public Finance Fact Sheet," Ministry of Finance, Government of Japan, 2016, 1.

44. "Hiroshima Commemorates Second Anniversary of Deadly Mudslides," *The Japan Times*, August 20, 2016.

45. "Landslides," United Nations University, January 18, 2008, 6.

46. R. P. Orense, "Soil Liquefaction and Slope Failures during the 2011 Tohoku, Japan Earthquake," 2012 New Zealand Society for Earthquake Engineering Conference, Christchurch, New Zealand, 2012.

47. "Tokyo-Osaka Maglev Train May Start Sooner than Planned," *Nikkei Asian Review*, May 26, 2016.

48. Bent Flyvbjerg, "What You Should Know About Megaprojects and Why: An Overview," *Project Management Journal* 45, no. 2, February 2014, 6–19.

49. "Japanese Public Finance Fact Sheet," 36.

50. "N. Korea Missile Lands in Pacific Ocean," NHK World, September 15, 2017.

51. "Nuclear Power in Japan," World Nuclear Association, December 28, 2016.

52. "A Look at Japan's History of Nuclear Power Trouble," Yahoo! News/AP, March 17, 2011.

53. "Outrage over Japan Nuclear Reactor Coverup," Reuters, March 15, 2007.

54. "Tepco Chairman, President Announce Resignations over Nuclear Coverups," *The Japan Times*, September 3, 2002.

55. Reiji Yoshida, "Japan to Scrap Troubled ¥1 Trillion Monju Fast-Breeder Reactor," *The Japan Times*, September 21, 2016.

56. "Monju Fast-Breeder Reactor Set for Decommissioning," Nippon.com, October 19, 2016.

57. Shinji Oikawa et al., "A Nationwide Survey of Outdoor Radon Concentration in Japan," *Journal of Environmental Radioactivity* 65, no. 2, January 1, 2003, 203–13.

58. "IG Report Finds Health Hazards in Japan Base Housing, Questions Pentagon Policy," *Stars and Stripes*, October 2, 2014.

59. Fumio Kondo et al., "Two Sensitive Sick-Building Syndrome Patients Possibly Responding to p-Dichlorobenzene and 2-Ethyl-1-Hexanol: Case Report," *Journal of Health Science* 53, no. 1, 2007, 119–23.

60. Tamami Suzuki et al., "Research into the Symptoms of Sick House Syndrome and/or Multiple Chemical Sensitivity Patients and Indoor and Outdoor Air Quality," *Japanese Journal of Applied IT Healthcare* 6, no. 2, 2011, 154–66.

61. Shigehisa Uchiyama et al., "Gaseous Chemical Compounds in Indoor and Outdoor Air of 602 Houses throughout Japan in Winter and Summer," *Environmental Research* 137, February 2015, 364–72.

62. Hiroko Nakaoka et al., "Correlating the Symptoms of Sick-Building Syndrome to Indoor VOCs Concentration Levels and Odor," *Indoor and Built Environment* 23, no. 6, October 1, 2014, 804–13.

63. Kondo et al., "Two Sensitive Sick-Building Syndrome Patients Possibly Responding to p-Dichlorobenzene and 2-Ethyl-1-Hexanol."

64. "Introduction to the Building Standard Law: Japanese Building Codes and Building Control System," The Building Center of Japan, 2013.

65. Tomoko Takigawa et al., "Relationship between Indoor Chemical Concentrations and Subjective Symptoms Associated with Sick Building Syndrome in Newly Built Houses in Japan," *International Archives of Occupational and Environmental Health* 83, no. 2, February 1, 2010, 225–35.

66. Koichi Harada et al., "A Review of Indoor Air Pollution and Health Problems from the Viewpoint of Environmental Hygiene: Focusing on the Studies of Indoor Air Environment in Japan Compared to Those of Foreign Countries," *Journal of Health Science* 56, no. 5, 2010, 495.

67. "Sick Building Syndrome Victim Wins Lawsuit in Japan," *The Yomiuri Shimbun*, October 3, 2009.

68. Masazumi Harada, "Minamata Disease: Methylmercury Poisoning in Japan Caused by Environmental Pollution," *Critical Reviews in Toxicology* 25, no. 1, January 1995, 1–24.

69. "Itai-Itai Victims Settle with Mitsui Mining," *The Japan Times*, December 17, 2013.

70. Mayumi Hori, Katsumi Shozugawa and Motoyuki Matsuo, "Hexavalent Chromium Pollution Caused by Dumped Chromium Slag at the Urban Park in Tokyo," *Journal of Material Cycles and Waste Management* 17, no. 1, January 2015, 201–5.

71. "Chemicals Exceeding Standards Again Are Detected at New Site of Fish Market in Toyosu," *The Japan Times*, January 14, 2017.

72. Eric Johnston, "Grounds of Universal Site Filled with Excessive Chemicals," *The Japan Times*, September 10, 1997.

73. "Sakai Park Off-Limits after Toxic Chemicals Found in Soil," *The Japan Times*, September 9, 2016.

74. Greg Rogers, "Japan's Brownfields Brought to Bear," Environmental Finance, October 2007.

75. "Current Status of the Brownfields Issue in Japan, Interim Report," Ministry of the Environment, Government of Japan, 2007.

76. Fumikazu Yoshida, "High-Tech Pollution in Asia," Ninth International Conference of Greening of Industry Network, Bangkok, 2001.

77. "Environmental Quality Standards for Groundwater Pollution," Ministry of the Environment, Government of Japan, 2012.

78. Jon Mitchell, "FOIA Documents Reveal Agent Orange Dioxin, Toxic Dumps, Fish Kills on Okinawa Base. Two Veterans Win Compensation, Many More Denied," *The Asia-Pacific Journal: Japan Focus,* October 5, 2015.

79. Masaaki Takahashi et al., "Ground Water and Soil Pollution near Ohyachi-Heizu Waste Disposal Site," *Yokkaichi University Journal of Environmental and Information Sciences* 11, no. 2, March 2008, 27–31.

80. "Current Status of the Brownfields Issue in Japan, Interim Report," 6.

81. K. Furuno et al., "Groundwater Management Based on Monitoring of Land Subsidence and Groundwater Levels in the Kanto Groundwater Basin, Central Japan," *Proceedings of the International Association of Hydrological Sciences* 372, November 12, 2015, 55.

82. Youichiro Takada and Yo Fukushima, "Volcanic Subsidence Triggered by the 2011 Tohoku Earthquake in Japan," *Nature Geoscience* 6, no. 8, July 1, 2013, 637–41.

83. Kazuo Konagai et al., "Maps of Soil Subsidence for Tokyo Bay Shore Areas Liquefied in the March 11th, 2011 off the Pacific Coast of Tohoku Earthquake," *Soil Dynamics and Earthquake Engineering* 53, October 2013, 240–53.

84. Kunio Tsunoda, "Improved Management of Termites to Protect Japanese Homes," Proceedings of the Fifth International Conference on Urban Pests, 2005, 33–37.

85. "Typhoon Isewan (Vera) and Its Lessons," Japan Water Forum, 2005, 7.

86. Teruko Sato, "Fundamental Characteristics of Flood Risk in Japan's Urban Areas," *A Better Integrated Management of Disaster Risks: Toward Resilient Society to Emerging Disaster Risks in Mega-Cities*, Terrapub, 2006, 23–40.

87. Teruko Sato, Teruki Fukuzono and Saburo Ikeda, "The Niigata Flood in 2004 as a Flood Risk of 'Low Probability but High Consequence,'" *A Better Integrated Management of Disaster Risks: Toward Resilient Society to Emerging Disaster Risks in Mega-Cities*, Terrapub, 2006, 177–92.

88. Weili Duan et al., "Anomalous Atmospheric Events Leading to Kyushu's Flash Floods, July 11–14, 2012," *Natural Hazards* 73, no. 3, September 2014, 1255–67.

89. Kazumasa Inoue, Moeko Arai and Masahiro Fukushi, "Dispersion of Radiocesium-Contaminated Bottom Sediment Caused by Heavy Rainfall in Joso City, Japan," *PLOS ONE* 12, no. 2, February 24, 2017.

90. H. Gotoh et al., "Flood Risk Management for Schools in the Lowlands of Tokyo, Japan," Proceedings of the 5th International Conference on Flood Risk Management and Response, 2016, 203–13.

91. Tomoko Otake and Tomohiro Osaki, "Tokyo at High Risk of Devastating Floods, Experts Say," *The Japan Times,* September 21, 2015.

92. Brett Israel, "Japan's Explosive Geology Explained," Live Science, March 14, 2011.

93. "Colossal Volcanic Eruption Could Destroy Japan at Any Time: Study," *The Japan Times*, October 24, 2014.

94. "Japan Enacts Bill on Volcanic Disaster Evacuation," Jiji Press, June 30, 2015.

95. "Kagoshima's Sakurajima Volcano Erupts, Spews Plume 5,000 Meters Up," *The Japan Times,* July 26, 2016.

96. "Volcano Grows Japanese Island," CNN, February 28, 2015.

97. "National Catalog of the Active Volcanoes in Japan," Japan Meteorological Agency, 2013.

98. "Colossal Volcanic Eruption Could Destroy Japan at Any Time: Study."

99. "Yakuza Decline Accelerates, Headcount Falls below 40,000," *The Asahi Shimbun,* March 16, 2017.

100. "The Yakuza: From Tattoos to Business Cards," *FTI Journal,* January 2016.

101. Peter Hill, "Heisei Yakuza: Burst Bubble and Botaiho," Sociology Working Papers, University of Oxford, 2002.

102. Andrew Rankin, "21st-Century Yakuza: Recent Trends in Organized Crime in Japan, Part 1," *Asia-Pacific Journal: Japan Focus*, February 11, 2012.

103. "Urban Planning System in Japan, 2nd Edition," Japan International Cooperation Agency, 2007, 66.

Choosing a Location

1. Dan Ariely, *Predictably Irrational: The Hidden Forces That Shape Our Decisions,* HarperCollins, 2009, 31.

2. Chihiro Shimizu, Kiyohiko G. Nishimura and Koji Karato, "Nonlinearity of Housing Price Structure: The Secondhand Condominium Market in the Tokyo Metropolitan Area," CSIS Discussion Paper, no. 86, University of Tokyo, 2010, 19.

3. Komine Takao, "Japanese Regions in the Face of Depopulation and the Trend of Compact City Development," Discuss Japan—Japan Foreign Policy Forum, May 7, 2015.

4. Chihiro Shimizu, Kiyohiko G. Nishimura and Koji Karato, "Nonlinearity of Housing Price Structure: The Secondhand Condominium Market in the Tokyo Metropolitan Area," CSIS Discussion Paper, no. 86, University of Tokyo, 2007, 34.

5. Isabel Reynolds, "Father of Four Tasked With Halting Japan's Population Decline," Bloomberg, October 7, 2015.

6. Ikuko Higuchi, "Day Care Center Goals Still Far Away in Japan," Asia-One/The Japan News, April 6, 2015.

Hokkaido

1. "Ainu History and Culture," Ainu Museum, November 4, 2010.

2. Philippa Fogarty, "Recognition at Last for Japan's Ainu," BBC, June 6, 2008.

3. "Experiencing Ainu Culture," Japan National Tourism Organization, Government of Japan, accessed August 25, 2017.

4. Philip A. Seaton, *Local History and War Memories in Hokkaido,* Routledge, 2016, 91.

5. "Household Projections by Prefecture in Japan: 2010–2035," National Institute of Population and Social Security Research, Government of Japan, 2014.

6. Hachiro Nishioka, "Population Projections by Prefecture in Japan: 2005–2035, Outline of Results and Methods," *The Japanese Journal of Population* 9, no. 1, March 2011.

7. "When Becoming New for a Landowner in a Forest, Notification Is Needed," Hokkaido Government, 2017.

8. "Tables of Climatological Normals (1981–2010)," Japan Meteorological Agency, May 8, 2015.

9. "Sexual Minority Partnership Oath System Newly Established on June 6," City of Sapporo, May 12, 2017.

10. Kenya Katayama, "Towards the Creation of an Eco-City," October 27, 2015, 5.

11. "Niseko Quasi-City Planning," Niseko Town Office, July 3, 2009.

12. "Foreign Tourism, Redevelopment Send Commercial Land Soaring," *Nikkei Asian Review,* March 23, 2016.

13. "JR Hokkaido Says It Can't Maintain Half of Its Railways," *The Japan Times*, November 19, 2016.

Greater Tokyo

1. "Japan Statistical Yearbook 2017—Chapter 2: Population and Households; 2-3 Population by Prefecture (1920 to 2015)," Statistics Bureau, Ministry of Internal Affairs and Communications, Government of Japan, 2017.

2. "Prefectural Economic Calculation," Economic and Social Research Institute, Cabinet Office, Government of Japan, April 3, 2017.

3. "The Japanese Real Estate Investment Market 2016," Nomura Research Institute, October 2016.

4. "Tokyo Statistical Yearbook," Tokyo Metropolitan Government, April 25, 2016.

5. "Shibuya Ward Plans Vote on Same-Sex Marriage," *The Japan Times,* February 13, 2015.

6. "Foreign Residents," City of Yokohama, March 1, 2017.

7. "A Guide to Living in Saitama," Saitama Prefecture, 2017.

8. "Population News of Major Cities," City of Yokohama, March 1, 2017.

9. "Haneda Monorail to Extend to Tokyo Station," *The Japan Times*, August 20, 2014.

10. "Tokyo to Get Two New Subway Lines amid Redevelopment Boom," Japan Today, July 13, 2015.

11. Kenji Irie, "Railroad Improvement in Tokyo Metro," Japan International Transport Institute Railway Seminar, March 4, 2015.

12. "Abe, Other Dignitaries Attend Groundbreaking Ceremony for Tokyo's New Olympic Stadium," *The Japan Times,* December 11, 2016.

13. "Tokyo 2020 Olympic Village to be hydrogen-powered: report," Yahoo!/AFP, January 5, 2015.

14. "2016 Annual Report," East Japan Railway Company, 2016, 30.

15. "Tokyo-Osaka Maglev Train May Start Sooner than Planned," *Nikkei Asian Review,* May 26, 2016.

16. "Yaesu 2-Chome North District Category-I Urban Redevelopment Project Overview," Mitsui Fudosan, April 10, 2014.

17. "Mitsubishi Estate announces Tokiwabashi District Redevelopment Project," Mitsubishi Estate, August 31, 2015.

18. "Tokyo's Tsukiji Fish Market Move on Ice," AsiaOne, November 18, 2016.

19. "Economic Impact of the Tokyo 2020 Olympic Games," Bank of Japan, January 21, 2016, 12.

20. "Revamping Shibuya: A Massive Redevelopment Project Gives the Station Area a New Look," Nippon.com, June 30, 2017.

21. "New Yamanote Line Station Eyed," *The Japan Times,* May 1, 2012.

Nagoya

1. "Population," City of Nagoya, June 13, 2017.

2. "Chubu Bureau of Economy, Trade and Industry," METI Chubu, July 5, 2017.

3. "About the Port," Nagoya Port Authority, 2017.

4. "Invest in Nagoya! The Perfect Place for Your Business!," City of Nagoya, March 18, 2015.

5. Akito Murayama, "Urban Landscape: Urban Planning Policies and Institutional Framework," *Labor Forces and Landscape Management,* Springer 2017, 61–71.

6. "Offering Circular: Central Nippon Expressway Company Limited U.S.$1,000,000,000 2.369 per cent. Bonds due 2018," Nippon Expressway Company, September 4, 2013, 46.

7. "Financial Condition of the City of Nagoya," City of Nagoya, October 2016, 13.

Kansai

1. Sophie Buhnik, "The Dynamics of Urban Degrowth in Japanese Metropolitan Areas: What Are the Outcomes of Urban Recentralisation Strategies?," *The Town Planning Review* 88, no. 1, January 1, 2017.

2. Hachiro Nishioka, "Population Projections by Prefecture in Japan: 2005–2035, Outline of Results and Methods," *The Japanese Journal of Population* 9, no. 1, March 2011.

3. "Kobe Masjid: Japan's First Mosque," Islam in Japan Media, September 9, 2016.

4. Robert Olshanksy, Laurie Johnson and Kenneth Topping, "Opportunity in Chaos—Rebuilding After the 1994 Northridge and 1995 Kobe Earthquakes," Department of Urban and Regional Planning, University of Illinois, Urbana-Champaign, IL, 2005.

5. "Efforts Underway to Better Support Foreign Nationals in Times of Disaster," *The Japan Times*, April 20, 2017.

6. "City of Kobe Investor Relations Materials," City of Kobe, December 2016.

7. Nishioka, "Population Projections by Prefecture in Japan: 2005–2035, Outline of Results and Methods," 10.

8. "Kyoto-Fu, Kyoto-Shi," e-stat, Portal Site of Official Statistics of Japan, 2015.

9. "Population of Kyoto City," Kyoto City, October 2017.

10. Daisaku Kadokawa, Mayors' Summit, MIPIM Japan, Osaka, Japan, September 9, 2016.

11. Kazuhisa Matsui and Mototsugu Fukushige, "Land Prices and Landscape Preservation Restriction in a Metropolitan Area: The Case of Kyoto City," *Review of Urban & Regional Development Studies* 24, no. 1–2, March 1, 2012, 17–34.

12. Akira Hatano, "Kyoto to open tip line to regulate illegal 'minpaku' tourist inns," *The Asahi Shimbun*, June 13, 2016.

13. Lisa Twaronite,"Old Machiya Houses in Japan's Kyoto given New Lease of Life by Niche Loans," Reuters, August 30, 2016.

14. Nishioka, "Population Projections by Prefecture in Japan: 2005–2035, Outline of Results and Methods," 10.

15. Tomoko Otake, "Tokyo's Ota Ward Approves First Short-Term, Airbnb-Style Home Rentals," *The Japan Times*, February 12, 2016.

16. Eric Johnston, "Osaka Referendum Causes Turbulence for LDP, Komeito," *The Japan Times*, May 19, 2015.

17. "Disaster Prevention Map: Protecting Lives from Tsunami and Floods," Office of Emergency Management, Osaka City, March 9, 2011.

18. "Osaka to Privatize Subway, Bus Operations in 2018, Achieving Hashimoto Goal," *The Japan Times*, March 29, 2017.

19. Carola Hein, Jeffrey Diefendorf and Yorifusa Ishida, *Rebuilding Urban Japan After 1945*, Palgrave Macmillan, 2003, 69.

20. David W. Edgington, "City Profile: Osaka," *Cities* 17, no. 4, August 2000, 310.

21. Julian Ryall, "Osaka is on the Brink of Bankruptcy; Financial Panel Aims to Revive Flagging Fortunes of Japan's Former Industrial Centre," *South China Morning Post,* June 17, 2004.

22. Hitoshi Kawata, "Appealing Investment in Osaka and Kansai Area," MIPIM Japan, Osaka, Japan, September 8, 2016.

23. Eric Johnston, "In Osaka, a Place the Homeless Call Home," *The Japan Times*, December 8, 2009.

24. Eric Johnston, "Timing, like Finances, Everything for Osaka's New Rail Links," *The Japan Times*, March 26, 2017.

25. "Plan for the Maintenance and Improvement of Historical Scenic Beauty of Kyoto," Kyoto City, 2012.

26. Eric Johnston, "Cabinet Gives the Greenlight to Osaka's 2025 World Expo Bid Proposal," *The Japan Times,* April 11, 2017.

Fukuoka

1. Paul Eason, "Forging Fukuoka: Locality and Development in Modern Japan," Princeton University, 2012, 1.

2. Eason, "Forging Fukuoka," 189.

3. Sae Naganuma and Yoshio Arai, "Planning and Conceptual Changes Relating to a Waterfront Development at Seaside-Momochi, Fukuoka, Japan," *Journal of Geography* 121, no. 6, 2012, 1030–42.

4. "Island City Turns 10; Popular with Families but Issues Remain," *Fukuoka Now,* September 25, 2015.

5. "Annual Report on Finance and Municipal Bonds of Fukuoka City," Fukuoka City, December 2015, 4.

6. "Annual Report on Finance and Municipal Bonds of Fukuoka City," 5.

7. "Damage to Kumamoto Castle Walls Linked to 1889 Meiji Temblor," *The Japan Times,* November 6, 2016.

8. "2016 Kumamoto Earthquake Survey Report (Preliminary)," Asian Disaster Reduction Center, June 21, 2016.

9. "Efforts Underway to Better Support Foreign Nationals in Times of Disaster," *The Japan Times*, April 20, 2017.

10. Eason, "Forging Fukuoka," 155.

11. "Fukuoka City Business Establishment Support Program," Fukuoka City, November 30, 2016.

12. "Singapore's Changi Airport Joins Fukuoka Bid Consortium," *Nikkei Asian Review*, April 5, 2017.

13. "Annual Report on Finance and Municipal Bonds of Fukuoka City," 15.

14. "Fukuoka Facts—The Tenjin Big Bang Project," Fukuoka City, July 7, 2015.

Okinawa

1. "Outline of Okinawa Prefecture," Executive Office of the Governor, Okinawa Prefecture, March 2016, 1.

2. "IR Presentation Document," City of Sapporo, November 2015, 10.

3. "The Basic Concept of the Okinawa Prefectural Peace Memorial Museum," Okinawa Prefectural Peace Memorial Museum, April 1, 2000.

4. Carola Hein, Jeffrey Diefendorf and Yorifusa Ishida, *Rebuilding Urban Japan After 1945*, Palgrave Macmillan, 2003, 133.

5. Jon Mitchell, "Battle Scars: Okinawa and the Vietnam War," *The Japan Times*, March 7, 2015.

6. Miya Tanaka, "U.S. Land Return Does Little to Soften Okinawa Anti-Base Stance," Japan Today, December 24, 2016.

7. Isabel Reynolds, "Japan Sees Chinese Groups Backing Okinawa Independence Activists," Bloomberg, December 26, 2016.

8. "U.S. to Start Moving Okinawa-Based Marines to Guam in 2024," *The Japan Times*, April 27, 2017.

9. Hideaki Tobe, "Military Bases and Modernity," *Transforming Anthropology* 14, no. 1, April 1, 2006, 89–94.

10. Linda Sieg, "Historians Battle over Okinawa WW2 Mass Suicides," Reuters, April 6, 2007.

11. Jon Mitchell, "The Battle of Okinawa: America's Good War Gone Bad," *The Japan Times*, March 30, 2015.

12. Andrew Pollack, "Marines Seek Peace With Okinawa in Rape Case," *The New York Times*, October 8, 1995.

13. Brendan McGarry, "'AmericaFest' Canceled for US Troops in Japan after Okinawa Murder," Military.com, June 10, 2016.

14. "Okinawa School Marks 50th Year since Deadly U.S. Fighter Crash," *The Japan Times,* July 1, 2009.

15. Jon Mitchell, "FOIA Documents Reveal Hot Spots, Fish Kills and Toxic Dumps on Okinawa Military Base," *The Japan Times,* September 29, 2015.

16. Jon Mitchell, "Contamination: Documents Reveal Hundreds of Unreported Environmental Accidents at Three U.S. Marine Corps Bases on Okinawa," *The Japan Times,* November 19, 2016.

17. Mark Manyin, "The Senkakus (Diaoyu/Diaoyutai) Dispute: U.S. Treaty Obligations," United States Congressional Research Service, October 14, 2016.

18. "Projected Number of Households by Prefecture," National Institute of Population and Social Security Research, Government of Japan, 2014.

19. Hachiro Nishioka, "Population Projections by Prefecture in Japan: 2005–2035, Outline of Results and Methods," *The Japanese Journal of Population* 9, no. 1, March 2011.

20. Jun Homma, "Revival of Failed Projects," *Nikkei Real Estate Market Report,* October 2016, 8.

21. Keiko Ujikane and Maiko Takahashi, "Abe Names Special Strategic Zones in Bid to Boost Japan's Allure," Bloomberg, March 28, 2014.

22. "Gov't Begins Seawall Construction off Henoko amid Okinawa Protests," *Mainichi Daily News,* April 25, 2017.

23. "Okinawa Prefecture Industrial Site Promotion Guide," Okinawa Prefecture, 2017, 22.

24. Keith Barrow, "Trains Set to Return to Okinawa," *International Railway Journal,* February 21, 2014.

Mortgages

1. "A Quick Look at Housing in Japan," The Building Center of Japan, 2017, 35.

2. Masahiro Kobayashi, "The Reverse Mortgage Market in Japan and Its Challenges," *Cityscape* 19, no. 1, 2017, 103.

3. "Presale: Japan Housing Finance Agency," Standard & Poor's Financial Services, January 23, 2017.

4. "Prevention of Discrimination: The Rights of Non-Citizens. Progress Report of the Special Rapporteur, Mr. David Weissbrodt (Addendum)," United Nations, June 3, 2002, 13.

5. Nobuyoshi Yamori and Kazumine Kondo, "How Has Japan Housing Finance Agency's Flat 35 Affected Regional Housing Loan Markets?," *Government Auditing Review* 15, March 2008, 64, 75.

Insurance

1. "2017 Annual Report: Introduction to Earthquake Reinsurance in Japan," Japan Earthquake Reinsurance Co., Ltd., July 2017, 25.

2. Philip Brasor, "Temblors in the Home Insurance Business," *The Japan Times*, July 4, 2015.

3. "2017 Annual Report: Introduction to Earthquake Reinsurance in Japan," 19–20.

4. "Quake Insurance Costs to Rise by 50% in Some Prefectures," *The Japan Times*, October 1, 2015.

Taxes

1. "Land Value Appraisal for the Public Purpose," Land Economy and Construction Industries Bureau, Ministry of Land, Infrastructure, Transport and Tourism, Government of Japan, October 31, 2017.

2. "Japanese Real Estate Statistics 2018," Mitsui Fudosan, December 2017, 27.

3. "Land Price in Ginza Once Again Rises to Record High," *The Asahi Shimbun*, July 3, 2017.

4. "Japan: Residence of Individuals," PwC, August 15, 2017.

5. "Taxation and Investment in Japan 2017," Deloitte, August 2017, 26.

6. "Learning More About Taxes," Ministry of Finance, Government of Japan, July 2017, 26.

7. Paul Previtera, "Tax Consequences of Cross-Border Investment in Japanese Real Estate," *Tax Notes International*, July 10, 2006, 157.

8. "2017 National Tax Agency Report," National Tax Agency, Government of Japan, 2017, 20.

9. John Darcy, *Japan Master Tax Guide 2015/2016,* CCH Asia Limited, 2015, 342.

10. "Comprehensive Handbook of Japanese Taxes 2010," Ministry of Finance, Government of Japan, December 2010, 150–51.

11. "Real Estate in Japan 2017," The Real Estate Companies Association of Japan, May 12, 2017, 54.

12. "Japan Real Estate Income, Capital Gain Tax for Non-Resident Individuals," Shimada & Associates, August 29, 2017.

13. "Taxation in Japan 2015," KPMG Tax Corporation, November 2015, 150.

14. "No. 12014: Real Estate Income of Non-Residents," National Tax Agency, Government of Japan, December 20, 2017.

15. "Taxation and Investment in Japan 2017," 29.

16. "Japan Gift and Inheritance Taxation Highlights for Expatriates on Assignment in Japan," PwC, October 2014.

17. "Japan: Significant Developments in Individual Taxation," PwC, August 15, 2017.

18. "Update: Japan Gift & Inheritance Taxation Reforms Affecting Expatriates on Assignment in Japan—Relief and More Exposure," PwC, April 2017.

19. "A Quick Look at Housing in Japan," The Building Center of Japan, 2017, 63.

20. Kazuya Wakimoto and Jon Salyards, *The Fundamentals of Japanese Real Estate*, Shuwa System, 2015.

A Custom-designed Home

1. Joseph G. Allen et al., "Green Buildings and Health," *Current Environmental Health Reports* 2, no. 3, September 1, 2015, 250–58.

2. "How Energy-Efficient Light Bulbs Compare with Traditional Incandescents," Department of Energy, United States Government, accessed November 25, 2017.

3. Philip Jodidio, *Architecture in Japan,* Taschen, 2006, 8.

4. "Kenchikushi: Architect/Building Engineers in Japan," The Japan Architectural Education and Information Center, 2016, 5.

5. Dana Buntrock, *Japanese Architecture as a Collaborative Process: Opportunities in a Flexible Construction Culture,* Taylor & Francis, 2002, 149.

6. "Introduction of Urban Land Use Planning System in Japan," Ministry of Land, Infrastructure, Transport and Tourism, 2003.

7. Jun Endo, "Jichinsai," Encyclopedia of Shinto, February 24, 2007.

Investment Property

1. "A Quick Look at Housing in Japan," The Building Center of Japan, 2017, 17.

2. "21-6: Dwellings Used Exclusively for Living and Area of Floor Space per Dwelling by Tenure and Type of Building (2008 and 2013)," Statistics Bureau, Ministry of Internal Affairs and Communications, Government of Japan, November 8, 2017.

3. Tatsuya Ishikawa, "The Current Situation of Japan's Housing Market, and Policy Implications of the Projected Population Decrease," NLI Research Institute, 2003, 10.

4. "Tenant Caused 'mental anguish' by Rent Collectors Awarded 50,000 Yen," *The Mainichi Daily News*, February 19, 2009.

5. Miki Seko and Kazuto Sumita, "Fixed Term Contracts versus Open-Ended Contracts in the Japanese Rental Housing Market," June 25, 2008, 3.

6. Masayuki Nakagawa, Makoto Saito and Hisaki Yamaga, "Earthquake Risk and Housing Rents: Evidence from the Tokyo Metropolitan Area," *Regional Science and Urban Economics* 37, no. 1, January 2007, 98.

7. Minoru Matsutani, "Shakeup in Tenant Terms," *The Japan Times*, August 1, 2009.

8. Yasuyuki Fukukawa, "Solitary Death: A New Problem of an Aging Society in Japan," *Journal of the American Geriatrics Society* 59, no. 1, January 1, 2011, 174–75.

9. Tomohiro Osaki, "Japan's Foreign Residents Offer up Insights in Unprecedented Survey on Discrimination," *The Japan Times*, March 31, 2017.

10. "Disposable Homes," The Economist Intelligence Unit, 2009.

11. Nakagawa, Saito and Yamaga, "Earthquake Risk and Housing Rents," 88.

12. Tomoko Kubo and Yoshimichi Yui, "Transformation of the Housing Market in Tokyo since the Late 1990s: Housing Purchases by Single-Person Households," *Asian Studies* 15, no. 3, December 1, 2011, 13.

13. Paul Previtera, "Tax Consequences of Cross-Border Investment in Japanese Real Estate," *Tax Notes International*, July 10, 2006, 152.

Other Opportunities

1. Takako Idee, Shinichiro Iwata and Teruyuki Taguchi, "Auction Price Formation with Costly Occupants: Evidence Using Data from the Osaka District Court," *The Journal of Real Estate Finance and Economics* 42, no. 1, March 5, 2009, 86.

2. "Summary Report of the 2010 Population Census," Statistics Bureau, Ministry of Internal Affairs and Communications, Government of Japan, 2013, 390.

3. "366,000 Seniors Waiting for Nursing Homes, Down 30% from 2013 Amid Tougher New Rules," *The Japan Times*, March 28, 2017.

4. "Over 15,000 Elderly People Found to Be Living in Unauthorized Nursing Homes across Nation," *The Japan Times*, May 1, 2016.

5. "Alleged Killings at Nursing Home Highlight Labor Shortage, Severe Working Conditions," *Mainichi Daily News*, February 17, 2016.

6. Hiroko Tabuchi and Stephanie Strom, "Conflict in Cargill Sale of 'Love Hotel' in Japan," *The New York Times*, October 1, 2012.

7. "'Love Hotels' Targeted for Conversion to Meet Lodging Shortage," *The Japan Times*, May 14, 2016.

8. Justin McCurry, "No Sex Please, We're Japanese: Love Hotels Clean up Their Act Amid Falling Demand," *The Guardian*, December 24, 2016.

9. "Don't Let a 'Minpaku' Bad Apple Ruin Your Travel Experience," Japan Today, July 31, 2017.

10. Alex Martin, "Beyond Airbnb: Minpaku Market Poised for Growth," *The Japan Times*, September 17, 2017.

11. "Japanese Towns Adopt Own Rules to Curb Home-Sharing," *Nikkei Asian Review*, December 9, 2017.

12. "Cabinet OKs Heavier Penalties for Unauthorized Private Lodging Operators," *The Japan Times*, March 7, 2017.

13. "No Evidence of a Post-Olympics Boom or Bust for Host City Real Estate Prices: UBC Study," UBC News, January 25, 2010.

14. "Resort Condos: An Option for Home Buyers," *The Japan Times*, August 6, 2016.

15. "Farm Land Policy and Agriculture Recovery after the Great East Japan Earthquake," Mizuho Securities, November 1, 2012, 4.

16. "Monthly Statistics of Agriculture, Forestry and Fisheries," Ministry of Agriculture, Forestry and Fisheries, Government of Japan, November 24, 2017, 100.

17. "Rural Land without Identified Owners a Puzzling Concern for Urban Planners," *The Japan Times*, June 7, 2017.

18. "About 11% of Land in Japan Is Unclaimed," Bloomberg, November 29, 2017.

19. "Farm Land Policy and Agriculture Recovery after the Great East Japan Earthquake," 4.

20. Chico Harlan, "In Japan, New Policy Spurs Solar Power Boom," *The Washington Post*, June 4, 2013.

21. "Japan's Solar Power Feed-in Tariff to Fall 20% or More in 3 Years," *Nikkei Asian Review*, April 2, 2016.

22. "Solar Shambles," *The Economist*, November 27, 2014.

23. "Sun Setting on Japan's Solar Energy Boom," Phys.org, November 30, 2016.

INDEX

To minimize duplication, only section headings from the "Information Sources" chapter are included in this index. The "Property Buyer's Checklists" are excluded from the index.

ABOUT THE AUTHOR

Christopher Dillon is an award-winning writer and entrepreneur based in Hong Kong.

In 2002, he bought and renovated a floor in an office building in Hong Kong's Central business district. Since then, he has purchased and refurbished a luxury apartment on the west side of Hong Kong Island

and transformed a derelict steam laundry into a multimedia studio. He began investing in Tokyo real estate in 2010.

That experience inspired four books: *Landed Hong Kong* (2008), *Landed Japan* (2010), *Landed China* (2013) and *Landed Global* (2014), which includes case studies and data from more than 110 countries and territories. A second edition of *Landed Hong Kong* was published in 2015.

A native of Canada, Dillon lived in Tokyo from 1989 to 1992. He appears regularly in the international media, as both a contributor and a guest.

www.ingramcontent.com/pod-product-compliance
Lightning Source LLC
Chambersburg PA
CBHW061127220326
41599CB00024B/4197